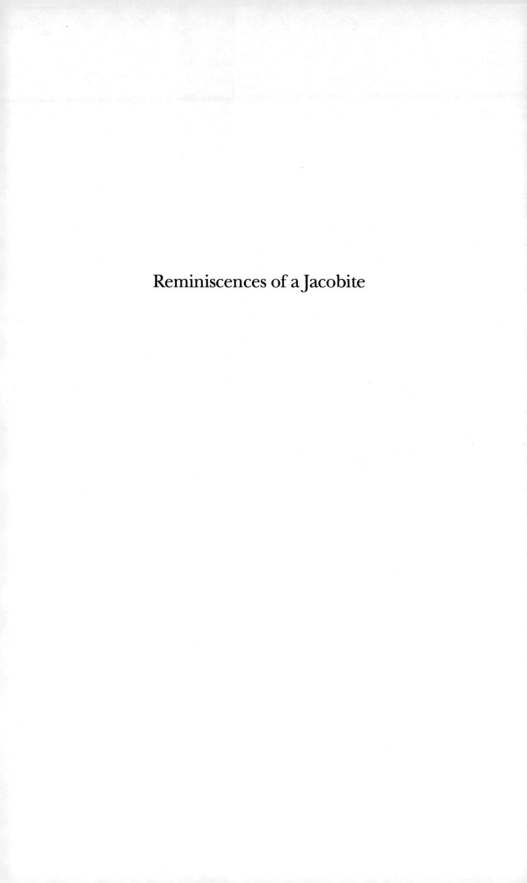

Reminiscences of a Jacobite

To those we have loved who are with us no longer,
And to those we have loved who are with us still;
And may God bless them all
Wherever they may be.

Reminiscences of a Jacobite

The Untold Story of the Rising of 1745

Michael Nevin

ORIGIN

First published in 2020 by
Origin
an imprint of Birlinn Ltd
West Newington House
10 Newington Road
Edinburgh
EH9 1QS

www.birlinn.co.uk

ISBN 978 1 83983 009 9

British Library Cataloguing in Publication Data
A catalogue record for this book is available
from the British Library.

Designed and typeset by Mark Blackadder

Printed and bound by Clays Ltd, Elcograf S.P.A.

Contents

List of Illustrations

List of Plates

vii

List of Figures

Stuart Family Tree

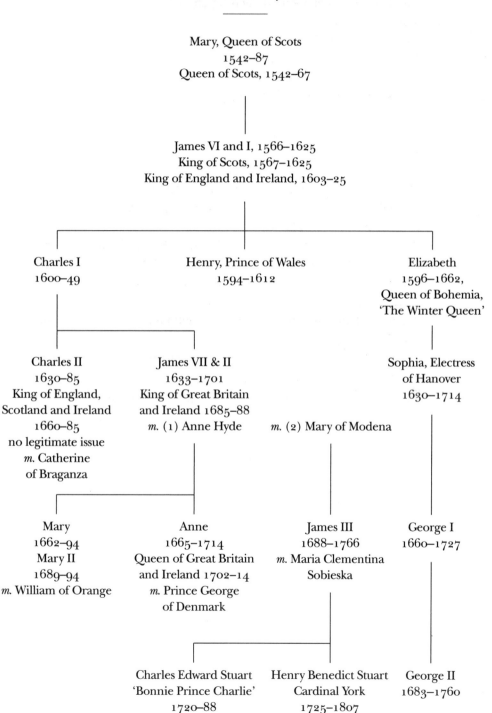

Mary, Queen of Scots
1542–87
Queen of Scots, 1542–67

James VI and I, 1566–1625
King of Scots, 1567–1625
King of England and Ireland, 1603–25

Charles I
1600–49

Henry, Prince of Wales
1594–1612

Elizabeth
1596–1662,
Queen of Bohemia,
'The Winter Queen'

Charles II
1630–85
King of England,
Scotland and Ireland
1660–85
no legitimate issue
m. Catherine
of Braganza

James VII & II
1633–1701
King of Great Britain
and Ireland 1685–88
m. (1) Anne Hyde

m. (2) Mary of Modena

Sophia, Electress
of Hanover
1630–1714

Mary
1662–94
Mary II
1689–94
m. William of Orange

Anne
1665–1714
Queen of Great Britain
and Ireland 1702–14
m. Prince George
of Denmark

James III
1688–1766
m. Maria Clementina
Sobieska

George I
1660–1727

Charles Edward Stuart
'Bonnie Prince Charlie'
1720–88

Henry Benedict Stuart
Cardinal York
1725–1807

George II
1683–1760

To Begin at the Beginning . . .

In May 2002, my eye was caught by an article reporting that a letter written by Prince Charles Edward Stuart to King Louis XV of France in November 1746 was shortly to be sold by auction in London. The letter included a memorandum by the Prince to the French King, appealing for his support to go back to Scotland and finish what he saw as the unfinished business of the Rising of 1745.

This struck me as odd. The way I understood it, the Prince had completely abandoned Scotland after the failure of the Rising, never to return. The Battle of Culloden in April 1746 marked the end of his hopes of a Stuart Restoration and the total destruction of his cause. That was what the history books said. So what was the Prince doing, writing to King Louis as if he still had every expectation of going back to continue his campaign?

Intrigued, I contacted the auction house and arranged to bid by phone. Anticipating that the lot would come up at around two o'clock in the afternoon, one o'clock found me enjoying one of Masons' excellent meat pies for my lunch in Newhaven on Edinburgh's seafront. At that moment my mobile rang. On the line was the auctioneer with news that the letter was now up for sale. Caught unawares, I found myself, meat pie in one hand, mobile phone in the other, bidding sight unseen for Bonnie Prince Charlie's own account of his campaign, written in his own hand. As I put in my top bid, the signal cut out. So it was only five minutes later, when the auctioneer rang back, that I learned that my final bid had been successful.

And so I became the proud possessor of a letter and memorandum that had lain, ignored and forgotten, in the archives of the Marquis d'Argenson, King Louis' Minister of War, for almost three centuries. A letter that gave Prince Charlie's own account of the turbulent year during which he had led the most audacious attempt in history to win the British throne.

According to Prince Charles, far from being doomed from the outset, the Rising had been, as Wellington was to say of Waterloo, 'the nearest run thing you ever saw'. Indeed, the Prince asserts his cause would surely have triumphed, if only he had secured a little more support from France at three critical moments during the campaign: at the battles of Prestonpans, Falkirk Muir and Culloden.

If only . . .

Never mind, he continues, it is still not too late. If King Louis can see his way to conferring on him a corps of 20,000 professional soldiers, he will go back and finish the job, with the support of his partisans in Scotland, who will surely rise once again.

When I mentioned my acquisition to Siân Johnson, a friend and colleague from my days in the City, she told me of an historical association founded many years before to study the Jacobite period, whose members would be most interested to see the Prince's memorandum. So I got in touch with these latter-day keepers of the Jacobite flame. As Siân had intimated, they were indeed interested in the Prince's own account of his campaign. I wrote an article translating it from the original French for *The Jacobite* magazine, beginning a long involvement with the 1745 Association. Over the years, friends and colleagues in the Association helped me to piece together a complex story of the Rising. They included the historians Christopher Duffy and Norman MacDonald, and collectors of Jacobite memorabilia such as Peter Lole (glass), Dr Martin Kelvin (militaria), Peter Elsea MacDonald (tartan), Professor Edward Corp (portraiture), Michael Sharp (coins and medals), and, latterly, Roderick Tulloch, who built up an important private collection of Jacobite letters, portraits, clothing and militaria.

During annual gatherings of the Association, usually held over the first weekend in September, I was able to discuss different aspects of the campaign with these authorities, who were willing to share their knowledge and expertise generously and freely, and with other experts on different aspects of Jacobite history. They included Stephen Lord, who had written a book describing how he had retraced the Prince's journeys during 1745 and 1746 only to discover that many of them were extremely arduous and gruelling, and could only be undertaken by an extremely strong and fit individual – certainly not by the effete weakling portrayed by Hanoverian propaganda. I began to see that the Prince was a far more charismatic and courageous – and enigmatic – figure than is portrayed in popular fiction.

In 2015, our Italian colleagues Stefano Baccolo and Benedicta Froelich organised a wonderful trip to Rome, where we visited the places where the Prince was born and brought up. Another with whom I formed an enduring friendship, notwithstanding our generational difference in years, was the Association's long-standing secretary, Christian Aikman, author of the *Muster Roll of the Jacobite Army*, which sought to collate the names of the men who had risen for the Prince in 1745, their regimental affiliations and, so far as was known, the ultimate fate of each of them.

A further source of information was *The Jacobite*. In 2018, I put together a catalogue of 157 editions of the journal, going back to 1954. They provided first-hand accounts in the form of letters, diaries and memoranda written by those caught up in the Rising, many never previously published and never cited in any histories of the period.

All these sources offered invaluable evidence about what really happened, undistorted by anti-Jacobite propaganda or the prism of academic histories written long after the Rising was over. This evidence enabled me to solve a series of mysteries and paradoxes about the Rising: how Prince Charles Edward Stuart had succeeded in persuading the Highland clans to support his campaign in the face of overwhelming odds against its success, and why experienced and intelligent men with much to lose, such as Lord George Murray and the Duke of Perth, threw in their lot with the Prince. What had convinced them to back the Prince? Likewise, where did he get the money for his campaign, which cost many millions of pounds in today's values?

The Jacobites, with victory seemingly within their grasp, decided to turn back at Derby, but why? And why is it that today the defeated Jacobites are still remembered with respect, while none of the victorious Government regiments include Culloden among their battle honours?

The Prince's own account of his campaign became the start of my quest. History, as Churchill once observed, is the version of events written by the winners. By contrast, this was the version of events written by the loser in the immediate aftermath of his defeat.

And so began my journey through the mists of time, from a pie shop in Newhaven in the early twenty-first century to the mountains and glens of the Highlands in the Year of our Lord 1745.

Monsieur Mon Frere et Cousin

J'ai eu l'honneur d'ecrire a Votre Majesté
avant mon depart de fountainebleau et je prens
la liberté de vous representer a cette heure
que je viens d'achever un petit memoire de
mes affaires, et que je souhaite fort d'avoir
l'honneur de le remettre a sa Majesté en
main propre. Le platot sera le meilleur.
J'attendrai avec impatience ses Ordres, pour
le jour et la Mantiere, qu'elle jugera a pro-
pos de m'accorder ce plaisir la. Si Votre Majesté
trouve bon que je m'en aille en cachette, je
pourrois bien le faire avec une personne,
et me rendre a l'endroit qu'elle aura la bon-
té de me marquer, a l'Insu de toute le
Monde. Comme je me flatte d'avoir
l'amitié d'un si grand Roy, je ne veux —
rien faire sans prendre la liberté de
demander son avis, en tout et partout.
J'ay l'honneur d'etre,

Monsieur Mon Frere et Cousin
de Votre Majesté
Le bon Frere et Cousin
Charles. P.

a Chihy Le 5.
Novembre, 1746.

Letter from Prince Charles Edward Stuart to King Louis XV of France,
5 November 1746

My dear brother and cousin,

*I have had the honour of writing to Your Majesty before my
departure from Fontainebleau, and I am taking the liberty
of writing to you once more at this hour as I have just
completed a little memorandum of my affairs, and I greatly
wish to have the honour of submitting it to His Majesty in
my own hand. The sooner the better. I await with impatience
his instructions of the date and the manner that he will
judge it appropriate to accord me that pleasure. If Your
Majesty prefers that I come in secret, I would be happy to do
so with a single person, and make my way to the place that
he would have the kindness to receive me without anyone's
knowledge. As I am privileged to have the friendship of such
a great King, I do not wish to do anything without taking
the liberty of requesting his opinion on all matters. I have
the honour of being the dear brother and cousin of Your
Majesty.*

Your good brother and cousin

Charles P.

Clichy, 5 November 1746

PART 1
Genesis of a Revolution

1

The Rise and Fall of the House of Stuart

I started my quest to unlock the mystery of the '45 in London. In the end, the Jacobites never made it that far, except as prisoners. Yet many of the events that led to the Jacobite Wars occurred there, and the character of many of the leading actors in the drama that unfolded are captured in the great collection of Stuart and Jacobite portraits at the National Portrait Gallery.

This collection includes a famous portrait which may be that of the greatest dramatist who ever wrote in the English language, William Shakespeare, painted around 1610, seven years into the reign of King James in England and Ireland, and more than forty years after he had, as a baby, succeeded his mother Mary, Queen of Scots, to the Scottish throne.

Commentators on Shakespeare's work have argued that his tragedies reveal him to have been a social conservative. In his plays, those who seek to upset the established order – from Cassius and Brutus in *Julius Caesar*, through *Macbeth* and *Richard III* – invariably come to a sticky end.

Some would argue that Shakespeare had to take this line because if he'd written any plays suggesting that rebellion against authority was a good idea it wouldn't have gone down too well in the courts of Queen Elizabeth and King James. While this is undoubtedly true, I don't think that Shakespeare presented this view because he was afraid of upsetting an English monarch. I think he did so because he believed it was true – that it is almost always better to support established authority and seek to make existing relationships work, no matter how imperfect they may be, than to seek to destroy them.

Shakespeare was such a great dramatist that his observations about human nature and the nature of human conflict transcend the time and place in which he lived. Yet Shakespeare was also a child of his time. He lived through a period of great social and political turbulence, including the execution of Mary, Queen of Scots in 1587, the Spanish Armada in 1588, and various plots and counter plots, most famously Guy Fawkes' 1605 Gunpowder Plot, which unsuccessfully attempted to blow up King James and his entire Parliament.

What Shakespeare and his generation desperately sought was political stability and the opportunity to be left to enjoy their lives in peace.

The accession of King James to the throne, uniting the crowns of Scotland and England for the first time, offered the possibility of peace and stability. It is well known that King George II was the last English king to lead an army into battle. What is less well known is that James was the first English king, other than boy kings such as Edward VI who never reached maturity, never to have led an army into battle.

In the 1621 portrait by Dutch artist Daniel Mytens that hangs today in the National Portrait Gallery (Plate 1), King James is projected as a calm father figure, offering reassurance to the nation. Clearly, this is a man of substance and power. But he's also a man of peace – there is no evidence of weaponry in the portrait. This man could pass as a judge or even a cleric. The message seems to be, here is someone who governs not by force of arms but by the rule of law, whose authority is upheld not by military might but by consent of the governed.

So I think this is a king of whom Shakespeare would have approved, knowing that a world without rule of law would be one in which, in the philosopher Thomas Hobbes's phrase, life would be 'nasty, brutish and short'.

King James was the first man to unite the crowns of Scotland and England: good, Shakespeare would have said, in bringing an end to constant conflict between the two nations. He introduced a common currency in the two countries; excellent for the merchant classes from which Shakespeare came, as it would facilitate trade between Scotland, England and Ireland. He introduced a common flag, combining the cross of St George of England and the cross of St Andrew of Scotland; another tick in the box, in promoting reconciliation between two ancient enemies.

He commissioned the first English translation of the Bible – the King James version – which over the 400 years since has perhaps been the most influential book ever published in the English language. Again, this would have met with the approval of Middle England, in promoting a code of conduct understandable to the common man and woman, preaching peace and tolerance.

A case could be made that only a monarch emerging from the Scottish tradition of Kings or Queens of the Scots, ruling with the consent of the governed, could have successfully united the crowns of the three nations and successfully govern through legal authority rather than force of arms. Yet, as Shakespeare also wrote, 'uneasy lies the head that wears the crown'. King James was under constant threat of assassination, and not just from Guy Fawkes. He is reputed to have packed his coat with straw in order to protect himself against the daggers of potential assailants, accounting for its unusual bulk in his portraits. He was also criticised for what was seen, in less tolerant times, as his moral turpitude, and in particular his relationship with George Villiers, Duke of Buckingham (Plate 2).

Born in Leicestershire in 1592 the son of a minor gentleman, Villiers ascended rapidly in the court of King James. He was appointed as a gentleman of the bedchamber to the King in 1615, where his duties were, as the title suggests, to attend to the King's needs – duties that he fulfilled with such proficiency that in 1623 he was elevated to the Dukedom of Buckingham.

His rapid advance was viewed with suspicion by jealous courtiers and he was blamed for Britain's involvement in costly and unpopular foreign wars during the 1620s. He did not long survive the passing of his mentor King James in 1625, being stabbed to death in the Greyhound Pub in Portsmouth aged just thirty-five in 1628.

According to the account given by Alexander Dumas in *The Three Musketeers*, his assassination was organised by the manipulative Milady de Winter, serving the purposes of Cardinal Richelieu in seeking to destabilise England and advance French interests. The official version of events is rather more prosaic. Buckingham was stabbed by an army officer by the name of John Felton who believed that he had been passed over for promotion by Buckingham. By the time of his death, Buckingham was so unpopular that Felton was widely acclaimed as a public hero. Sadly for Felton, this didn't prevent him from being hanged for Buckingham's murder in November 1628, although perhaps it might have come as some consolation to him that when his corpse was put on public display it became an object of public veneration.

Despite his preference for his gentlemen of the bedchamber, James did manage to marry and produce an heir and a spare. His heir was Henry Frederick Stuart, Prince of Wales, born at Stirling Castle in 1594, trained in naval and military matters and by all accounts a young man of great promise and sound judgement, who might have made a very successful king.

Sadly, it was not to be. The curse of the Stuarts struck and Henry was carried away by typhoid at the age of just eighteen in 1612. One wonders how different history might have been had he survived and succeeded his father. As it was, his brief life is just another sorry tale of 'what might have been' in the story of the Stuarts.

Following the death of Prince Henry, his younger brother Charles, seen in a 1630 portrait by Daniel Mytens, the same artist who had painted his late father ten years earlier, became the heir. It had never been envisaged that Charles would become King. He had been largely neglected during childhood, not benefiting from an education in statecraft as his elder brother had.

Robin Nicholson, author of *Bonnie Prince Charlie and the Making of a Myth: A Study in Portraiture* and currently executive director of the Telfair Museums in Savannah, Georgia, made the following comments on the portraiture of King Charles:

> Charles I attempted to control his self-image to a far greater extent than his father . . . As his country collapsed around him, portraiture literally became a mask behind which the King could hide, a desperately overconfident, even arrogant, demand for loyalty; betrayed only by the haunted look of the eyes.

Many of these features are evident in his portrait by Daniel Mytens (Plate 3). A weak and sickly child, his speech development was slow and he had a stammer all his life. Unlike his brother Henry, who during his brief life appears to have been someone who sought consensus and reconciliation, Charles sought to establish his divine right to rule, stating that 'princes are not bound to give account of their actions but to God alone'. Charles did not recognise the right of Parliament to restrict his activities. When Parliament sought to limit the taxes that Charles wished to raise in order to pay for Continental wars, instead of working with his Parliament, he prorogued it and sought to govern directly. This disastrous strategy led directly to the English Civil War, when the King fought unsuccessfully against Parliamentary forces under Oliver Cromwell.

There are a number of clues offered in Mytens' portrait as to why Charles's attempt to impose absolute rule ended in disaster. In the portrait, Charles bears a curious resemblance to another failed autocrat, his distant relative Nikolai Romanov, the last Tsar, striking a diffident and slightly built figure whose weak chin is barely disguised by his beard.

Unlike the most notorious tyrant in British history, the powerfully built King Henry VIII, who had reigned a century earlier, Charles was not a man whose mere physical presence could strike fear into those he sought to command. He thus lacked the tyrant's most potent tool – terror.

There are other sharp contrasts between Charles and Henry VIII. While Charles had a long and loving relationship with his queen, Henrietta Maria, Henry VIII showed no compunction in ridding himself of his wives once he had tired of them, whether by divorce or execution. Where Charles was loyal to his advisers and tried to make peace with his enemies, Henry VIII sought the death of any who failed to do his bidding. Thomas More and Thomas Cromwell both met their ends on the scaffold, their last mortal remains mingled together to this day in the locked vaults of the Church of St Peter ad Vincula in the Tower of London. The same fate would have befallen Cardinal Wolsey had he not died before Henry's axeman reached him.

Charles was never going to be a successful tyrant like Henry VIII. And the problem with being an unsuccessful tyrant is that if your enemies don't lose their heads, then you are likely to lose yours.

*   *   *

In 1660, the Stuart dynasty was restored under Charles II and over the next quarter of a century Great Britain enjoyed a period of stability and prosperity, as the King worked to heal the wounds of the Civil War. There was a poem written about Charles II, which ran:

> *Here sits a great and mighty King*
> *Whose word no one relies on.*
> *For he never said a foolish thing*
> *Nor ever did a wise one!*

When this ditty was reported to him, Charles readily accepted its accuracy. 'While my words are my own,' he said, 'my actions are decided by my ministers!' As his response suggests, unlike his unfortunate father, Charles II sought to rule through Parliament rather than seeking to overrule Parliament. He accepted that his ministers could tell him what to do, even if, on occasion, he believed their advice to be foolish.

Something of his character is captured in the famous and rather intriguing portrait of Charles II by Thomas Hawker that hangs in the

7

National Portrait Gallery (Plate 5). In general, seventeenth-century artists sought to portray their subjects in a favourable light, if for no other reason than to make sure they got paid. Yet Hawker's portrait doesn't show Charles in a favourable light at all. The painting reveals an ageing roué: sensuous, overweight, with a cunning glint in his eyes. Morally easy-going though this figure may be, the portrait says this is not a man to be trusted.

Given the unflattering depiction of the King, it seems unlikely that this portrait was the result of a commission from the King himself. This, then, begs the question, just why was it painted?

I did some research on the artist to whom it is attributed, Thomas Hawker, and discovered a few facts that might shed some light on the mystery. Hawker worked in the studio of Sir Peter Lely. After Lely died in 1680, Hawker moved into his house and sought to become the new head of his practice, hoping to take over his customer base and perhaps also Sir Peter Lely's title as Painter in Ordinary to King Charles. Instead, that post was given to Sir Godfrey Kneller.

My guess is that Hawker may have been a little irritated at being passed over for the post of Court Artist and took his revenge on the King, not with a dagger like the assassin of the Duke of Buckingham, but with a paintbrush, by portraying him as a venal and untrustworthy rascal.

Having said that, unlike many of his Stuart predecessors who met their end on the block or on the battlefield, Charles II did die in his own bed, which was a not insignificant achievement in the atmosphere of the time.

Charles II's survival was assisted by his wisdom in leaving affairs of State to his ministers, rather than seeking to impose his own policies on a recalcitrant Parliament as his father had. This strategy had the incidental benefit of leaving Charles II to pursue his own private affairs. Not that he emulated Henry VIII by cutting off the heads of his wives once he had tired of them. No, Charles had just one wife, the long-suffering Catherine de Braganza, to whom he stayed married until the day he died, although she did not deliver him a surviving heir.

Charles himself had no problem in producing children – at least fourteen of them, five of whom were by Barbara Villiers, portrayed by Sir Peter Lely (Plate 4). She was described by the diarist John Evelyn as 'a vulgar mannered, arrogant slut'. In appreciation of these qualities, the King awarded her the title of Duchess of Cleveland.

Lely's infamous portrait shows the Duchess with one of her children by King Charles in the guise of Madonna and Child, which scandalised the good Christian folk of England. While they might have tired of the oppressive puritanism of Oliver Cromwell's Protectorate, there were many who felt that the Merrie Monarch had gone too far in commissioning an almost sacrilegious portrayal of his mistress and illegitimate son as the Immaculate Conception. Conception there had undoubtedly been, but immaculate? Perhaps not so much.

Among those whom the Duchess sought to promote within the Restoration Court was a young man by the name of John Churchill, who was to play a key role in the events surrounding the succession to Charles II.

John Churchill was the product of the impoverished gentry. His father, the original Winston Churchill, had been reduced to penury when he was fined three times his annual income as a punishment for supporting King Charles I during the Civil War.

After the Restoration, the sixteen-year-old John Churchill gained a post as a page to James, Duke of York, Charles II's younger brother. He secured a second income when he gained a commission as an army officer. A third income was reputedly earned for services rendered to King Charles II's mistress, Barbara Villiers, Duchess of Cleveland, of whom John Evelyn was such a big fan and who certainly seems to have been very generous with her favours.

When his patron, the Duke of York, became King, John Churchill advanced further, only to be faced with a difficult decision when William of Orange crossed the Channel to oust James from the throne. Waiting to see which way the wind was blowing, Churchill, it is reported, switched his allegiance from King James to William of Orange when William promised to grant him the title of Earl of Marlborough.

It is curious to reflect that the great Churchill dynasty was founded by the toy boy of one of Charles II's mistresses, who made his way in life by double-dealing and opportunism. In the words of a popular jingle of the day:

Many a beau without a shilling;
Many a widow, not unwilling;
Many a bargain if you strike it –
This is London – how do you like it!

*   *   *

In the initial years of James's reign, Churchill was loyal to his patron. Churchill's role in defeating Charles II's illegitimate son, the Duke of Monmouth, at the Battle of Sedgemoor in 1685 helped to secure James on the throne.

Unlike his older brother Charles II, King James II and VII actively professed his Catholic faith, provoking fear among the English Whigs that he might seek to emulate his father, Charles I, in asserting the dogma of the Divine Right of Kings and the supremacy of the King over Parliament.

At that time, under the laws of England, Catholics could not practice their religion, nor hold public office, or vote or sit in Parliament. James wanted to end the discrimination against Catholics and other religious minorities, and in 1687 proposed a new Act for the Liberty of Conscience. In a speech to persuade Parliament to pass this Act, King James said:

> Suppose there should be a law made that all black men be imprisoned, it would be unreasonable, and we have as little reason to quarrel with other men for being of different religious opinions as for being of different complexions.

To us today, King James's stand against racial and religious discrimination would seem laudable. Indeed, it was supported by other minorities who also suffered religious discrimination in 1688, including Quakers, Baptists, Jews, Congregationalists and Episcopalians – and even one minority religion not generally regarded as particularly sympathetic to the Jacobites, the Presbyterians.

But not the State Church, the Church of England. When James ordered Anglican bishops to read his Declaration of Indulgence from their pulpits, seven of them refused to obey. In response, James did something that even today, more than 300 years later, seems unbelievably stupid. He charged them with treason. This at a time when the memory of Anglican martyrs burnt at the stake by Mary Tudor was still very much alive. The seven bishops were acquitted of the charges against them, but the damage had been done. The Anglican bishops appealed to his son-in-law, William of Orange, to overthrow King James.

Up until that time, a fragile peace had been maintained by the expectation that, in the fullness of time, James would be succeeded by his two Protestant daughters, Mary and Anne, by his first wife, Anne Hyde, who had died before James had acceded to the throne. John Churchill's wife, Sarah, née Jennings, was Anne's closest friend and confidante, so as long as Anne remained loyal to her father, Churchill's loyalty as the leading military commander could also be assured.

A crisis in the ruling family was precipitated by the birth on 10 June 1688 of James Francis Edward Stuart, the son of James by his second wife and Queen, the Catholic Mary of Modena. James Francis Edward was baptised a Catholic, and if his legitimacy was recognised he would displace Mary and Anne in the line of succession.

We are faced with classic second marriage syndrome. The children of the first marriage don't entirely approve of their step mum. What they particularly dislike is her giving birth to a baby boy who stands to inherit the estate and take the fortune that they thought was coming to them, along with a few other minor baubles like the Crown Jewels and the thrones of Scotland, England and Ireland.

In response, Mary and Anne put about a scurrilous rumour that their baby half-brother was not truly the son of the Queen but an impostor smuggled into her bedchamber. They thus lent their support to the move by the Whigs to depose their own father from the throne.

When Anne turned against her father, so did her best friend, Sarah Jennings, and Sarah's husband, John Churchill. Churchill's support was crucial in deposing King James II and replacing him with the joint monarchy of Anne's older sister Mary and her husband, William of Orange. In return, William of Orange elevated him to the peerage as Earl of Marlborough.

There is a popular myth that the last time that England was conquered by a foreign invader was in 1066. This myth was challenged by Lucy Worsley in the second episode of her 2017 series *British History's Biggest Fibs*, when she demonstrated that the so-called Glorious Revolution of 1688 was, in fact, a foreign invasion of our islands. Earlier historians have made the same point. Writing in 2000, Count Nikolai Tolstoy commented:

> In 1688, the King of England was driven from his throne by his son-in-law, the Prince of Orange, who invaded and conquered England with the most powerful foreign fleet and army ever seen in Northern waters. Until the Spring of 1690, London remained under rigorous Dutch military occupation, no English regiment being permitted within twenty miles of the capital . . . The cabal of English traitors who collaborated with the invader could no more have affected the so-called "Glorious Revolution" unaided by enemy troops than could Dr Quisling have governed Norway in the absence of the German Army.

Anne's support for the rebellion led by her brother-in-law caused her father great distress. His daughter's betrayal seems to have precipitated a nervous breakdown. King James II fled from London for the Continent, leaving the Crown vacant for William of Orange to seize.

What has been termed the 'Glorious Revolution' was neither glorious nor a revolution; it was nothing more nor less than a squalid family split driven by the conflicting ambitions and financial interests of different family members.

But since the family in question was the ruling dynasty of Britain, it was to have profound consequences for all of its citizens.

2

Remembering Dunkeld

When great dynasties fracture, ordinary people suffer. The family disputes between King James II, his two daughters and his son-in-law were to have repercussions far beyond the gilded corridors of St James's Palace and led to the deaths of many thousands of soldiers in remote fields of battle of the realm, which are today long forgotten.

I had hardly heard of Dunkeld when, in the autumn of 2019, my friend and colleague on the Council of the 1745 Association, Kevin Smith, suggested we should commemorate the battle that had been fought there 330 years previously.

Up until that time, I had also laboured under the misapprehension that the smallest city in Great Britain was St David's in Pembrokeshire, with a population of just over 2,000, and that the smallest city in the world was the Vatican. Dunkeld, a cathedral city which today has a population of a thousand people, is smaller than either of them. But few know about Dunkeld, for this once great city was razed by fire on a single day in 1689 that witnessed terrible slaughter from which it has never recovered.

Dunkeld is the Orphan Battle of the Jacobite Wars, forgotten and neglected, literally fatherless after the Jacobite leader Bonnie Dundee was taken out by a sniper at Killiecrankie a month before and not belonging to any family of battles. It is quite unlike any other battle of the Jacobite Wars, in that it was fought in an urban environment with brutal street-to-street fighting. By the end of the fight, Dunkeld was utterly destroyed. Only the cathedral and three houses adjacent to it remain today of the buildings that stood before 1689.

As I researched, my studies threw up new questions. Records of the battle are very poor, meaning that we don't know basic details, for example even approximately how many soldiers fought. The battle ended at twelve o'clock, but does this mean midday or midnight? I wondered why were there so many gaps in official accounts of the battle, why the records had been hidden, suppressed or destroyed. Call me cynical, but the suspicion when official sources provide very little information about an event is that officials have something to hide. But what could that be?

The Williamites decided to try and halt the Jacobite advance at Dunkeld, of all places, but why would they select an exposed position in a low-lying valley lacking any defensive wall, so obviously exposed to attack from the surrounding hillsides? Why not choose an elevated position, or even the fastness of Stirling Castle, occupying a position so impregnable that it could not be reduced by a siege lasting several weeks, as the Jacobites discovered in 1746?

Another anomaly was the defensive position, chosen with a river running behind it. The silvery Tay may seem very calm and serene today, but back in 1689 it was a trap for the defenders because it restricted their freedom of manoeuvre and, more fundamentally, it cut off their only possible line of retreat.

Having decided to defend Dunkeld, why did the Williamites then send in an inexperienced militia formed just three months before? Surely, if they were serious about holding the city, it would have made more sense to deploy a crack regiment of regulars to do the job, not a bunch of amateurs. The Cameronians were not commanded that day by their regimental commander, the Earl of Angus. He was deployed elsewhere, along with a third of his regiment, leaving just 800 men to hold Dunkeld against the might of a battle-hardened Jacobite Army, which a few weeks earlier had scored a stunning victory at Killiecrankie. Could it be that the Earl, as a noble lord, was deemed too valuable to be sacrificed in what looked likely to be a suicide mission?

Command of the Cameronian Regiment was delegated instead to the inexperienced twenty-eight-year-old officer Lieutenant-Colonel William Cleland. Why were the men under Cleland's command so poorly armed, being issued, according to contemporary accounts, with just 400 outdated firelocks, 400 pikes and forty halberts – just one inadequate weapon for every man defending the city?

Finally, why, two days before the battle on 19 August 1689, were two troops of horse and three troops of dragoons under Lord Cardross, which had been sent to reinforce the Cameronian infantry, suddenly withdrawn without explanation?

You don't need to be Sherlock Holmes to work out a possible answer to these questions. The Cameronians were being set up to fail. The Williamites didn't seriously expect them to hold Dunkeld against the advancing Jacobites at all. Their mission was merely to blunt the Jacobite advance, softening them up while the main Williamite army prepared to meet the Highlanders at a more propitious location.

And if the Cameronians were slaughtered during their defence of Dunkeld, that was deemed by those in authority to be a price worth paying.

This gives rise to two further questions: why were the Cameronians, uniquely among the Williamite Regiments, deemed to be so expendable, and how did they escape their expected fate?

*   *   *

The Cameronians were Covenanters – adherents to the National Covenant signed in Greyfriars churchyard in Edinburgh in 1638. The Covenanters didn't need Charles I and his bishops to tell them what to believe or how to interpret the Bible, particularly since, during the reign of Charles's father, the Bible had been translated into English, in what remains to this day the most widely read book ever published in English – the King James Version. The Cameronians went beyond more moderate Presbyterians, who only wanted to be left in peace to practise their religion, according to their consciences.

Their founder, the Reverend Richard Cameron, denounced the King as a tyrant. In 1680, he called for a war against Charles II and demanded the exclusion of his brother, James, from the succession. This extract from his last known sermon, delivered at Kype Water in East Kilbride on Sunday, 18 July 1680: 'The gates of Rome shall be burnt with fire . . . [We] shall overthrow the throne of Britain, and all the thrones of Europe!'

Unsurprisingly, the authorities took a rather dim view of this call for violent insurrection. The Scottish Privy Council declared Cameron and his supporters 'open and notorious traitors and rebels', and sent a posse to bring him to justice. They caught up with him four days after his Kype Water sermon, on 22 July, at Airds Moss near Cumnock.

The Reverend Cameron did not give himself up peaceably to the forces of the law. Why should he, when he didn't recognise their authority in the first place, having, as he believed, a direct line to the Almighty?

What followed was a shoot-out that makes the Gunfight at the O.K. Corral look like a children's tea party. By the end of it, the Reverend

Cameron lay dead and his supporters were dispersed.

At this point, some Government official came up with the bright idea, just to discourage any further nonsense from the Cameronians, of cutting off the head and hands of the late Reverend Cameron and putting them on public display at the Netherbow Port in Edinburgh. This particular piece of political genius immediately transformed the late Reverend Cameron from being regarded as a reckless militant extremist in his life-time to being revered as a holy martyr after his death.

So, when William of Orange led a rebellion against King James nine years later, the Cameronians were first in line to raise a regiment in his support, in May 1689, under the command of James Douglas, Earl of Angus.

Under the principle of 'my enemy's enemy is my friend', the Williamites welcomed the Cameronian Regiment into their ranks. However, their commander in Scotland, General Hugh Mackay, regarded them with a very wary eye. How would the Cameronians, with a track record of advocating the violent overthrow of the established order, behave when King William consolidated his grip on the throne?

So when the Williamites were defeated by the Jacobites at Killiecrankie and began their retreat south, it occurred to General Mackay that the Cameronians might be the ideal regiment to blunt the Jacobite advance. After all, if they were willing to be martyrs for his cause, why would he want to disappoint them? And if they took out a few Jacobites in the process, so much the better. It might conveniently kill two birds with a single stone.

It isn't just me who suspects that the Cameronians were being set up. It was the opinion of the Cameronians themselves. They were so worried as they watched Lord Cardross and his cavalry ride off into the sunset the day before the battle that one of their number went to their commander, Lieutenant-Colonel William Cleland, to express their concerns that Cleland himself and his fellow officers would get on their horses and ride away, leaving them abandoned to their fate, just as Lord Cardross had done.

Cleland assured them that they would not do this. When pressed on the matter, Cleland looked the soldier in the eye and told him that to prove his commitment he would personally shoot the officers' horses. In the end, that did not happen. The men placed their trust in their colonel's word of honour.

*   *   *

The battle can be split into four phases: the Jacobite onslaught, the siege, the counter-attack and finally the Jacobite withdrawal.

When the Jacobites advanced at dawn, the Cameronian officers did indeed stand shoulder to shoulder with their men, and several among them were to make the ultimate sacrifice that day. As they watched the Jacobites march and then break into a slow run down the hills towards Dunkeld, one thought must have run through the minds of each man among them: will this be the day that I die?

It was the day that Lieutenant-Colonel William Cleland died. Leading his men from the front, he was hit in the liver and the head. Aware that he was fatally wounded, he crawled out of the sight of his men so that they would not give up as they watched him die.

Command of the Regiment fell to his second-in-command, Major James Henderson, but he was also taken out in the first wave of the attack. So, too, was Lieutenant Henry Stewart of Livingstone, manning the barricades at the Dunkeld Cross.

Command of the Cameronian Regiment then fell to Captain George Munro of Auchinbowie.

By this time, around half past eight in the morning, the Jacobites were closing in for the kill. However, their advance was impeded by the buildings before them. The traditional Highland Charge works best in open countryside, with Highlanders running at an increasing pace downhill to achieve maximum speed at the moment of impact against an enemy exposed on open ground. By contrast, at Dunkeld, the Cameronians were well dug into houses around the cathedral, which protected them against the full ferocity of the Highland Charge. The Jacobites set fire to the houses in which the Cameronians were positioned, which were mostly of wooden construction with thatched roofs and thus highly flammable. Those Cameronians who were able to evacuate their positions withdrew to their central defensive position in five buildings: the cathedral itself, the rectory, the manse and the Dean's House that served the cathedral, and, in a nearby field, Dunkeld House, the mansion of the Marquis of Atholl. All these buildings were of solid stone construction with lead roofs and therefore difficult to set aflame.

In these buildings, with the doors locked, the Cameronians were, for the moment, safe from the initial Jacobite onslaught.

Some accounts state that the battle lasted well into the night. Others state that it was over within four hours. My own view is that the latter version is correct and the battle was over by midday. This is based on the following evidence.

Firstly, the nature of the Highland Charge itself. It was a shock tactic: a sudden, rapid advance on to the enemy position, concluding in close quarters engagement that either broke the enemy line or would be broken within a matter of fifteen minutes, certainly no more than half an hour, as was to be shown at three battles of the '45 – at Prestonpans, Falkirk Muir and Culloden. Even allowing for the fact that the Highland Charge at Dunkeld was blunted by the buildings in which some of the defenders were positioned, we know that the first phase of the battle was over not long after eight o'clock in the morning, by which time the Cameronian officers Cleland, Henderson and Stewart all lay dead or dying, and the Cameronians had been forced to withdraw to their core defensive position.

Secondly, we know that the Cameronians had very little ammunition and, trapped inside the cathedral and Dunkeld House, they would have had very little water as well. They were so desperate that they stripped lead from the roofs to manufacture makeshift shot. Under these circumstances, could they really have held out until midnight?

Thirdly, I have undertaken a visual inspection of the cathedral walls, as can others today. Yes, there is evidence of musket shot pitting the walls, but the damage is not extensive, and certainly not consistent with a prolonged, sustained attack on the cathedral. That suggests to me that the second phase of the battle – the siege of the cathedral and Dunkeld House – must have been relatively brief, lasting no more than a couple of hours.

A fourth piece of evidence that we have to consider is the mindset of the surviving Cameronians themselves. Trapped in the cathedral and Dunkeld House, running short of ammunition and making their desperate last stand, Captain Munro and the surviving officers must surely have concluded fairly soon that their only hope of survival was to attempt a break-out and launch a counter-attack, otherwise their fate would be sealed.

And that it exactly what they did, armed with pikes mounted with blazing faggots to set alight the roofs of the houses in which the Jacobite musketeers were positioned. And it worked, though only at the cost of reducing the once great city of Dunkeld to ashes. Here is a vivid account of what happened by James Browne in his *History of the Highlands and the Highland Clans*, published in 1840:

> The whole town was in a conflagration, and the scene which it now presented was one of the most heartrending description. The din of war was no longer heard, but a more terrific sound had succeeded, from the wild shrieks and accents of despair which issued from the dense mass of smoke and flame which enveloped the unfortunate sufferers. The pike men had locked the doors of such of the houses as had keys standing in them and the unhappy intruders, being thus cut off from escape, perished in the flames. No less than sixteen Highlanders were burnt to death in one house. With the exception of three houses possessed by the Cameronians, the whole town was consumed.

At this point, the Jacobites suddenly and unexpectedly withdrew from the town.

The Cameronians' reaction to their withdrawal presents the fifth and, for me, the clinching piece of evidence that the battle ended at around midday, not at midnight. *If the Jacobites had withdrawn late into the night, it would have been no surprise at all* – indeed, the Cameronians might even have expected disengagement when darkness fell, with the possibility of re-engagement the following morning.

And yet every account of the battle refers to the surprise and joy felt by the Cameronians when they saw their enemies retreat. This response can only be consistent with a withdrawal in broad daylight. Withdrawal deep into the night would not have elicited such a response.

So why did the Jacobites retreat so peremptorily? Their commander, Colonel Alexander Cannon, stated that it was because they had run out of ammunition. However, this statement has been challenged as self-serving since it would absolve Cannon of any blame for the Jacobite retreat just when they were on the point of victory.

A more convincing explanation is that the Jacobites were spooked by seeing their comrades burned alive under the ferocity of the Cameronian counter-attack. 'We can fight with men, but not with devils,' they said. This is echoed in the most enduring poem about the battle:

You lie, you lust, you break your trust,
And commit all kinds of evil;

Your say your Covenant makes you a Saint,
But you are the very Devil.

In murders too, like demons true,
Of others' blood you've drunk well;
You fought like devils, your only rivals,
When we met you at Dunkeld.

So what is the legacy of the Battle of Dunkeld?

First and most obviously, it swung the tide of the Civil War of 1689 in Scotland decisively against King James and in favour of William of Orange. After the battle, Jacobite forces in Scotland steadily dwindled. The Jacobite Army in Scotland never regained its former strength, and the Jacobite threat in Scotland was finally snuffed out at the Battle of Cromdale in 1690. James's attempt to regain the throne then switched to Ireland but was extinguished by his defeats at the Battle of the Boyne in 1690, and finally at the Battle of Aughrim on 12 July 1691, where it is estimated that between 6,000 and 7,000 men died, making it the bloodiest battle fought in the Jacobite Wars. James never was to regain his throne.

A second legacy of Dunkeld is that it demonstrated the immense advantages enjoyed by defenders in an urban battle, even when heavily outnumbered. They can select the strongest defensive positions, dig themselves in and inflict huge losses on their attackers, who inevitably are more exposed as they advance.

The final, and perhaps most important, legacy of Dunkeld is that it reminds us of the dangers of intransigence and intolerance, especially in matters of personal belief, which can lead to escalating violence when those convinced of their own rectitude seek to impose their views on others by force.

By remembering, respecting and honouring those on both sides who fell at Dunkeld on that fateful day in August 1689, and whose last mortal remains lie there still, we may express the hope that never again in this country will our lives, liberty and happiness be threatened by civil war.

3

The Tragedy of Queen Anne

In Gallery No. 1 of the Scottish National Portrait Gallery in Edinburgh hangs a beautiful portrait of Anne, the last of the Stuart monarchs, painted shortly after the death of her uncle Charles II in 1685 (Plate 6).

Anne was aged just twenty at the time of the portrait and is revealed as an elegant, even glamorous, young Princess on the threshold of her adult life, with great prospects ahead. On the death of Charles II, her father had ascended to the throne as James II of England and VII of Scotland, with Anne as his heir presumptive. She was not the heir – that was her older sister, Mary – nor was she the heir apparent, defined as someone whose claim cannot be set aside by the birth of another. In Anne's case, if her sister Mary had a child, she would be demoted in the line of succession. This would also be the case if her father had a male child by his second wife, Mary of Modena. However, by 1685 Mary of Modena had suffered a series of miscarriages and still births, and her five children born living had all died in infancy (Catherine Laura, nine months; Isabella, four and a half years old; Charles, Duke of Cambridge, one month; a daughter, unnamed, born and died 1678; Charlotte Mary, two months). So the chances of Mary of Modena giving birth to a healthy baby boy were considered remote.

If neither Mary of Modena nor her sister Mary gave birth to another child, then it could be presumed that Anne would one day ascend the three thrones of England, Scotland and Ireland.

This, then, was the prospective Queen captured by Willem Wissing and Jan van der Vaardt in their 1685 painting. Their portrait is replete with references to Anne's role as prospective monarch and the woman who would continue the Stuart line.

At Anne's feet lies a King Charles spaniel, a symbol of fealty to the memory of her uncle, King Charles II, who had restored the Stuart dynasty. Above her left shoulder are roses, while her hand points to her stomach, both allusions to Anne's fertility and her role as a mother who would bear the children to ensure a Stuart succession.

Seventeen years after the Wissing portrait, Anne ascended the throne. The image we have of the later Queen Anne is very different from the glamorous young Princess of Denmark in 1685. Twenty years on, the Queen, as portrayed by Michael Dahl, in her fortieth year (Plate 7), looks distinctly matronly and was not particularly healthy. From then on, things only got worse for Anne.

There is an old adage: be careful what you wish, for it may be granted to you. By 1702, Queen Anne had gained the thrones of Scotland, England and Ireland, but only at the cost of splitting her own family. A house divided against itself cannot stand, and she had, unwittingly, already sowed the seeds of the destruction of the House of Stuart. She had betrayed her own father to secure the succession for herself and her children. It proved a bad bargain. Although Anne fell pregnant no less than seventeen times, not one of her children survived to full maturity.

The last of Anne's children to die was William, Duke of Gloucester, born in 1689 and carried away by smallpox aged just eleven in 1700. His death removed the last hope of a smooth Protestant Stuart succession to the British throne and precipitated a constitutional crisis. For who would now succeed Queen Anne?

The English Parliament addressed the issue of Anne's succession by passing the Act of Settlement the year after the death of the young Duke of Gloucester, prohibiting a Catholic succession and decreeing that the throne of England would pass to Sophia, Electress of Hanover, and her Protestant heirs.

This Act applied only in England. Scotland's separate parliament remained loyal to the ancient Scottish Stuart dynasty. So there arose the nightmare possibility of a fracture of the Union of the Crowns.

The solution devised by Queen Anne and her ministers was to prorogue the Scottish Parliament and unify the Scottish and English Crowns under the Act of Union of 1707. Henceforward, the identity of the King of the Scots would be determined at the Palace of Westminster. Problem solved!

Well, not quite. Not everyone in Scotland was happy with an Act that transferred the sovereign powers of the Scottish Parliament to the remote Palace of Westminster in London. A plot was hatched to depose Queen

Anne, replace her with her half-brother, James Francis Edward, and restore the Scottish Parliament.

The plan devised by James's supporters to put him on the throne involved landing 5,000 French troops in north-east Scotland, where they would support a rising by the Jacobite Highland clans and seize control of the country. The plan fell apart when the French expeditionary force was intercepted by Royal Navy vessels commanded by Admiral George Byng and forced home. A couple of months later, Anne withheld royal assent from the Scottish Militia Bill, concerned that any militia raised in Scotland might give their loyalty to James rather than to her. This was to be the last time that any British monarch vetoed a parliamentary bill.

Although the Jacobite Rising of 1708 had been thwarted, war with France over the succession to the Spanish throne dragged on. The Duke of Marlborough might be scoring Continental victories over the French, but the expenses associated with his campaigns were causing growing disquiet among the Tory squires and landowners who had to pay for them.

In October 1708, Anne's husband, Prince George of Denmark, died. It was a devastating blow. Prince George had been the one person who had shared Anne's family tragedies, suffered alongside her in the loss their children and stood by her as they both sought to recover afterwards.

Anne's closest friend and courtier Sarah, Duchess of Marlborough, was less than sympathetic, telling her to pull herself together, attend to her duties and remove her husband's portrait from her bedchamber. Sarah's intervention may have been well meant, but it did not go down well with the bereaved Queen. The two women fell out and Sarah was finally dismissed from royal service in January 1711. Not long after, the Duke of Marlborough also lost his job as commander-in-chief of the British Army and was replaced by an Irish soldier, James FitzJames Butler, 2nd Duke of Ormonde.

Butler was born in Dublin in 1665 into an old Anglo-Irish family. He was the grandson of the 1st Duke of Ormonde, who had led Irish Royalist forces against Cromwell. Butler had served in the army of King James II in putting down the Monmouth Rebellion during the summer of 1685 and succeeded to the title of Duke of Ormonde on his grandfather's death in 1688. As a new member of the House of Lords, he voted against the motion to declare that James II had abdicated and to place William of Orange and Mary on the throne in his stead. However, after the supporters of King James were outvoted, Ormonde joined the army of

William of Orange as a colonel, commanding the Queens' Troop on the Williamite side at the Battle of the Boyne in July 1690. He continued to serve as a senior officer in King William's Army and was taken prisoner fighting the French at the Battle of Landen in July 1693. The fact that he was captured on the battlefield suggests that he was in the thick of the fighting.

He was exchanged by the French for the Duke of Berwick, James II's illegitimate son, in 1694. Following his release, Ormonde was promoted to lieutenant-general. Ormonde was a Tory with Jacobite leanings and, during the period of Tory government in the early years of Queen Anne's reign, served as Lord Lieutenant of Ireland between February 1703 and April 1707.

As commander-in-chief of British forces during the last years of the Queen's reign, Ormonde was in close contact with Jacobite leaders seeking a Stuart succession to Queen Anne. His Jacobite links led to his removal from military command on the accession of King George I in 1714. In the following year, he was accused of supporting the Jacobite Rising and was impeached for High Treason in June 1715.

Some historians have expressed the opinion that he should have stayed and faced trial on the grounds that he would have been exonerated. My own view is that this would have been extremely risky, and could have ended in his execution, and that it was entirely understandable that he fled to the Continent. I would have done exactly the same in his shoes. However, the fact that he had fled was taken as *prima facie* evidence of his guilt and in August 1715 he was attainted, his estates forfeited and his honours extinguished.

His fall was spectacular and complete, and, at the age of fifty, his career as a military and political leader in Britain was at an end.

Great Britain's war with France was ended by the Treaty of Utrecht in 1713, under which King Louis XIV of France recognised the Hanoverian succession in Britain. However, Anne refused any of her Hanoverian cousins permission to visit or move to England, and the suspicion was that she was seeking to engineer the succession of her half-brother James with the help of Ormonde and other Jacobite sympathisers. However, by the time of her death that decision was not hers to make.

In later life, the tragic Queen came to believe that the death of her children, and the ill health that she had suffered throughout her reign, were curses visited upon her by the Almighty for her betrayal of her own father.

Nevertheless, I find it difficult not to feel some sympathy for Anne, who was caught up in circumstances not of her making, faced with dilemmas not of her choosing, and forced into decisions that she never wanted to take, which were to have profound consequences for her, her family and her nation.

When Anne died, the throne passed to the next Protestant claimant, her German second cousin George, Elector of Hanover, who had become the heir following the death of his mother, Sophia, two months before Queen Anne. An attempt by Anne's half-brother, James Francis Edward, to reclaim what he saw as his birthright in 1715 failed.

In any act of betrayal, and particularly family betrayal, there is likely to be a sting in the tail. So it proved. The deposed King James's elder daughter, Mary, passed away at the age of just thirty-two in 1694. Mary's husband, William of Orange, died after being thrown from his horse when it stumbled on a molehill in 1702. The last of the Stuart monarchs, Queen Anne, died in 1714, a prematurely aged and disappointed woman, leaving no heirs.

By that time, Anne had learned the bitter truth of the ancient biblical adage: 'She that troubleth her own house shall inherit the wind.'

4

Glen Sheil: the Forgotten Battle

After the failure of the Rising of 1715, James Francis Edward Stuart realised that his only hope of winning back the British throne was to secure the backing of a major European power prepared to commit significant resources to his cause.

His opportunity came in 1718, when war broke out between Spain on the one hand and the Quadruple Alliance of Great Britain, France, Imperial Austria and the Dutch Republic on the other, in a struggle for control of the Mediterranean. An attempt by Spanish forces to dislodge the British from Sicily ended disastrously in August 1718, with the Spanish Navy annihilated by Admiral Byng off Cape Passaro.

Shortly afterwards, James Francis Edward Stuart received an approach from the Chief Minister of King Philip V of Spain, Cardinal Alberoni. In October 1718, Alberoni invited the Duke of Ormonde to Madrid to mastermind an invasion of Great Britain with the aim of restoring James to the throne.

The plan they devised involved a dual attack on Britain: Ormonde would land with a force of 5,000 men in south-west England, while a Highland Army would be raised under the command of William Murray, Marquis of Tullibardine, sometimes described as the Jacobite Duke of Atholl.

Ormonde's attempt to sail to England ended in disaster in early May 1719, when his fleet encountered heavy storms off Cape Finisterre and was driven back to Spain badly damaged. However, a few Highland chieftains, including Tullibardine and his younger brother, Lord George Murray, did succeed in reaching Scotland, along with a Spanish regiment of 320 Galician regulars under the command of Lieutenant-Colonel Don Nicolas Bolaño.

The Galicians, from north-west Spain, have a dual heritage – both Spanish and, as their name suggests, of Gaelic heritage – which is why they were hand-picked by Alberoni to support the Highland expedition.

The Jacobites chose as their headquarters the castle of Eilean Donan, ancient seat of the Clan MacKenzie, located on a small tidal island in the western Highlands which commands views over three sea lochs – Loch Duich, Loch Long and Loch Alsh.

On 10 May 1719, three Royal Navy warships lying in Loch Alsh sailed up to the castle and dispatched an officer with a flag of truce to demand its surrender. His boat was refused permission to land; indeed, the MacKenzies gave their traditional greeting to those whom they wished to encourage to go forth and multiply. Firing on the Royal Navy didn't prove to be the smartest thing that the MacKenzies had ever done. The warships had several times the firepower of the castle. At about 8 p.m. on 10 May, the three ships began to bombard the castle walls, which were soon breached. A storming party then landed, and, meeting with little resistance, took the garrison's defenders prisoner and seized 300 barrels of gunpowder, most of which they kept for themselves, other than the amount required to reduce Eilean Donan to a beautiful but forlorn ruin on the Kyle of Lochalsh.

The Jacobites were now in a tight spot. Their headquarters had fallen, their access to the sea had been cut off, they had lost most of their ammunition stores, and Government forces in Scotland were being rapidly reinforced. On 5 June 1719, the Hanoverian Major-General Joseph Wightman marched from Inverness with a force of approximately 1,100 men to engage Tullibardine's Jacobite Army. Wightman's army was supported by artillery in the form of four light Coehorn mortars.

The Jacobites decided to wait for Wightman in Glen Shiel at a location where the road crosses the River Shiel by a stone bridge. On the afternoon of 10 June, the two armies came in sight of each other about half a mile apart. Wightman halted and deployed his troops in preparation for an attack.

What happened next is captured in a painting of the battle by Flemish painter Peter Tillemans (Plate 8). It is a very fine artwork, but more importantly, for expository purposes, it is an outstanding work of military draftsmanship. Tillemans has reduced to just two dimensions the four dimensions of height, breadth, depth and time – for the events depicted did not all happen contemporaneously.

The most obvious point to note about the Tillemans painting is that we are observing the battle from a Hanoverian perspective. We are standing behind the redcoat lines, looking across to the Jacobites, who are depicted as the enemy. The hero of the painting, just slightly off centre, is the Hanoverian commander Major-General Joseph Wightman, seen with his sword aloft, urging on his troops. Alongside him is his second-in-command, Colonel Jasper Clayton (Acting Brigadier at the time of the battle), a trusted confidante alongside whom Wightman had served at the Battle of Sheriffmuir three and a half years earlier.

Anticipating the imminent arrival of Government forces, the Jacobites had spent 9 June building a strong defensive formation.

As shown in the Tillemans painting, the Jacobite centre was naturally protected by the River Shiel to its right and a ravine to its left, while to the front the terrain is rugged and steep, affording natural protection against a redcoat advance. Added to this, the Jacobites had built barricades in the form of dry-stone walls to waist height, protecting their troops while optimising their firing positions. This was the position held by the Galician Regiment of approximately 300 regulars under Lieutenant-Colonel Bolaño which formed the core of the Jacobites' central defence.

Before the event commemorating the 300th anniversary of the battle in June 2019, I climbed the hill to position myself behind one of the walls and scan the valley below. Had I been a soldier in the Galician Regiment lying flat, musket trained on the enemy, in June 1719, I would have felt very confident indeed, observing Wightman's troops advancing below me. The position gives a superb panorama of the valley and provides a commanding position for any soldier firing on enemy troops advancing up the hill towards them.

However, I would only have felt this confidence until I became aware of the power of the enemy's mortars.

To the left of the Galician position, as shown in the Tillemans painting, on the hill known as Sgurr a'Chuilinn, or Crag of Holly, were positioned 150 MacKenzies under the command of Lord George Murray.

To the right, positioned on the hill known as Sgurr na Ciste Dhuibhe, stood 250 Seaforth MacKenzies under the Earl of Seaforth.

In support in the second line were 150 Camerons under Lochiel, 150 Glengarry MacDonalds, eighty MacGregors led by Rob Roy MacGregor and eighty men of the Clan MacKinnon.

This, then, was the formidable crescent-shaped defence that faced General Wightman when he arrived at Glen Shiel.

To make a direct advance against such a defensive formation would have been little short of suicidal. Wightman's redcoats would have been shot at by Lord George's men to their left, strafed by the Seaforths to their right, and faced relentless fire from the Galician Regiment and the other forces dug in behind barricades in the centre.

So, what was Wightman to do? Well, we know exactly what he did from his account of the particulars of the engagement sent by him from Glen Shiel on 11 June 1719: 'About four in the afternoon, I came up within a mile of the rebel's camp, at a place called Glensheels, such a strong pass that is hardly to be paralleled; I took about an hour to view their situation.'

So, for an hour Wightman did absolutely nothing. As you would expect of a man commended by no less an authority than the Duke of Marlborough as 'a very careful and diligent officer', he assessed the position like a chess grandmaster faced with a particularly complex and difficult problem – how to crack his opponent's apparently impregnable defensive formation.

And then he made his decision.

He writes in his account: 'Without loss of a moment, I made my disposition. About five I began the attack, which lasted about three hours and a half of continual fire and hazardous dispute.'

The battle plan that Major-General Wightman had devised was based on the principle of divide and rule. First of all, he attacked Lord George Murray's position. Instead of a full frontal onslaught, this was his initial move in picking off each of the Jacobite units in turn. He utilised his four portable mortars to lob high explosives into the air, beginning with a bombardment against the most exposed Jacobite division on the Sgurr a'Chuilinn, and sending his men to advance up the hill against them.

To begin with, Lord George succeeded in fending off their attack. Wightman then sent in further reinforcements, the Munros, so that Lord George was now heavily outnumbered.

Why did Tullibardine not also deploy reinforcements to help his younger brother? It is a question that remains unanswered in Tullibardine's rather bland account of the battle. Applying the Occam's Razor principle – that in the absence of any other evidence one should accept the simplest and most obvious explanation for any event – one suspects that the reason was that Tullibardine simply wasn't a very nimble battlefield commander and was caught flat-footed by Wightman's dynamic battle plan. Accounts of Tullibardine's character describe him as a most affable gentleman. Translated into the vernacular, I interpret this as implying that he wasn't the brightest of individuals, and certainly lacked sharp military intelligence of his younger brother, Lord George Murray.

By this time, the shells shot from the Coehorn mortars had set fire to the dry bracken on the crag, blinding the Jacobites with smoke so that they could not clearly see their enemies approaching. Worse still, Lord George himself received a deep leg wound in a third attack from an exploding mortar shell and was finally forced to withdraw.

The character of Lord George Murray, which Tillemans captures so well in his depiction – his raw courage, his stubbornness, his desire always to lead his men from the front and his resolute refusal to retreat, even in the face of relentless enemy fire, until, so badly wounded, he could fight on no more – which made Lord George such an outstanding, and indeed inspiring, battlefield commander, also made him, to be perfectly frank, sometimes a rather difficult individual with whom to work outside of battlefield conditions, as Prince Charles Edward Stuart was to discover.

But, as Lord George Murray limped off the battlefield of Glen Shiel to live to fight another day, all that lay in the future.

Having dislodged Lord George Murray's division, Wightman now turned his attention to the MacKenzies under the Earl of Seaforth on the Sgurr na Ciste Dhuibhe, the outermost peak of the mountain range. Seaforth called for reinforcements, and Rob Roy's MacGregors moved in to reinforce him, but by this time Seaforth's men were retreating under intensive shelling and the Earl himself was badly wounded in the arm. The Sgurr na Ciste Dhuibhe translates as 'the Crag of the Black Coffin', and it did indeed almost become a black coffin for Seaforth, who was forced to withdraw under heavy fire.

Only now did Wightman redeploy his mortars to attack the Jacobite centre. His troops formed a pincer movement converging on the centre from each flank. The Galicians held firm against this pincer movement and successfully covered the retreat of the Highland regiments. But why were the Galicians the last Jacobite Regiment to leave the field? Was it because they were the bravest, most professional and most disciplined?

Well, it may be the case that, as regular soldiers, the Galicians were more disciplined than the Highlanders. However, it must also be remembered that the Galician Regiment had a very different risk–return profile than the Highlanders. The Galicians were professional soldiers in the service of the King of Spain, a sovereign nation at war with Great Britain and, as such, if they were captured they would be treated as prisoners of war. By contrast, if captured, the Highlanders would have been treated as traitors and faced execution.

Once the Highlanders were safely off the field, the Galician Regiment retreated across what is known to this day as Beulach-na-Spainnteach – Spaniard's Pass.

In his account of the battle, Wightman wrote:

> Towards the end of the action, I observed some Spaniards left in the Pass to defend it, which obstructed our finishing the affair . . . The Highlanders were better climbing the rocks than we were in their retreat, so that we have few if any prisoners except the Spanish Captain and their physician.

Of course, Wightman's statement is the truth, but is it the whole truth? I wonder.

It is certainly true that the redcoats failed to capture any of the fleeing Highlanders, and Wightman's story that they were simply quicker and nimbler than his men across the rocks conveniently absolved him from any possible accusations of dereliction of duty in failing to take prisoners. But, at the very least, one must conclude that his men showed no great enthusiasm in chasing after them. So much so that one wonders whether they really wanted to capture them at all.

It would appear that Wightman wasn't prepared to risk much loss of life in the effort. If his men pursued the retreating Highlanders into the hills, they would be in mortal danger of being taken out by snipers, as Bonnie Dundee had been after Killiecrankie a few years previously. And even if they succeeded in capturing a few stragglers and executing them, what strategic advantage would be served? The grass grows green on the battlefield, but not on the scaffold. It is not the fate of those who fall on the field of battle that leaves a legacy of bitterness, rather the summary execution of prisoners of war and innocent civilians who pose no threat at all. Whether by accident or design, Wightman avoided this risk by the simple contrivance of failing to lay a finger on a single Highlander.

Luckily for Wightman, the Government officials, safe in their offices back in London, were not inclined to ask too many questions about how he had failed to capture a single Highlander. After all, their strategic objective had been achieved. The following day, 274 Galicians under the command of Lieutenant-Colonel Don Nicolas Bolaño formally surrendered and were taken to Edinburgh Castle for imprisonment. Four months later, they were put on a ship in Leith and sailed back to Spain. The Rising of 1719 was at an end.

So, what final conclusions can be drawn from the story of the Rising of 1719 and the Battle of Glen Shiel?

Don't fight wars you cannot win. The moment that the Marquis of Tullibardine learned that Ormonde's expedition had ended in failure, he should have dispersed his forces and sent the Galician Regiment back to Spain. There was no way from then on that the Jacobites had any hope of winning the war. In such circumstances, the best option is to cut your losses and live to fight another day.

In any battle, unity is strength. As the saying goes, 'United we stand, divided we fall.' Tullibardine's strategic error in continuing his campaign was compounded by his inadequacies as a battlefield tactician. Although the Jacobites' initial defensive deployment at Glen Shiel was sound, they then failed to adapt to Wightman's tactics. While the Government forces were under Wightman's unified command, as Tillemans' painting shows, the Jacobites operated as multiple separate units – Lord George Murray's men on the Jacobite right, the Earl of Seaforth's men on the left, the Galician Regiment in the centre, and the clan regiments supporting them all acted independently at the battle, with little co-ordination between them. At no point did the Jacobites deploy as a single, coherent, integrated army, and Wightman was able to exploit these divisions between the different Jacobite regiments very effectively.

Never be a pawn in someone else's game. As has happened so often in history, the Highlanders were treated as expendable cannon fodder to be sacrificed in someone else's political interests – in this case, those of the King of Spain. It seems likely that many of them realised this, and this may help to explain why their resistance crumbled after Lord George's position had been lost.

A victory is only complete if it leaves no lasting legacy of bitterness. Here, wherever one's personal sympathies may lie, one must commend the constraint and discipline of the Hanoverian Government forces in victory. Unlike the 'Butcher' Cumberland after Culloden, they did not pursue a scorched earth policy of vengeance and slaughter. Instead, they followed the precepts of just war laid down by St Augustine and St Thomas Aquinas many centuries before, applying proportionate force in achieving their objectives. The result was that military casualties were relatively light – just twenty-five dead and 139 wounded on the Government side, according to the official list. We don't know how many casualties there were on the

Jacobite side. If you had been a Jacobite soldier wounded at Glen Shiel, it would not have been a good idea to go around advertising that fact, with the redcoats combing the mountains looking for you! Nevertheless, most historians conclude that the Jacobite casualties were, if anything, even less than on the Government side. There were no civilian deaths and little collateral damage. After Glen Shiel, the volatile and turbulent Highlands of Scotland enjoyed a quarter of a century of relative peace, with law and order maintained within their territories by great clan chieftains like Simon Fraser, Lord Lovat, who at that stage in his long and picaresque career was a loyal supporter of King George.

The ultimate credit for Glen Shiel must rest with the commander of the Government army that day. Today, people passing the great Tillemans painting that hangs in the Scottish National Portrait Gallery may briefly pause to appreciate its melancholy splendour and wonder how it was that such an important battle came to be fought in such a remote and hostile environment 300 years ago, knowing little about the men who fought there, or why they fought, or what became of them. Few will know anything at all about the leader of the victorious army that day, even his name. But perhaps, all things considered, Peter Tillemans and the grateful Hanoverian Government officials who commissioned his painting were not so very wrong when they made Major-General Joseph Wightman the hero of their story.

While circumstances change, the choices we face as human beings do not.

If a victorious leader treats those he has defeated with restraint and respect, as Wightman did, he can lay the foundations of rapprochement and peace. However, if a victorious leader acts like a criminal in seeking vengeance as Cumberland did, then he will leave a legacy of enduring bitterness and resentment.

As Shakespeare observed:

The evil that men do lives after them;
the good is oft interred in their bones.

5

Queen Clementina's Cavinet

What was going on in the mind of James Francis Edward Stuart after the failure of the Rising of 1719? His birth had been the cause of his own father's fall from power and flight into exile. Imagine how that knowledge would have made a young boy feel.

He had then lost his father when he was just twelve years of age. Not yet a teenager, he is elevated to the status of 'the King over the Water', bearing the hopes of all who wish to see a Jacobite restoration, a terrible burden to place on a young boy.

Then, just as he reaches adulthood in 1712, he loses his sister, Princess Louisa, his closest friend and confidante, to smallpox.

As a young man, he and his supporters seek to regain the throne from those they regard as usurpers, in 1708, 1715 and then again in 1719. All three attempts end in abject failure.

Little wonder, then, that he is nicknamed 'Old Miseriguts' and 'Old Mr Misfortune' – and those are just two of the gentler epithets ascribed to this rather depressed and pessimistic figure, carrying so much baggage as he enters his thirties, still unmarried.

In a 1719 portrait by Italian painter Francesco Trevisani (Plate 11), there is a faraway look in James's eyes and a rather sad expression on his face, as if he is already detached from the role that he has been called by fate to play. Perhaps he is already resigned to the possibility that he will never fulfil the hopes and dreams of his followers. Would his final failure be to die unmarried, leaving no heirs, the last of the Stuart line?

His Counsellors are desperate to find him a bride and, at last, that same year they find a young lady who is deemed a suitable match. Princess Maria Clementina Sobieska is captured in a fine portrait also by Trevisani, dating from 1719, the partner to the portrait of her future spouse (Plate 12).

'So, James Edward Stuart, what first attracted you to millionaire Clementina Sobieska?'

It is not difficult to work out the answer. James had never actually met Clementina before they wed. This was a dynastic marriage, bringing together the exiled House of Stuart and the immensely wealthy Sobieski dynasty of Poland. 'Whom political expediency has joined together, let no man put asunder!'

The immediate impression of the Trevisani portrait of Clementina, aged just seventeen, is of an attractive and, above all, a very wealthy young lady, dressed in beautiful clothing adorned with jewels. And of all the jewels she wears, the most remarkable is the ruby pinned into her hair directly above the centre of her forehead (Plate 12).

It calls to mind the biblical proverb (King James version, naturally):

Who can find a virtuous woman?
For her price is far above rubies.

This is not just any ruby. This is the Great Ruby of Poland, a ruby of such exquisite quality and beauty that it was unrivalled in Christendom; indeed, it was an icon of the very survival of Christendom. For this is the legendary Sobieski Ruby – the ruby won by Clementina's grandfather, King Jan III of Poland, from the leader of the Ottoman Turks, whom he defeated at the Siege of Vienna in 1683, when he was hailed by the Pope himself as the Saviour of Christendom.

For all her wealth, Maria Clementina is not a free woman. She is not free to choose her husband. She is an asset to be traded in the market of international politics, sold to the most promising bidder in a dynastic alliance.

And that bidder was James Edward Stuart, now aged thirty-two, almost twice the age of his young bride.

'Those who do not remember the past are condemned to relive it,' wrote Santayana. It is perhaps unfortunate that, almost three centuries later, others did not recall that this marriage between an older, rather introverted prince and a much younger bride with very different interests did not bring either of them any great happiness.

*   *   *

Their marriage on 3 September 1719, just three months after the Battle of Glen Shiel, is commemorated and celebrated in a major painting by Agostino Masucci (Plate 13). The most significant point to note about this commemoration of the marriage of James and Clementina is that it was not painted in 1719. It was, in fact, commissioned by James in 1735, sixteen years after the marriage.

By that time Clementina was dead.

As to why it was commissioned, no one can be absolutely sure. It was no doubt partly in homage to his late wife. But it could also have been inspired by a sense of guilt. Perhaps an attempt by James to portray the marriage as a successful alliance, which was very far from being the case.

Clementina fulfilled her principal duty as James's consort in producing an heir – Prince Charles Edward Stuart, born in 1720 in Rome.*

Prince Charles's younger brother, Henry Benedict, was born in 1725.

However, shortly after Henry's birth the marriage broke down and Clementina fled from the court to find sanctuary in a convent. James's supporters placed the blame for the marital breakdown squarely on Clementina. She was suffering from post-natal depression, they said, and had always been a highly strung and at times almost hysterical woman. What they did not mention is that Clementina had a number of legitimate grievances against her husband.

A devout Catholic, she was unhappy that he had entrusted Charles's education to Protestant tutors, and, more seriously, Clementina was unhappy with James's relationship with the woman standing behind them in Masucci's painting of the solemnisation of their marriage – Marjorie Hay – the wife of one of James's leading courtiers, the Earl of Inverness, and sister of another, the Earl of Dunbar. Clementina may even have suspected her husband of infidelity.

There is no evidence that James had a physical affair with Majorie Hay, however what is undoubtedly true is that he had a far closer rapport with Marjorie Hay than with his own wife, securing from her emotional support that he never got from Clementina. There were three people in the marriage – and, as far as Clementina was concerned, that was one too many.

The crisis came to a head in 1725, when James removed Clementina's

* Charles's date of birth is generally recorded as being 31 December 1720, according to the New Style (NS) Gregorian calendar, which had been adopted in Rome more than a century before. The date of his birth in the Old Style Julian calendar, then in use in Great Britain, and which is used to date all other events in this account, would have been 20 December 1720.

closest confidant, Mrs Sheldon, as the governess of Prince Charles and replaced her with Marjorie Hay's brother, the Earl of Dunbar.

Alone and isolated in a foreign land, no longer on speaking terms with her husband, and with her closest friend and confidante now expelled, Clementina fled from the court to the Convent of St Cecilia, where she was reunited with Mrs Sheldon. From there, Clementina wrote to her sister to explain what had happened:

> I am in such a cruel situation, that I had rather suffer death than live in the King's Palace with persons that have no religion, honour nor conscience, and who, not content with having been authors of so fateful a separation between the King and me, are continually pressing him every day to part with his best friends and most faithful subjects.

To help her through this difficult time, Clementina created a work of art, a Cavinet or devotional image (Plate 10), dedicated to the Sacred Heart of Jesus and Mary. It is small, showing a remarkable delicacy and attention to detail in its execution. It's so small that perhaps it was intended to mark a page in her missal or Bible, highlighting a passage to give her guidance through her time of troubles in the Convent of St Cecilia.

In those faraway days before the age of psychoanalysis, medication or pills, men and women had to find different ways of dealing with crises in their lives. Clementina used the power of prayer, and created her devotional image as a source of comfort and inspiration.

The Sacred Heart is one of the most powerful motifs in Christianity, a universal symbol of unconditional love and the foundation of life. The Sacred Heart of Jesus on the left is encased in a crown of thorns, recalling that mockingly placed upon the brow of Jesus. The Immaculate Heart of Mary on the right is pierced by a lance, recalling that which pierced Christ as he was dying on the cross. Above both hearts is the symbol of the cross on which Jesus was crucified on Mount Calvary. The two hearts are surrounded by shining light and framed by a wreath of eight red roses. Below the image, Clementina has written '*Cor Jesu, Cor M*' (Heart of Jesus, Heart of Mary). On the reverse are the words:

> *Prego la Cara Mar di racomandar la figlia nel lo cor di Jesu et di Maria.*
> I pray to Dear Mary to recommend her daughter to the sacred heart of Jesus and Mary.

After more than two years, following the intervention of the Pope, Clementina returned to her husband on her own terms, when James agreed to dismiss the three courtiers whom Clementina believed had been responsible for the rift in their marriage.

Thereafter, Clementina dedicated her life to religious devotion, fasting, and good works among the poor, the infirm and the dispossessed of Rome. Clementina never did become Queen of any earthly realm. She passed away in January 1735 at the age of just thirty-three, her early death possibly accelerated by her ascetic lifestyle and frequent fasts. Other accounts state that she died of tuberculosis.

Her funeral procession was attended by several thousand mourners and she was laid to rest in the vault of St Peter's Basilica in the Vatican. Pope Benedict XIV commissioned Pietro Bracci to sculpt a monument to her memory, showing Clementina being cast up to heaven by cherubs. The sculpture was placed in the Basilica, at the heart of the Vatican, where it can be seen to this day.

6

Keeping the Flame Alive

When Prince Charles Edward Stuart was born in 1720, it was said that a new star had appeared in the firmament above Rome. To be more precise, it was said by *Jacobite courtiers* that a new star had appeared. Strange to relate, no such observation was recorded by independent astronomers or scientists.

The story of the new star is, of course, so much moonshine. It formed part of a well-organised campaign presenting Charles as the rightful heir to the throne, sustained by a steady stream of stories and portraits of the Prince and his younger brother, Henry Benedict, from their birth in the 1720s through their youth and adolescence during the 1730s and into the 1740s.

In his book *The King Over the Water*, Professor Edward Corp writes: 'The portraits were an essential ingredient in a long campaign of political propaganda which the exiled Jacobite court maintained without a break from 1689 until the late 1740s.'

He goes on to observe: 'Most people in England and Scotland would not have seen the oil portraits themselves, but there were a very large number of popular prints derived for mass circulation from these original images.'

Thus, the portraits helped keep alive the memory of the exiled Stuart dynasty for their supporters in Great Britain and reinforced the hope that one day the King Over the Water might return.

The 1725 painting of the baptism of Prince Charles by Antonio David (Plate 14) has an almost religious aspect about it, recalling paintings of the *Adoration of the Magi* at the birth of Christ. It represents Prince Charles as the great hope for the future, a man of destiny born to rule. His father by this time cut a rather pessimistic figure, debilitated by fissures in his marriage to Clementina and his three failed attempts to reclaim the throne. The hopes of many Jacobite supporters increasingly focused on his older son. Reports from Rome, as he grew from childhood to adolescence, represented Charles as a young man blessed with energy and intelligence, who was developing into a competent hunter, swordsman and soldier.

In a presentation to the 1745 Association in Rome in 2015, Professor Corp made the point that earlier portraits of Prince Charles Edward Stuart emphasised his claim to the English throne but made little allusion to his claim to the throne of Scotland. It is only as he reaches maturity that he is represented as a Scottish Prince.

Thus, in the pair of portraits of Prince Charles and Prince Henry, dating from 1732, by Antonio David (Plates 16 and 17), which today hang in the Scottish National Portrait Gallery in Edinburgh, the two Princes are shown with the garter sash across their coats, proclaiming their membership of the English Order of the Garter, and below the Garter can be seen the Cross of St George, patron saint of England. Similarly, the pair of portraits dating from 1737 by Jean-Etienne Liotard prominently display the Garter and also the English Cross of St George pinned over Prince Charlie's heart.

By contrast, the William Mossman portrait of Prince Charlie, which dates from the 1740s, shows him dressed in a tartan coat with a blue bonnet decked with a white cockade, the unifying emblem of his Jacobite Army. So, in the portraits of Prince Charlie as a boy, commissioned by his father, he is shown as an English Prince, whereas in the portraits of him as a man he is represented as a Scottish Prince. By the early 1740s, it would appear that the Prince regarded himself not primarily as an English Prince but as Scottish, as the idea began to germinate in his mind that the road to a Stuart Restoration lay through Scotland rather than England.

*　　*　　*

The Jacobite flame in Great Britain was also kept alive through the Jacobite Clubs, remembered today primarily through the glasses with which their members raised their post-prandial toasts to the cause.

Prior to 1675, glass was a rare and expensive luxury, mostly imported from the Continent, designed *à la façon de Venise* and manufactured from fragile soda glass, which shattered easily unless handled with considerable care.

The growth of a distinct English glassmaking industry dates from 1674, when George Ravenscroft discovered that the addition of lead oxide to traditional Venetian glass considerably enhanced its solidity and durability, producing a lead crystal suitable for engraving.

Eighteenth-century English glassmakers separately produced a bowl, stem and floor (base), which were then moulded together to create a single glass. An alternative method involved manufacturing a trumpet-shaped bowl and stem blown as a single unit, which was then melted with the base to complete the glass.

The earliest English glasses were heavy baroque balusters commonly dated to the reign of Queen Anne. Perhaps reflecting their scarcity and cost, these were used rather like chalices today, as communal drinking vessels to be passed around after the main meal, with each diner taking a sip.

As the eighteenth century progressed, English glasses became smaller. Wine glasses had a standard capacity of 75 ml, compared to today's standard glass of 175 ml, and were designed for use by a single drinker. The gradual change in drinking habits from communal to individual consumption was not universally popular. My friend Peter Lole, whom I succeeded as treasurer of the 1745 Association in 2005 and who was one of the world's leading authorities on Jacobite glass, was fond of telling the story of a disgruntled mid-eighteenth-century connoisseur who grumbled, 'How standards have declined! In Queen Anne's day, we drank twelve bottles a night from but a single glass; now, under King George, we drink but a single bottle from twelve glasses!'

The development of Jacobite glass as a distinct subset of eighteenth-century English glass is associated with the growth of the Jacobite Clubs, a loose network of groups of gentlemen of status and influence within their local communities who shared a common desire to see the restoration of King James. They met at regular intervals to exchange information and intelligence over dinner, followed by toasts to the 'King over the Water' and other members of the exiled Stuart dynasty. For this purpose, many clubs commissioned glasses engraved with Jacobite symbols, most commonly the Jacobite six-petalled white rose and the 'stricken oak', recalling Charles II's refuge in the Boscobel oak after his defeat at the Battle of Worcester.

In total, Peter estimated that between 1,500 and 2,000 Jacobite glasses have survived to this day, which he classified (see Figure 1).

Peter challenged a common misconception that such a Club evening

Figure 1: Classification of Jacobite glasses.

Type	Number
Amen glasses*	36
Portrait glasses	100
Glasses engraved with a Rose alone	450
Glasses engraved with a Rose and FIAT	350**
Glasses engraved with a Rose and other emblems	450
Glasses engraved with other emblems (but not a Rose)	350

*Since Peter published this analysis in the 1990s, a further Amen glass has been discovered, bringing the total number of Amen glasses known to be in existence at the time of writing to 37.
**FIAT glasses were associated particularly with the Cycle of the White Rose, the most famous of the Jacobite clubs, formed in Wrexham on White Rose Day, 10 June 1710. It moved its headquarters to Wynnstay in or shortly after 1720.

would end with its members roaring drunk. His thinking was as follows. A typical Club evening might comprise a dozen diners, each of whom would be called upon to raise a toast after the meal. So each member may drink twelve toasts, each a maximum of 75 ml, the standard capacity of a wine glass of the day. In fact, the average toast would be less than this, as the glass might be no more than half full, or the toast might be drawn from a squat 'firing glass', so-called because its strong base could be rapped on the table to make a noise like a gun being shot to signal the drinker's approbation for the toast raised. So a drinker imbibing a full twelve toasts would consume perhaps the equivalent of two-thirds of a bottle of wine on a full stomach after a good dinner. Plus, the alcoholic content of wine in the 1740s would likely be less than today. So, by the end of the evening, the loyal Jacobites would be pleasantly merry rather than blind drunk and more than capable of calling for their carriages home in good humour, reassured by the fellowship they had enjoyed that the cause was still alive and kicking.

Peter's research, building on pre-war research by Muriel Steevenson, identified a total of 143 separate Jacobite Clubs operating at some time during the eighteenth century. Of these, forty-seven were in the north-west of England and thirteen in Scotland, of which nine were in Edinburgh, the centre of Jacobite support in the Lowlands.

When they were put to the test in 1745, however, the Clubs played little part in mobilising support for the Rising. Sir Watkin Williams Wynn, Tory MP for Denbighshire and founder of the Cycle Club, was conveniently absent from his constituency. He was on parliamentary business in London when the Jacobite Army marched south from Manchester and thus unable to raise his Welsh Jacobites for the cause. Peter's conclusion was that Sir Watkin was deliberately keeping his head down and waiting to see how things would play out.

After the failure of the Rising, Prince Charles was reported to have caustically observed, 'I shall do as much for those gentlemen as they have ever done for me – and drink to their good health!'

Auction catalogues today typically date engraved Jacobite glasses as 'circa 1750', implying that most Jacobite glass was commissioned after the Rising as a sort of sentimental reflex. This is misleading, and fails to distinguish – as Peter, Geoffrey Seddon and other authorities on Jacobite glass do – between glasses engraved prior to 1747, commissioned when there was real hope of a Stuart Restoration, and those that post-date 1747, when the prospects of a Restoration had considerably diminished.

Dr Seddon makes a convincing case that most Jacobite glasses manufactured before 1747 were engraved by five identifiable individuals working in London, who between them accounted on his estimate for approximately 60 per cent of all surviving Jacobite glass. In *The Jacobites and their Drinking Glasses*, Dr Seddon observes:

> Jacobite engraving (by these five engravers) came to an abrupt end in 1746–47. A state of near martial law existed, and whether there was an official visit to individual glass sellers advising them of the likely consequences if Jacobite engravings continued to appear, or whether the engravers themselves became nervous as heads started to appear on the spikes of Temple Bar, may never be known. However, something occurred which caused all five of the major engravers to stop producing Jacobite glasses.

The 40 per cent of glasses which post-date 1746 were engraved by different individuals whom Seddon does not attempt to identify, and, from an historical viewpoint, are less interesting than those engraved before or during the Rising. For that reason, I would encourage auction houses to make more effort to offer a catalogue opinion as to whether a Jacobite glass is pre- or post-1747.

It is not difficult to distinguish between the two. In addition to the engraving, there are two other indicators. The first is style of the glass, with a clear distinction between the heavier, plainer glasses manufactured before the 1745–46 Glass Excise Act and lighter glasses manufactured afterwards, sometimes with an enamel stem not liable to the new excise duty. The other indicator is weight. A comparison of a pre-1747 trumpet-bowled glass with a plain stem and a post-1747 bucket-bowled glass with an opaque air-twist stem revealed that the former weighed 213 grams (7.5 oz), while the latter weighed just 150 grams (5.3 oz).

The 1745–46 Glass Excise Act was introduced by the Hanoverian Government as a means of generating additional revenues to pay for its Continental wars and the army raised to quell the Jacobite Rising. The new duty was levied at a rate of a penny per pound (lb) of glass. The move towards lighter stems and smaller bowls post-1746 was a response by glass manufacturers to reduce the amount of tax they had to pay. Based on the weights given above, the tax that would be saved on a commission of a dozen glasses would be a full two pennies. In the values of the day, this was a significant saving. As a point of reference, the pay of an ordinary infantry soldier at that time was between 6d and 8d a day.

Peter's view was that owning a standard Jacobite glass decorated with a six-petalled rose or stricken oak would not in reality have posed a great risk for its owner, particularly after 1750, and indeed he could find no record of anyone ever having been tried for mere possession of such a glass. As the Prince himself observed, their owners seemed unlikely in practice to do anything more than raise a toast to the increasingly unlikely return of the King over the Water, so they hardly posed a threat to State security.

The Amen glasses were a different matter. These glasses are engraved not with subtle Jacobite symbols, such as roses, stars and oak trees, but with words explicitly calling for the overthrow of the House of Hanover and the restoration of King James. Peter wrote:

> The main purpose of these glasses is to honour James VIII, and they all carry his cipher, surrounded by a royal crown and followed by the word AMEN. Most of them have two, three or occasionally four verses of the Jacobite National Anthem and all are engraved in diamond point . . . which calls for considerable calligraphic skills; they seem to date from the 1740s.

He concluded: 'The Amen glasses are virtually the only form of Jacobite glass that are so explicit in their support for King James VIII as to be legally treasonable.'

There are a total of thirty-seven Amen glasses of established provenance in existence today, of which thirty-five are separately listed and described in *The Jacobites and their Drinking Glasses* and a further two validated subsequent to its publication, including the Gask Amen glass. Peter regarded the finest surviving example as the Traquair Amen glass, which, he wrote, 'with its dedication of *Prosperity to the family of TRAQUAIR* is the only Amen glass to remain today in its true and original home.' He noted that he could find no Bill of Sale for this glass, but stated that this was understandable, as the engraver – believed to be the same individual for all thirty-seven Amen glasses – would not have wished to leave any evidence of his identity that could be traced by Hanoverian law enforcement agents.

The last glass which Peter acquired was at the Lyon & Turnbull Scottish silver auction of August 2017. As a discerning collector, he was not interested in replicating examples of glasses already in his collection. I submitted a successful bid for a classic rose-engraved pre-1747 glass, for which Peter did not bid, as it was similar to a glass already in his collection. He did, however, put in a successful offer for a more unusual item engraved with a sunflower. As ever, I benefited from his observations on the features and quality of the different glasses up for auction.

He passed away in November 2018 and I then put together this synthesis of his thoughts, papers and articles on Jacobite glass to provide a record of his advice and insights on a fascinating and important manifestation of Jacobite support.

Peter's entire Jacobite collection was sold through Bonhams' Scottish Auction the following year and I acquired a 1719 Clementina medal from it, a valued memento both of the Jacobite Queen and my old friend (Plate 9).

The front of the medal shows Clementina as Queen and is engraved with the words '*Clementina M Britan Fr et Hib Regina*' (Clementina, Queen of Great Britain, France and Ireland). The reverse shows Clementina triumphantly arriving in Rome in a chariot, Boudicca-like, and is engraved with the words '*Fortunam Causamque Sequor*' (I follow the fate of the cause).

*　　*　　*

Despite the fracture in her marriage, Clementina remained close to both her sons, and particularly close to her elder son, Charles. He was only just fourteen when his mother passed away on 18 January 1735. It is recorded that during the days following her death, 'the Princes were both sick with weeping and want of sleep'.

The pair of portraits by Jean-Etienne Liotard of Prince Charles and Prince Henry, painted in 1735, not long after her passing, tell us little of their emotional reaction to their mother's early death.

The absence of emotion is entirely deliberate. These portraits are not intended to reveal the character of Charles and Henry; they are works of propaganda in which the princes are mannequins playing a role, the role of legitimate heirs to the throne of England, as symbolised by the Garter sash and cross of St George, and the throne of Scotland, symbolically represented by the thistle.

There they dutifully sit, as directed by their father, playing their role as royal princes, giving little away about what they are thinking. And yet, each of them sought to fulfil the legacy of their dead mother in their own way.

Most obviously, Prince Henry. He followed his mother's religious vocation, becoming the longest-serving Cardinal in the 2,000-year history of the Roman Catholic Church. In the end, in 1797, Prince Henry sacrificed the Sobieski Ruby itself – his mother's most valuable material possession, passed down to him after his father's death – to try and save the Vatican, where she is interred, and the Church to whose highest principles she, and he, dedicated their lives, and which, for Prince Henry Benedict Stuart, did indeed have a value far above rubies.

Henry gave the ruby to Pope Pius VI as part of a tribute that the Pope paid to Napoleon Bonaparte to prevent him from sacking Rome. Napoleon took the tribute, and the ruby disappeared forever from history, its fate unknown. My guess is that it fell into the hands of lapidaries who cut it into smaller pieces to disguise its origins prior to onward resale. If I am correct, we will never see the Sobieski Ruby again.

Alas, Henry's sacrifice was in vain. In the following year, Bonaparte sacked Rome anyway, imprisoned Pope Pius, who died shortly afterwards in French captivity, and forced Prince Henry, Cardinal York, to flee from Rome to Venice. He was saved from utter penury only by the intervention of Cardinal Borgia, who helped to secure a pension for him from King George of England.

So, in a bizarre twist of fate, the last of the Stuarts was saved from destitution by a combination of the Borgias and the Hanoverians. Who would ever have thought that they would turn out as the good guys at the end?

But what of Clementina's elder son, Charles Edward Stuart?

Psychologists say that children who lose a parent, and perhaps particularly their mother, during adolescence may be vulnerable to anxiety, depression and a range of other problems later in life because of the intense feelings of loss and fear that they experience as a result.

In 2017, the current Prince Henry (more familiarly known as Prince Harry) reflected on the twentieth anniversary of the death of his mother, Princess Diana, when he was just twelve years old, even younger than Prince Charles Edward Stuart when he lost his mother.

Losing his mother had, said Prince Harry, resulted in him 'shutting down all my emotions for the last twenty years . . . My way of dealing with it was sticking my head in the sand and refusing to ever think about my mum, because why would that help? It's not going to bring her back . . . There was all this grief I'd never processed. So from an emotional side, I said, right, don't ever let your emotions be part of anything.'

Prince Harry was able to speak about his emotions, but during the very different environment of the eighteenth century I have been able to find no record of Prince Charles ever speaking about his mother after her death. It is as if Clementina had never existed. She had been airbrushed out of his existence.

Prince Charles appears to have done what Prince Harry said he did: he suppressed the memory of his dead mother, trying never to think of her, because the memory would be too painful. Instead, he tried to deal with his grief by channelling his energies into doing something positive – seeking to right what he saw as an historic injustice and reclaim the British throne for his father.

And he used the jewels that his mother left him – the diamonds in which she is adorned in Trevisani's 1719 portrait – as collateral to raise funding for his expedition.

He is impatient for action. Even Prince Charlie's most ardent supporter would acknowledge that his venture was extremely high risk; indeed, it is the most audacious attempt in history to seize the British throne. Others might say it was reckless, as if he was driven by a fear that time was not on his side, that everything might suddenly be taken away from him, as his mother was.

He did not seek approval for his expedition from his father or the King of France. Why? Because he already knew what their answer would be – he would be told to wait until circumstances were more propitious, until the tide turned in his favour and he had more support.

But Prince Charlie didn't want to wait. He feared that the time would never be right, as far as his father and King Louis were concerned.

Life was too short, as his mother had proved.

And, at first, events seem to vindicate his decision.

PLATE 1. King James I of England and VI of Scotland by Daniel Mytens, 1621
The National Portrait Gallery, London

Mytens' 1621 painting portrays King James as a calm father figure, whose dress and posture suggests a man who seeks to govern by rule of law rather than force of arms, offering stability and order welcomed by the Jacobean dramatists, including the greatest of them all, William Shakespeare.

PLATE 2. George Villiers, 1st Duke of Buckingham attributed to William Larkin, 1616
The National Portrait Gallery, London

King James's flamboyant favourite did not long survive the passing of his mentor.
He was assassinated in 1628, aged just thirty-five.

PLATE 3. King Charles I by Daniel Mytens, 1631
The National Portrait Gallery, London

The King who sought to govern as an absolute monarch by Divine Right is portrayed as a slightly built man with an unimposing physical presence – hardly the stuff of which successful tyrants are made.

PLATE 4. Barbara Palmer (née Villiers), Duchess of Cleveland with her son, after Sir Peter Lely, *c.* 1664
The National Portrait Gallery, London

This painting, portraying the king's mistress and illegitimate son as the Madonna and Child, scandalised Restoration England when it was unveiled just four years after the end of Cromwell's Puritan Commonwealth.

PLATE 5. King Charles II, attributed to Thomas Hawker, *c.* 1680
The National Portrait Gallery, London

This distinctly unflattering portrait reveals an ageing, overweight roué with a cunning glint in his eye. It seems unlikely that this was the product of a court commission. My theory is that Hawker was moved to paint Charles II as an untrustworthy scoundrel following the failure of his attempt to become the King's court artist.

PLATE 6. Anne as Princess of Denmark by Willem Wissing and Jan van der Vaardt, 1685
The National Galleries of Scotland

This portrait, painted shortly after the death of her uncle King Charles II, reveals Anne, now heir presumptive to the thrones of Scotland, England and Ireland, as an elegant young princess with the world at her feet and the hopes of the Stuart dynasty in her hands.

PLATE 7. Queen Anne by Michael Dahl, *c.* 1702
The National Portrait Gallery, London

Almost twenty years on, the now Queen Anne is portrayed as a matronly lady who
cuts a very different picture from the glamorous young princess of twenty years earlier.
'What does it profit a woman if she gains the whole world yet loses her own soul?'

PLATE 8. The Battle of Glen Shiel by Peter Tillemans, 1719

The National Galleries of Scotland. Purchased with assistance from the National Heritage Memorial Fund and the Art Fund 1984

Tillemans' painting is a superb piece of artistic draftsmanship that brilliantly captures the full action of the battle over several hours in a single image.

PLATE 9. Queen Clementina Medal of 1719.

From the Author's Collection

The medal, struck in 1719 to commemorate Clementina's marriage, shows the head of the Jacobite queen on one side, and her arrival in Rome, Boudicca-like, in a chariot, on the reverse, engraved with the words Fortunam Causamque Sequor ('I follow the fate of the cause.')

PART 2
The Rising of 1745

7

The Road to Prestonpans:
the Quartermaster's Story

John William O'Sullivan, Quartermaster-General of the Jacobite Army, was one of the 'wild geese' – Irish soldiers-of-fortune exiled from their own country by virtue of their religion and loyalty to the House of Stuart. Forbidden from owning land in their native country, barred from Government office and severely restricted in their ability to pursue conventional careers or professions, they left Ireland to join the army of King Louis in France.

O'Sullivan hailed from County Kerry, where his family owned lands that had been confiscated from them and placed with Protestant trustees until such time as the O'Sullivans were willing to renounce their own religion. So far from doing this, O'Sullivan's father sent his son to Rome to train for the priesthood. While there, O'Sullivan decided his true vocation lay not with the Church but with the Army. His surviving writings reveal a direct, robust and vigorous style more attuned to a man of action than a man of the cloth, and his military career progressed well. Following a varied career during which he served with the French Army in Italy, on the Rhine and in the campaign in Corsica in 1739, he joined Prince Charles's household in Paris in early 1745, serving as his major domo, with responsibility for the day-to-day management of the Prince's household affairs. His appointment met with the approval of the Prince's father. In a letter to his son on 25 March 1745, James Francis Edward Stuart wrote:

> I am glad to find O'Sullivan is now with you. When a gentleman is capable of such detail and drudgery as that of family expenses, you will find it both of ease and advantage to you . . . And on all accounts it behoves you not to outrun your small income.

O'Sullivan thus followed in a long tradition of army officers appointed to senior positions in the Royal Household for their organisational skills, charged with keeping the domestic affairs of young Princes in good order.

In the foreword to her book *1745 and After* (1938), Henrietta Tayler refers to a 'most interesting manuscript, entirely in the handwriting of O'Sullivan, found among the Stuart papers at Windsor . . . [which] throws a good deal of light on the daily incidents of the Prince's campaign of 1745 and his wanderings'.

When I read O'Sullivan's account, doubts began to surface regarding whether he had actually written it down on paper is own hand, as Henrietta Tayler believed. I agree with her that the manuscript does indeed represent O'Sullivan's own record of the campaign; however, I do not agree with her view that O'Sullivan personally wrote the account. I think that he dictated it to a third person. Indeed, this is suggested by its description in the catalogue of the Stuart Papers as the *Narrative* rather than memoir.

There are a number of reasons for this conclusion. First of all, throughout the text he is referred to in the third person as 'Sullivan'. This, as Sherlock Holmes might observe, is suggestive but not conclusive.

Second, several passages suggest that it was written by someone other than Colonel O'Sullivan. Consider, for example, this account of events after the battle at Clifton in December 1745: 'I forgot to tell you that the Duke of Perth, who, as I told you before, acted no more as general officer, desired the Prince's leave to go to Perth.'

Surely, if Colonel O'Sullivan was writing this account himself, he wouldn't use the phrase 'I forgot to tell you'. This phrase only makes sense if he was telling his story to someone else. Several other parts of his account also only make sense if they were recorded by a third party.

But who was this third party? The evidence suggests that he or she was a secretary to the exiled King James VIII and III in Rome, who commissioned O'Sullivan to give his account of the events of the '45. It could have been the King's personal secretary, James Edgar. It is also possible that Edgar delegated someone within the Stuart court-in-exile to sit with O'Sullivan and take down his story in one of the basic shorthand systems of the day during the weeks between 15 March and 18 April 1747, when it is recorded that O'Sullivan was in Rome at King James's request. Or perhaps different people – probably including James Edgar – sat at different times with Colonel O'Sullivan to take down his account, as he recalled the events of the campaign.

I briefly discussed this matter with my immediate predecessor as chairman of the 1745 Association, Dr Christopher Duffy, after he had delivered the Annual NTS/1745 Association Lecture at Culloden in April 2018. Christopher immediately concurred that it was obvious that the *Narrative* had been dictated rather than written.

The same individual who took down O'Sullivan's account later interviewed the Prince himself. The dates are not given, but most probably it would have been shortly after O'Sullivan left Rome in late April or early May 1747. Towards the end of the *Narrative* it is reported:

> I had the honour to pay my court to the Prince one day at Clichy. Finding him alone, I took the liberty to ask him whether he suffered as much after he left the isle of Uist [where O'Sullivan and the Prince parted ways] as he did while Sullivan was with him.

Again, these words only make sense if their author was someone other than O'Sullivan. The writer then goes on to record the Prince's own account of what happened to him after he parted from O'Sullivan.

Once the account is read as a conversation between Colonel O' Sullivan and a Secretary, rather than written on paper by O'Sullivan, it starts to make sense. It also explains the staccato style of the *Narrative*, which at times reads as a stream of consciousness delivered in the present tense, with frequent grammatical errors and composed in language that is archaic and colloquial, a stark contrast to the more elegant literary style of O'Sullivan's written correspondence. In order to make O'Sullivan's account easier to understand, I have therefore rendered quotations from his *Narrative* into modern English.

Although he had a central role in the administration of the Prince's household, O'Sullivan's *Narrative* reveals that he was not privy to his decision to initiate the Rising. This decision was taken without any consultation between the Prince, his father in Rome or the King of France. O'Sullivan was perhaps kept in the dark because the Prince saw him as being too close to his father, whom he knew would try and dissuade him from undertaking the expedition.

As preparations continue, O'Sullivan states that he 'knew nothing of the matter', but questions put to him by Sir Thomas Sheridan asking how he could procure arms 'made Sullivan believe that there was something abrewing'.

The Prince secured two ships, the *Elizabeth* and the *Du Teillay*. The *Eliz-*

53

abeth engaged with the Royal Navy warship HMS *Lyon* during the crossing to Scotland and was forced to limp back to France, severely damaged, along with most of the Prince's men and munitions. In *Ships of the '45*, John Gibson quotes official records of the engagement, which state that forty-seven men were killed and 107 wounded on board the *Lyon*, while the *Elizabeth* suffered fifty-seven men killed, including the commander, Captain Dau, and a further 176 wounded.

This naval battle, the first action of the '45, marked a significant setback for the Prince and could have ended his campaign before it began. However, undeterred, he decided to press on and the *Du Teillay* landed on the Hebridean island of Eriskay on Tuesday, 23 July 1745. At this point, the Prince experienced what psychologists term 'cognitive dissonance', as the notions in his head came into sharp conflict with the reality on the ground. The first two clan chieftains that he met, Sir Alexander MacDonald of Sleat and Norman MacLeod, 19th Chief of Clan MacLeod, were blunt in their assessment.

O'Sullivan's *Narrative* relates that they told the Prince:

> If he came without troops, there was nothing to be expected from the country, that not a soul would join with him, and that their advice was that he should go back and wait for a more favourable occasion.

O'Sullivan's *Narrative* continues:

> Everybody was struck as with a thunderbolt, as you can imagine, to hear that sentence, especially from MacLeod, who was one of those who, it had been said, would be among the first to join the Prince even if he came alone. Everybody was for his going back except His Royal Highness, Walsh, and Sullivan.

So the only one of the Seven Men of Moidart who supported the Prince's decision to continue his campaign was John William O'Sullivan himself. O'Sullivan sets out his rationale for supporting a continuance of the campaign:

> The Prince ran as great a risk in going back as he did in staying. If he went back, the Court of France would have good grounds for saying that they were imposed upon and that the King (James) had

no support at all in the country. That could ruin the King's case (for further French support) and greatly undermine the Prince's reputation.

So they press on, and on 18 August 1745 the Stuart standard is raised at Glenfinnan. The core of the Jacobite Army is formed from 700 Cameron men led by Lochiel and 350 men under MacDonald of Keppoch.

O'Sullivan states that he was charged with organising the embryonic army. He says:

His proposition was to form the Army into companies of 50 men, assigning a captain, a lieutenant and four sergeants to each company. But that structure could not be followed, they must go by tribes. One tribal chief had 60 men, another 30, another 20 more or less. They would not mix nor separate, and would have double officers – that is, two Captains and two Lieutenants – to each company, strong or weak.

Notwithstanding the practical constraints placed upon the Jacobite Army structure by clan and tribal loyalties, as it marched south it picked up more recruits, including 500 MacDonalds under Young Glengarry, 350 men under Cluny MacPherson and a substantial cavalry regiment raised by Lord Ogilvy.

But now another problem arose: how to pay the men?

The embryonic Jacobite Army was almost out of money when it reached Perth in early September, by which time, O'Sullivan tells us:

I don't believe that the Prince had ten guineas in the world. The Duke of Perth sent him in money or bank bills two or three hundred pounds. In seven or eight days there was a reasonable sum gathered up, which friends who did not appear sent in.

In other words, rather than volunteering men to the cause, many of the townspeople contributed money. They didn't want to get involved. O'Sullivan comments laconically, 'The town in general was not well disposed.'

Despite the generally cool reception that the Prince received in Perth, he did secure two important recruits there. The first was the Duke of Perth, who contributed between £200 and £300 to the cause, according to O'Sullivan, equivalent to approximately £50,000 in today's values. The second was Lord George Murray, who brought with him a regiment of Atholl men.

From the outset, it is clear that Lord George is not at the top of O'Sullivan's Christmas card list. Here is how he introduces him:

Though his character was not of the best, and his own friends and relations were afraid of him, and some of them spoke openly, especially a lady, warning the Prince that he could not be trusted and that he would sooner or later ruin the King's cause, his presence nevertheless was thought necessary to determine the Atholl men to join, as I don't doubt but it did, though few or none of them had confidence in him in the beginning.

This comment doesn't make sense. If the Atholl men had so little confidence in Lord George, how did he manage to persuade them to follow him? In fact, O'Sullivan's observation says more of his own feelings about Lord George than how Lord George was regarded by his own Atholl men. And even O'Sullivan has to concede that Lord George had some plus points. His *Narrative* continues:

But to render him justice, Lord George was a very active stirring man, he knew the country perfectly well and gave himself a great deal of pains. As he was a Brigadier in the Year 1719, the Prince made him a Major General. A day or two later, when he found out that the Duke of Perth was a Lieutenant General, he insisted that he should be one too, and so the Prince made him one.

The frictions between Lord George and O'Sullivan were to continue throughout the campaign. However, over the following few days the two men's differences were forgotten in the common purpose of continuing the advance. On 17 September, the Jacobites entered Edinburgh and, by O'Sullivan's account, received a better reception there than they had in Perth, with 'demonstrations of joy . . . the roads so crowded for near upon a mile before he came to the Canongate that the Prince could hardly make his way'.

It seems that the citizens of Edinburgh were happier to give practical support to the Prince than their compatriots in Perth. O'Sullivan's *Narrative* records:

His Royal Highness sent Sullivan orders to make the strictest search he possibly could for arms and ammunition, and to proclaim the King the next day (September 18), which was done in all form at the Cross. The Heralds of Arms in their robes, the King's declarations were read, and all the windows of that fine street [the High Street of Edinburgh] were full of men and women at every storey. When the Heralds had finished, there was a continual cry of "God bless the King" from both sexes, and the ladies presented themselves at the windows with white handkerchiefs in their hands, waving them about.

O'Sullivan reports that he found 1,200 stands of arms and some ammunition 'which were much wanting to us'. These provided the basic weapons which the Jacobites were then able to deploy at Prestonpans.

Armed and refreshed, the Jacobite Army then advanced to the King's Park, where they struck camp. The Prince himself lodged just along the road from the Sheep Heid Inn, and, says O'Sullivan, 'was employed that night in visiting the posts and sending out scouts, to be well-informed of Cope's motions and force'.

On the evening of 19 September, O'Sullivan's account relates:

The order of battle was regulated, and instructions given to each Colonel and Major regarding their conduct in different eventualities, inspiring them to inform their men that they would run little danger from a cavalry attack, provided they kept in a body, managed their fire, and made use of their bayonets.

These instructions proved to be timely and sound. These were exactly the tactics that the Jacobites were to successfully apply during the battle.

*   *   *

On the morning of 20 September 1745, the Jacobite Army mustered in the King's Park and the Prince gave them a stirring address, his words recalled by O'Sullivan:

'You are all agreed upon your ranks, and the order and conduct you are to observe this day. Our good success depends very much on it. I can assure you, as I often told you all before, that I wish that your delivery from slavery will be achieved as much by your own acts as by the King's or my own. Remember that you fight for a good cause, while our enemies' consciences will reproach them to fight against their King and Country and they will be half over-come. So God will protect us.' Upon which he drew his sword. 'Gentlemen, I have flung away the scabbard, and with God's assis-tance, I don't doubt of making you a free and happy people!'

At the conclusion of his stirring call to arms, the Jacobite soldiers cheered and threw their bonnets in the air, and the army began its march towards Tranent.

After a march of about three or four hours, they caught sight of the redcoats. O'Sullivan's *Narrative* continues:

We saw plainly the enemy forming in the plain near Preston Pans. Their position was very good. They had their right wing to Gardiner's house, with enclosures surrounded with stone walls, as almost all that country was; two large ponds and morasses at their left; and a deep ditch with morasses and enclosures to their front, between us and them.

Thus, the Hanoverians were dug into an excellent defensive position that was protected on all sides. 'This was not', O'Sullivan says, 'a proper situa-tion for Highlanders, for they must have nothing before them that can hinder them to run upon the enemy.'

While they pondered what to do next, the Jacobites positioned them-selves so that they were protected in the event of a Hanoverian counter-attack. In particular,

His Royal Highness ordered Sullivan to take the Atholl Brigade and post them, part on the road near the seaside that leads to Edin-burgh, and part on another road that goes by Edinburgh, fearing lest Cope should steal a march upon us in the night.

This manoeuvre caused ructions with Lord George, who was upset that the Prince should have given orders to his Atholl Brigade without first consulting him. The *Narrative* continues:

Sullivan obeyed his orders, but Lord George asked the Prince in a very high tone what had become of the Atholl Brigade. The Prince told him, upon which Lord George threw his gun on the ground in a great passion and swore God that he'd never draw his sword for the cause if the brigade was not brought back. The Prince, with his customary prudence, though sensible of the disrespect, gave orders that the brigade should come back, but Lord George, who by this time had calmed down thanks to Lochiel's intervention, prayed the Prince to send the brigade to their first destination.

This exchange throws an interesting light on the power structure within the Jacobite Army. Although, by O'Sullivan's account, Lord George over-reacted, he did have a point in complaining that the Prince had gone over his head by instructing O'Sullivan to give orders directly to his regiment. The Prince did not have his own army, so had to give commands through the Colonels who had recruited their own regiments. The Prince, to his credit, recognised this and this is why he accepted Lord George's objections.

The disagreement was soon forgotten. The Jacobite high command had more pressing concerns, as the moment of battle approached. Later that evening, a famer named Robert Anderson provided vital intelligence that there was a path across Riggonhead Farm along which the Jacobite Army could march to outflank the redcoats.

O'Sullivan reports:

The Prince, who happily was all night in motion, roused up every-body, and ordered them to march. He forgot what passed the day before, and was as great at Cup and Can with Lord George, as with all the Chiefs, who pleaded with the Prince not to expose himself, representing to him that if any accident happened to him, all would be lost, and that it was only his presence that kept them all united and encouraged the men.

With Lord George, the Prince and Colonel O'Sullivan all now friends again, the march to battle began. O'Sullivan states:

We began to march an hour before day, and happily for us, found no opposition, so that we had time to form before the enemy perceived us. The irregularity of the day before caused a general change in the order of battle, for the MacDonalds took the right, though they were to have the left by lot, and the Camerons, who were to have the right, had the left. But things did not go the worse for the changes, for every man did his duty, and no troops in the world could have shown more valour than the Highlanders that day. The Duke of Perth led the right flank, and Lord George the left. It was not yet day, so that we saw the enemy in good order of battle before they could see us; our dark clothes were advantageous to us.

The battle was over in less than half an hour. The Highlanders charged and, says O'Sullivan:

the dragoons answered with a very irregular discharge, and rode off as fast as they could, with the MacDonalds after them as fast as they could. The [Government] foot soldiers, finding themselves abandoned by their horse, flinched immediately after, so that there was a general rout, such as I have never seen in any action before. The left, composed of the Camerons, Stewarts of Appin and the Duke of Perth's Regiment who were almost all MacGregors, behaved most gloriously, for they rushed in with such fury upon the enemy, after their first discharge, that they had not time to charge their cannon. Then the broadswords played their part, for with one stroke arms and legs were cut off and heads split to the shoulders. Cope escaped with a few who followed him through the breaches he made in the stone walls near Gardiner's House and it was there where the greatest slaughter occurred. The poor soldiers who could not get through the breaches because the dragoons had filled them up were cut to pieces. The dragoons themselves were pursued so closely by Clanranald, Keppoch and Glengarry's men that they were obliged to abandon their horses and throw themselves into the parks where most of them were taken.

The battle was over. O'Sullivan reports that eighty-four Hanoverian officers and about 1,400 men were captured. There was joy in the Jacobite ranks, but when the Prince was urged to rest, he replied:

'I can't rest until I see my own poor men taken care of, and the other wounded too, for they are the King's subjects as well, and it's not their fault if they were led on blindly' . . . He told the surgeons, first to dress the Highlanders, and afterwards to neglect nothing for the others; neither would he eat nor drink until he saw people setting about this.

It will be noted that the Prince's conduct after Prestonpans with respect to the enemy wounded was very different from the conduct of the Duke of Cumberland after Culloden when, so far from showing compassion for the enemy wounded, Cumberland ordered their summary execution in what many regard to this day as an act of murder.

While surgeons were tending to the wounded on both sides, the commander of the Hanoverian Government forces, General Sir John Cope, was riding off down the road that to this day still bears his name, not stopping until he reached Berwick-upon-Tweed, and so becoming, as the town's Governor caustically remarked, the first commander in history to bear the news of his own defeat, mocked in a popular song of the day:

Hey, Johnnie Cope, are you waking yet.
Or are your drums a-beating yet?
If they were beating, then I would wait
To gang to the coals in the morning.

8

Decision at Derby

Following Sir John Cope's exit off into the mists of history – one in a long list of English commanders who made the fatal error of underestimating the Scots – why didn't the Jacobites press home the advantage they had gained at Prestonpans?

After the battle, the Jacobites did very little for six weeks. The ladies attending the balls at Holyrood celebrated the Prince's victory with beautiful fans created for the occasion (Plate 18) and brought elegance to the ancient palace with the elegant dresses they wore (Plate 19). If you enjoyed parties and dancing, Edinburgh was the place to be in late September and October 1745. However, while the Jacobites partied, their enemies were being given time to regroup.

Here's how Prince Charlie explained the delay in his memorandum to Louis XV a year later: 'With three thousand regular troops, I could have penetrated England immediately after defeating General Cope at Prestonpans, and nothing would then have opposed my arrival in London.'

Thus, according to the Prince, the reason the Jacobites did not advance immediately after Prestonpans was because they weren't strong enough. Other accounts, including the *Narrative* of Colonel O' Sullivan, confirm this. The Jacobites needed time to consolidate, to build up their army with new volunteers, secure arms, munitions and supplies, and above all mobilise the funds they needed to advance into England.

But there was another reason why the Jacobites failed to advance.

The fact was that Lochiel and the other clan leaders didn't want to. They were, in modern parlance, Scottish nationalists: quite happy to see a Stuart Monarch restored in Scotland, but with no desire to attack England. They wanted the Act of Union signed forty years earlier to be revoked and Scotland to separate from England.

The problem was that this policy was not viable. The Prince's grip on power was tenuous. He didn't even control Edinburgh. The castle remained in Government hands, while the Royal Navy commanded the seas. Even worse for the Jacobites, news came that King George was withdrawing his regiments from Flanders, where they were fighting the French, in order to redeploy against the Jacobites, and he was raising a further 50,000 Dutch and German mercenaries to launch a counterattack. If the Jacobites simply waited in Edinburgh, they would be sitting ducks.

In October 1745, the Jacobites secured the agreement of the King of France to support the Rising under the Treaty of Fontainebleau. With this support, and the men and money raised since Prestonpans, Prince Charlie was able to persuade the clan chieftains to advance into England at a crucial Council of War held at Holyrood at the end of October 1745 on the basis of two promises.

The first was that if the Jacobite Army moved south, they would gain additional support among English and Welsh Jacobites. In the event, this didn't happen. Over the five weeks of their advance, the Jacobites only managed to raise 200 men in Manchester.

The second was that once the Highlanders advanced from the north, the French would simultaneously cross the Channel and advance on London from the south, forming a pincer movement converging on the capital. On this, Prince Charles was correct. As the Highlanders marched southwards in November 1745, a large French force under the titular command of his younger brother, Prince Henry, was massing on the northern coast of France, preparing to embark for England and only waiting for fog to give them cover from the Royal Navy and a fair wind to carry them across the Channel.

However, the clan leaders had no way of knowing this. As the Jacobite Army advanced rapidly southwards, there was no means of communication between Prince Charlie's Scottish Army and the French Army under his brother Prince Henry.

*   *   *

Of all the paintings in the care of the Scottish National Portrait Gallery, perhaps the most intriguing is that of Prince Henry Benedict Stuart by Maurice Quentin de la Tour (Plate 20), acquired by the gallery in 1994.

The portrait shows Prince Henry in the armour of a military commander, and for many years it was believed to be a portrait of his elder brother. One can understand why. We don't usually think of Prince Henry as a soldier.

However, in 2009, art historian Dr Bendor Grosvenor demonstrated that it was, in fact, a portrait of Prince Henry, and this was subsequently accepted by Professor Edward Corp, the leading living expert on Jacobite portraiture.

But when, where and why was it painted?

The Scottish National Portrait Gallery dates it as being painted in 1746 or 1747, but I would question this dating. It would not have been painted after July 1747, for in that month Henry was ordained as a Cardinal Deacon of the Roman Catholic Church. I also think that it is highly unlikely that it would have been painted in the months leading up to that occasion, which seems to rule out 1747 altogether. That brings us back to 1746, but there are problems here too. Is it really credible that Prince Henry would have commissioned such a portrait in the aftermath of Culloden, with his brother on the run from the redcoats and under threat of his life? I would suggest that, during that period, Prince Henry would have been more concerned with the safe return of his brother from Scotland than with dressing up in armour to get his picture painted. There is nothing that we know of the character of Prince Henry, who seems to have been a gentle and compassionate individual, to suggest that he would have been capable of such an insensitive and even callous act.

So that means the portrait was probably painted *before* rather than after the Battle of Culloden.

This leads to the second question – where was it painted? I could find no evidence that La Tour travelled to Rome in 1746 or 1747. He was admitted as a member of the prestigious Academie de Peinture et de la Sculpture in Paris in 1746, which is where his studio was located, so it seems reasonable to conclude that he spent most of that year in Paris. Applying the principle introduced earlier of Occam's Razor, that if in doubt we should accept the simplest explanation, it seems most likely that Prince Henry had his portrait painted in La Tour's studio in Paris.

We can place Prince Henry in Paris in late 1745, when he was travelling northwards from Rome to persuade King Louis XV to back his brother's expedition.

On 29 August 1745, Prince Henry left Rome in secret. A cover story was put about that he had smallpox and, for that reason, could receive no visitors. This gave him a vital few days' head start over British spies seeking to intercept him and on 3 September he arrived in Genoa, from where he sailed to Antibes, successfully evading the Royal Navy to reach the French coast. From Antibes, Prince Henry travelled 150 miles westwards to find safety in Avignon at the home of the elderly Duke of Ormonde, erstwhile commander-in-chief of the British Army under Queen Anne and commander of the abortive Rising of 1719.

Prince Henry, who was barely twenty at the time of these tumultuous events, was something of a creaking door, a rather sensitive young man, of delicate constitution, who forever seemed to be falling ill of one ailment or another, but eventually outlasted most of his contemporaries and lived to a ripe old age.

Whether it was the stress of the journey, the risks he had faced or the excitement of the adventures that lay before him, it is reported that Henry collapsed with exhaustion when he reached Avignon and was unable to continue his journey. There he languished for several weeks. During this period, news reached him of his brother's decisive victory at Prestonpans and this doubtless assisted his recovery, aided perhaps by a warming pan in his bed and the finest French wines and cuisine!

Restored to full health, he was ready to travel northwards to Paris, where, in October 1745, he met King Louis XV and persuaded him to sign the Treaty of Fontainebleau. Under the terms of the Treaty, the King gave French support to Prince Charlie's campaign. Louis then committed an expeditionary force of 11,000 men, artillery and ships to the Rising under the operational command of the Duc de Richelieu, with Prince Henry himself in nominal command.

It was in order to celebrate this event, I believe, that Prince Henry commissioned his portrait from Quentin de la Tour.

This dating would explain the serene optimism of the Prince's countenance in the portrait. It explains the position of his arm, pointing over the Channel to England, in the hope and expectation that he would shortly return to the land of his fathers. It also explains why the portrait was then lost from view after 1745. Following the failure of the Rising, it would have been only natural for Prince Henry Benedict to put away this portrait as a painful reminder of what might have been, as he underwent a personal metamorphosis from military to religious leader, concluding in his ordination as a Cardinal of the Roman Catholic Church.

When I put forward this dating of the La Tour portrait in 2016, 1745 Association Member Joyce MacKenzie commented: 'It certainly seems plausible – even probable – that Henry sat for the portrait in 1745. Henry's social connections in Paris in late 1745 connect him to La Tour. He was living in a house loaned to him by the Princesse De Conti. Her brother, the Compte de Clermont, was painted by La Tour earlier that year.'

This dating is also supported by pastel expert Neil Jeffares, who wrote in a 2016 article, 'La Tour's Stuart Copyists':

> The portrait was likely to have been made after Henry's arrival in Paris, shortly after the victory at Prestonpans in September 1745, while Henry was trying to raise support for the Jacobite rebellion, but before his departure for Boulogne in December 1745.

If this is the case, this portrait was painted not in commemoration of the *failure* of the Rising of 1745 but rather in anticipation of the Rising's imminent *success*. It is this which makes this painting one of the most important and poignant Jacobite portraits of all.

The month after his portrait was painted, in December 1745, Prince Henry proceeded to Boulogne at the head of the 11,000 French troops King Louis had committed to the campaign to prepare to cross to England.

By this time, the Duke of Ormonde was dead. He passed away at the age of eighty on 16 November 1745. I like to think that, at the moment of his passing, he believed that his own reputation and the fortunes of his house were about to be restored, the news having come through that Prince Charles had scored a sensational victory at Prestonpans and was marching south on to London.

Perhaps it is as well that Ormonde did not live long enough to learn that the French force never crossed the Channel, and that Prince Charlie's Army never got to London, instead turning back at Derby three weeks after Ormonde's death.

As for Prince Henry, he remained on the French coast until news arrived of the Jacobite retreat, when the French abandoned the attempt to cross the Channel. As they prepared to leave, the Duc de Richelieu is reported to have turned to Henry, who was gazing forlornly over the Channel, and said, 'You may win the keys to the gates of heaven through your prayers, but I fear that you shall never win the British Crown.'

*   *   *

The narrative perpetrated by Whig historians is that the Rising never had a chance of success. That's obviously not what Lord George Murray, the Duke of Perth, John William O'Sullivan and the Prince's other supporters thought – all experienced and intelligent men. And as the Prince advanced on London, it wasn't what King George thought either – he was busy loading a ship with treasure and preparing to evacuate his family back to Hanover.

Nor did the ordinary citizens of London think this in early December 1745, when there was a run on the banks, as they desperately sought to withdraw their gold, and panic swept the city. In an effort to stem the run, it is said that banks redeemed their notes in silver sixpences rather than golden guineas in order to slow down the rate of withdrawal, while the Bank of England minted new sixpences to supply them, so that depositors were given new silver coins still hot from the presses.

On the evidence now available to us, I believe that, had the Jacobite Army continued its advance from Derby to London, there would have been at least a fifty-fifty chance of a Stuart Restoration. Instead of which, and despite the Prince's desperate entreaties, the Council of War held at Derby on 5 December 1745 voted to retreat.

Why did the Jacobite high command make what, in retrospect, looks like such a catastrophic mistake?

First, they didn't know that Prince Henry and a French expeditionary force were awaiting only favourable winds and tides to cross the Channel and advance on to London. There were no means of communication between the two armies.

Secondly, Prince Charlie had confidently predicted a major Jacobite Rising in England when his army advanced from Scotland. That hadn't happened and his own credibility had been damaged as a result.

Thirdly, Lord George Murray and many of the clan leaders had never wanted to leave Scotland in the first place, so they were keen to return.

Also, it's easy to forget that when he sat down at the Council of War in Exeter House in December 1745 Prince Charles Edward Stuart was just twenty-four years old. Lord George Murray, the leader of the camp opposing the Prince's proposal to continue the advance on to London, was more than twice his age. He was fifty-one, a veteran of the Battle of Glen Shiel and many other battles, and immensely more experienced as a battlefield commander than the young Prince. As a military commander, he had greater credibility among many of the clan chieftains than the young Prince.

Lord George was concerned that the Jacobite Army risked being squeezed in a pincer between three Hanoverian armies: Cumberland's to the east, Wade's to the west and a great army supposedly amassing to the south, barring their advance on London. The only way out of the trap, argued Lord George, was to retreat back to Scotland and seek reinforcements there. He was supported by Lord Elcho and Lord Ogilvy, who declared that the Jacobite Army could not defeat two or three armies in succession and, if they tried to do so, Prince Charles himself would be captured or killed.

The Prince showed no concern for his personal safety. The army's morale was high, he said, and its strategic position was excellent. The English Jacobites would come out in their support if they marched on to London. The French would cross the Channel and advance from the south coast.

Lord Elcho then said that he would support a march on London only if Charles had written proof that this was what the English Jacobites had requested. Of course, Charles had no such proof.

Charles was initially supported by Ranald Clanranald and the Duke of Perth. He also managed to persuade the Marquis of Tullibardine to march on.

It was at this juncture that Dudley Bradstreet is reported to have entered the Council with the information that there was an army of 9,000 soldiers standing between the Jacobite Army and London, assembled at Finchley, which would surely destroy the Jacobites.

It wasn't true. Bradstreet was, in fact, a double agent in the pay of King George. But his intervention succeeded in convincing the clan leaders that their only option was to retreat.

On that day, Bradstreet recounted in his memoirs, he saved the House of Hanover. One has to concede that he may well have been right. Charles is reported to have said, 'That fellow will do me more harm than all the Elector's Army.'

In the light of this supposed intelligence, Clanranald and Tullibardine dropped their support for an advance. In the end, only James Drummond, Duke of Perth, still supported the Prince's case for a continued advance.

What differentiated the Duke of Perth from the other Jacobite leaders was his gambling instinct. An aficionado of horseracing, he knew intuitively what modern mathematics has proved rigorously – namely, that when the odds are stacked against you, the optimal strategy is what mathematicians term the Strategy of Maximum Boldness. In simple English, you go for broke. The Duke understood that Prince Charlie was right, and that the only viable strategy for the Jacobites at Derby was to boldly continue the advance on to London. There was a chance that a rapier thrust to the heart of the Hanoverian kingdom would succeed. That chance was now lost.

Prince Charles's fears of the consequences of retreat were fully vindicated by events. As the saying goes, no one is afraid of an army that runs away.

There are many lessons to be learnt from the Rising of 1745. One of the most important is that once you've decided on a strategy, your best course of action is likely to be to stick with it. If you lose your nerve and abandon it halfway through, like the Jacobites at Derby, the outcome may be disastrous. In the words of the Gaelic lament:

Cha'n e buaidh ach bàs bha 'n dàn dhuinn.
Not victory but death was our destiny.

9

Return to Scotland

In the weeks that followed the Council of War at Derby, the Jacobites showed a great deal of tactical skill in outmanoeuvring Hanoverian forces under the Duke of Cumberland. They successfully forded the River Esk to return to Scotland and by late December had reached the town of Dumfries without serious losses.

By this time the Jacobite Army was weary and footsore, having marched a thousand miles to Derby and back, and many of the soldiers were barefoot. To this day, the town of Dumfries seems to have an unusual preponderance of shoe shops, as if awaiting the return of shoeless Jacobite warriors seeking to salve their blistered feet.

From Dumfries, the Jacobite Army withdrew to Glasgow. An early nineteenth-century writer told this story of their stay there, passed down to him from his mother:

> The rebels entered Glasgow on December 25th 1745, and my mother informed me that she had a good opportunity of seeing the different Highland regiments while they lay in Glasgow and marched daily through the centre part of the city. My mother further mentioned to me that one day, when Prince Charles was marching at the head of one of these detachments, she stood so close to him that she could have touched him with her hand. She stated that he was a handsome good-looking man, but that his countenance seemed rather sombre and melancholy. I remember when a boy that we had a bust of Prince Charles standing in our lobby, but, having received some damage, it was laid aside, and I never could learn what became of it.
>
> The Chevalier, having extorted from the citizens a levy of shirts,

shoes, hose, waistcoats and bonnets, and having clothed his ragged troops with them, treated the inhabitants of Glasgow with a grand review on the City Green of his newly clothed ragamuffins, who marched to the Green by way of the Saltmarket in splendid military array, with colours flying, drums beating, and the skirling notes of the Highland piobaireachd resounding from the pipes of every clan. On the next day, being the 3rd of January 1746, the Prince, with his motley crew, evacuated Glasgow.

(Reproduced in *Quarterly Notes of the 1745 Association*, No. 55, Summer 1984)

The Prince's Army moved off in two columns, a Highland Division under Lord George Murray marching towards Falkirk, and a Lowland Division led by the Prince himself taking a more northerly route to Kilsyth and then advancing towards Stirling.

The Prince stopped at Bannockburn House, home of Sir Hugh Paterson, which he made headquarters. While there, he met Sir Hugh's niece, Clementina Walkinshaw, for the first time. After the Rising, she was to become his mistress and the mother of his only child, his daughter Charlotte.

The Prince deployed some 1,200 men from his division to continue the advance to Stirling under the Duke of Perth. They duly took the town and laid siege to Stirling Castle, which continued to hold out.

The Highland Division under Lord George took the town of Falkirk. However, when news came through that the Hanoverian Army was advancing on the town, Lord George withdrew and joined the main corps at Bannockburn.

The Prince consolidated his forces at Bannockburn, where the troops who had returned from England were reinforced by more than 3,000 men, including the regiment raised by Lord Lewis Gordon, which on 23 December had inflicted a defeat on Hanoverian forces under MacLeod of MacLeod at the Battle of Inverurie. Jacobite forces were also strengthened by the Irish Piquets, who had landed from France the previous month. By mid-January 1746, approximately 7,000 Jacobite soldiers were encamped in and around Bannockburn.

On 6 January 1746, Lieutenant-General Henry Hawley arrived in Edinburgh to take overall command of Hanoverian Government forces in Scotland. True to his nickname of 'Hangman' Hawley, his first act on arriving in Scotland's capital was to erect gallows in the Grassmarket for the express

71

purpose of executing the rebel Jacobites whom he confidently expected to capture. 'I do and always shall despise these rascals,' he announced.

On 13 January 1746, his second-in-command, Major-General Huske, was dispatched to Linlithgow with an advance guard, followed over the next few days by the main body of the Hanoverian Army and by Hawley himself, who arrived in Falkirk and took up residence at Callendar House on 16 January.

At this stage, the two armies were at maximum strength and just five miles apart. The Hanoverians were encamped in and around the town of Falkirk, while Jacobite forces were scattered around Bannockburn.

So ended the prelude to the largest battle, in terms of number of combatants, fought in Scotland during the Jacobite Wars between 1688 and 1746. On one side were Prince Charles and his 'ragamuffin army' of some 6,700 men, short of money, munitions and supplies. Ranged against them were 9,400 well-armed and funded professional troops under General Hawley.

Yet the following day, Prince Charlie's ragamuffins were to inflict a decisive defeat on Hawley's redcoats.

It was the greatest victory of the Jacobite Wars.

It also proved to be the last Jacobite victory.

*   *   *

Between 3 a.m. and 4 a.m. on the morning of Friday, 17 January 1746, Prince Charles Edward Stuart was aroused from his slumbers at Bannockburn House with some alarming news.

The Prince was informed that the sound of drums had been heard in the distant town of Falkirk, beating a call to arms to Hanoverian forces in preparation for a dawn attack on his Jacobite Army.

The Prince's forces were scattered far and wide in farms, barns and cottages around Bannockburn – anywhere, indeed, where they could find shelter from the bitterly cold winter's night. If the redcoats were to attack, his men were in no position to defend themselves. The Prince sent scouts to find out what movements there were in the Hanoverian camp and was relieved to be told that there was no sign of a general assembly. The report had been a false alarm.

Nevertheless, the Prince was well aware of how vulnerable his men were. The Hanoverian Army could assemble and mobilise much more rapidly than his own. As dawn broke, he ordered a general assembly of his army on Plean Muir, a couple of miles from Bannockburn House, where they had drawn up in battle order the previous day, when it had taken until midday for them to assemble. It took almost as long for Prince Charles to gather his scattered forces together that morning. Fortunately for the Jacobites, there was no early Hanoverian onslaught.

While waiting for his regiments to assemble, the Prince called a Council of his senior officers to determine what to do next. Lord George Murray, his most senior commander and the man who had led the opposition to the Prince at Derby, was on this occasion in complete agreement with the Prince. Both men agreed that they could not simply stay and wait for the Hanoverians to make the first move. As Lord George recounted in his memoir, *Marches of the Highland Army*:

> On January 14th we went to Bannockburn as we were ordered. For three days thereafter, the army drew up in line of battle to the east of Bannockburn (on Plean Muir). On the 17th, as all the men we expected were come up (with the exception of those under the Duke of Perth left at Stirling, being about 1,200), it was proposed to march to the enemy. We had been told they designed to have marched towards us that day, but they were still in their camp on the west side of Falkirk, as they had been for two days before.
>
> The officers being called into His Royal Highness's presence, I observed how difficult it was to bring our men together from so many different cantonments for several miles round. We found it was always midday before we could be assembled; whereas the enemy, being encamped, had nothing to do but strike their tents. They could march by break of day, and so could be in the heart of our quarters before we could make head against them, in which case I was afraid that we would be in great confusion.

Lord George's account is corroborated by another member of the Jacobite Council that day, Lord Elcho, who described how it was decided to advance in two columns: one under Lord John Drummond, marching directly towards Falkirk through the Torwood, where it would be clearly visible to the Hanoverians; the other, under Lord George, following a more westerly route on lower ground, where their advance would be hidden from the Hanoverians encamped at Falkirk.

The Jacobite Council of War decided that the Highland Division under Lord George Murray should advance to pass close by Dunipace, crossing the Carron Water and approaching the town of Falkirk from the west. Their march would be through low-lying land where, it was hoped, their progress would go unobserved by the Hanoverians.

The dictionary definition of a feint is 'a movement made in order to divert an adversary; an attack aimed at one point as a distraction from the real point of attack'. The plan devised by the Jacobite high command to mislead the Hanoverians involved sending a second column, led by Lord John Drummond, on a more direct route through the Torwood towards Larbert, approaching the town of Falkirk from the north.

The Jacobites hoped that the Hanoverians would mistake Lord John Drummond's column for the main corps of the Jacobite Army, so that the larger Highland division under Lord George could outflank them unobserved. As Lord Elcho recalls in his account of the battle:

> It was decided that Lord John Drummond would go forward upon the straight road to Falkirk with his own regiment, the Irish Piquets and all the horse, in order to cover Lord George Murray's march. Lord George Murray was to gain the top of the hill to the south of Falkirk with the rest of the army before General Hawley knew anything of his march.
>
> The appearance of Lord John Drummond and his corps upon the road from Torwood led General Hawley and his army to believe that the Prince's whole army was marching that way . . .

The planned route of the two columns is shown in Figure 2.

The larger western column under Lord George Murray, comprising the Highland clan regiments and his own Atholl Brigade, would advance across low-lying land not visible from Falkirk through Dunipace and across the Carron Water. The eastern column under Lord John Drummond, although smaller in numeric terms, could move more rapidly than Lord George's division, comprising as it did the cavalry and the most experienced infantry regiment in the Jacobite Army, the Irish Piquets.

Lord John's division advanced along the route of the current A9 from Bannockburn to Falkirk, through Plean and Torwood and onwards towards Larbert. The two columns advanced about 200 yards apart from each other, with Prince Charles and his Adjutant-General Colonel John William O'Sullivan riding between the two lines.

Although Lord John's division was less than half the size of Lord George's division, its numbers were not insignificant. According to the

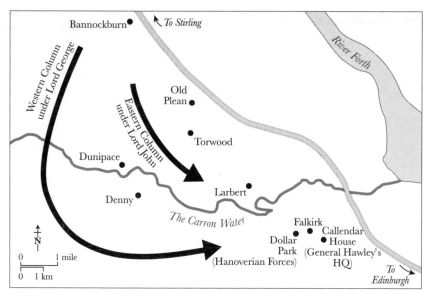

Figure 2: Map of the western/eastern columns of the Jacobite army advancing on Falkirk.

estimates provided by Lord Elcho, the total strength of the Jacobite Army that day was approximately 6,700 men, with approximately 2,000 men under the command of Lord John and 4,700 men under Lord George.

The regimental structure of the two divisions is shown in Figure 3, showing the strength of the two Jacobite columns.

The Irish Piquets were professional soldiers selected from the Irish Brigade and sent over by King Louis to assist the Rising after the signature of the Treaty of Fontainebleau – the so-called 'wild geese'. A few months earlier, in May 1745, the Irish Brigade had made a major contribution to the French victory over the Duke of Cumberland at the Battle of Fontenoy. Commenting on this victory, the French War Office had written that the Irish Brigade had 'distinguished itself in the most remarkable manner in the presence of the King and the Dauphin, and principally contributed to achieve the complete victory that was ultimately gained'. As events were to transpire, the Piquets were to play a crucial part in the Battle of Falkirk Muir.

As the two columns advanced, Colonel O'Sullivan became concerned that they might be observed and that it would be unwise to try to cross the Carron Water in full daylight. Between 1 p.m. and 2 p.m. in the afternoon, he rode up to Lord George and suggested that the advance should stop. Lord George relates what happened next:

Lord George Murray: Highland Infantry Regiments

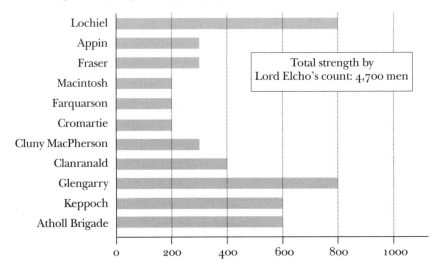

Lord John Drummond: Cavalry and Irish Piquets

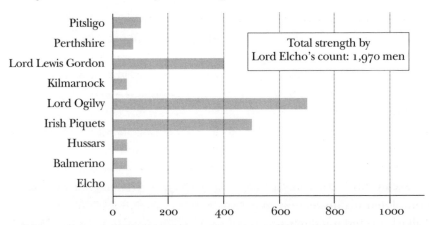

Figure 3: The strength of the two Jacobite columns at Falkirk Muir.

After I had marched about half a mile, Mr O'Sullivan came up to me, and told me he had been talking with the Prince, and that it was thought advisable to delay the advance until night, when we could do it unperceived.

This surprised me. I told him we would all pass the Carron Water in less than a quarter of an hour, and the place where we were to pass was four miles from the enemy. I did not halt, and he went back to His Royal Highness who was riding betwixt the two lines. The Prince came up soon after with Brigadier Stapleton [regimental commander of the Irish Piquets], Mr O'Sullivan, and some others. When I told him my reasons [for continuing to advance], that I thought we could not lie in the open fields all night in that season of the year, and that if we attempted it most of the men would shift for themselves so that we would be longer next day in getting them together than formerly. Therefore, I was of the opinion that we should either march forward or return to our quarters, for it seemed to threaten a very bad night.

Brigadier Stapleton said, to be sure, if the enemy were not near enough to dispute our passing, there could be no other objection. I told him, so far from disputing our passing, that we were now within half a mile of the water, which then was very low, and that the enemy were two full miles off, and could not see us till we were very near it, so that we must get up to the high ground before them.

His Royal Highness and the Brigadier were entirely satisfied. We had not stopped all the time, and Lord John Drummond had been sent to make a feint with horse below the Torwood.

So, despite Colonel O'Sullivan's intervention, the advance continued.

Lord John Drummond's division advanced ahead of the main column under Lord George, thus providing cover against any Hanoverian counter-attack and restricting the movements of Hanoverian scouts. As a result, the scouts failed to observe Lord George's division. Conversely, Lord John's cavalry was able to ride ahead and secure vital intelligence on the position and movements of the Hanoverian Government forces.

Meanwhile, back in the Hanoverian camp, General Hawley had completed his inspection of the Hanoverian troops at Dollar Park in Falkirk around midday, when he returned to his headquarters at Callendar House. Geoff Bailey, in *Falkirk or Paradise*, reports that upon his arrival at Callendar House Hawley was given a warm posset to take the chill off his chest by Lady Ann Livingston, the chatelaine of the house.

Lady Ann's solicitude for General Hawley's welfare may seem surprising in light of the fact that her own husband, the Earl of Kilmarnock, was a regimental cavalry commander in the Jacobite Army which was at that very moment advancing on Hawley's army.

There was undoubtedly an element of realpolitik in Lady Ann's hospitality to the Hanoverian commander. To preserve her own house, Lady Ann needed to be hospitable to its occupier. Moreover, Lady Ann's own loyalties were divided. There is little evidence that she encouraged her husband to join Prince Charlie's cause, having witnessed the destruction of her own father, the Earl of Linlithgow, because of his support for the earlier Jacobite Rising of 1715. He had lost his titles and estates and been driven into exile, dying shortly thereafter and leaving Ann fatherless at the age of just eight. Her oldest son and heir, James Lord Boyd, was serving as a junior officer in the Hanoverian Army, while her second son, William, was serving with the Royal Navy. Only her youngest son, Charles, then aged just seventeen, had enlisted with Prince Charlie's army alongside his father – he was serving with Lord Balmerino's Lifeguards.

The Rising of 1745 caused a devastating and ultimately irreparable split in the Boyd family, as in many other Scottish families. The Earl of Kilmarnock was to be executed for High Treason on Tower Hill on 18 August 1746. There is evidence that the emotional conflicts and immense stress under which Lady Anne laboured during those difficult times were a contributory cause to her own early demise at the age of just thirty-eight the following year, probably from stomach cancer, as related by Barbara Graham, in 'Did Lady Kilmarnock die of a broken heart?' (*The Jacobite*, No. 153, Spring 2017).

*   *   *

At approximately half-past two in the afternoon, Lord John's division reached the Torwood. There it halted, lit fires, flew the banner of the Royal Stuart, beat the drums and generally made so much commotion that someone watching the proceedings from Falkirk could have been forgiven for thinking that the entire Jacobite Army was encamped there.

Which was, of course, precisely the point.

Contrary to the fears of the Jacobite high command, General Hawley had no immediate plans of attack. Having arrived at Callendar House only the night before, his tactical position on that Friday was essentially defensive.

At Callendar House, he received regular reports from his officers regarding the advance of Lord John Drummond's division. He was sceptical as to whether the Jacobite advance was a prelude to a direct attack, and his principal concern was to counter a possible move outflanking his defending forces in Falkirk – not to the west, but to the east.

In his NTS/1745 Association Lecture at Culloden in April 2017, Christopher Duffy cited an unpublished account of the battle written by

General Hawley now lodged in the Royal Army Museum. In that account, Hawley stated that his primary concern that Friday was to cover the road to Edinburgh. His fear was that the enemy could by-pass his forces, advancing along the current route of the M9 towards Scotland's capital.

Scrutinising his maps at Callendar House, and with the intelligence at his disposal in the early afternoon of 17 January, Hawley's primary concern was to guard against the possibility that the Jacobite Army would suddenly swing eastwards and advance rapidly upon Edinburgh. Hawley followed reports of the advance of Lord John Drummond's column to the Torwood with interest. It was now mid-afternoon and he was still unaware of the existence of a second, larger column under Lord George Murray.

General Hawley did not believe that the Jacobite advance presaged a direct attack on his own army. Should the Jacobites decide upon such an attack, his opinion was that his men were well positioned to repel it.

When Lord John's column halted above the Torwood at around 2.30 p.m., it tended to confirm Hawley's opinion. As he pored over his maps in Callendar House, he was trying to read the Jacobites' most likely next move, and he concluded that they would try to outflank his forces to the east of Falkirk and then march on Edinburgh.

The threat that General Hawley was seeking to counter is shown in Figure 4.

The threat that Hawley feared was that the Jacobite Army would suddenly swing sharply eastwards and march rapidly on the capital,

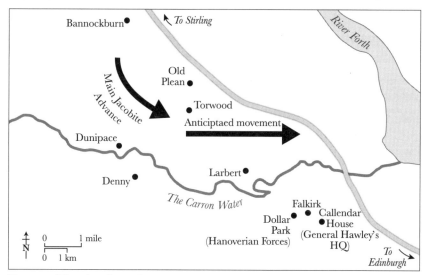

Figure 4: The view from the Hanoverian Camp at Falkirk Muir

completely outflanking his own Hanoverian forces, which would be unable to stop their advance. The Jacobite feint had been completely successful in wrong-footing the Hanoverian commander.

Only after Lord George's column had safely crossed the Carron Water did Hawley secure full intelligence on his enemy's movements. The Hanoverian scout John Wight arrived to find Hawley in discussion with his second-in-command, Major-General Huske, with a map of the Torwood spread before them.

> Wight told them that the rebels were approaching. They asked him in what posture they marched. He answered, in two lines. They asked him of their number, and if their motion was quick. He told them he believed there was about four or six thousand, and that they marched at a rate of four miles an hour. They asked him whereabouts they were when he came off, he told them a little to the west of Dunipace, that he believed it was the whole army for he had seen both the front and rear, upon which General Hawley said to General Huske: 'We are long enough here, then.' And they both took the door before them. (Quoted in Christopher Duffy, *Fight for a Throne.*)

At this stage of the proceedings, there is no evidence to suggest that General Hawley was unduly perturbed by the course of events. As far as he was concerned, his men were more than capable of defeating the advancing Jacobites.

As Napoleon later observed, 'a General will never be a great commander if he cannot see beyond his own map board'. Hawley was certainly not a great commander. His own brigade-major, the nineteen-year-old James Wolfe, wrote of Hawley: 'The troops dread his severity, hate the man and hold his military knowledge in contempt.'

Wolfe had good reason to dislike his commanding officer. It was Hawley who, three months later in the immediate aftermath of the Battle of Culloden, ordered Wolfe to execute a wounded Jacobite, Charles Fraser of Inverallochy, a Major in the Clan Fraser Regiment, in cold blood on the battlefield. Wolfe risked his military career by refusing to obey.

A dozen years later, when the now General James Wolfe fell mortally wounded on the Heights of Abraham outside Québec, it is said that he passed away in the arms of a Fraser Highlander.

They had not forgotten.

10

Falkirk Muir:
the last Jacobite Victory

James Wolfe's low opinion of Hawley's abilities as a commander are confirmed by the decisions that he took immediately after learning of the true strength and intentions of the Jacobite Army.

For the first time, Hawley realised that the point of attack of the Jacobite Army was not to the east but to the west. He also realised that, at the speed at which they were marching, there was no chance that his own infantry – positioned with the primary objective of guarding the road to Edinburgh – could reach the heights above Falkirk before the Highlanders.

Throughout the Rising, one key advantage that the Jacobite infantry possessed over the Hanoverians is that they could march much more rapidly, even over rough terrain. It seems likely that they were physically fitter than the redcoats, even after a march of a thousand miles to Derby and back.

Realising that the speed at which his infantry could march towards the top of the hill above Falkirk Muir was too slow to prevent the Highlanders reaching it first, General Hawley instead took the highly unorthodox decision of ordering his light cavalry – the dragoons – to advance first.

Hawley sent orders to Colonel Francis Ligonier to ride as fast as possible to the top of the hill with his own regiment of dragoons and those of Colonels Cobham and Hamilton. According to Lord Elcho's estimates, each regiment numbered about 300, giving a total command of some 900 horse. It is reported that Colonel Ligonier received this order 'with some surprise', as well he might, as it was contrary to all established battle tactics of the day. The invariable convention in battle was for the infantry to advance first and the cavalry to sweep in behind them in a second wave of attack. The reverse tactic now being employed by General Hawley carried the obvious risk that the first line of cavalry would be entirely exposed to a musket volley without any infantry protection.

Hawley's crack professional regiments were deployed on his right (eastern) flank, covering the road to Edinburgh, so the closest infantry regiment he could deploy in support of the dragoons were the Glasgow Militia, a volunteer regiment of some 1,500 men who were probably the least experienced and disciplined unit in his entire army.

Ligonier asked for confirmation of the command and, having received it, notwithstanding his personal reservations, as a loyal officer he followed the order and began the advance. As events transpired, it was to be the last order that the brave Colonel Ligonier was ever to obey.

This was the first time in history that a cavalry charge preceded the infantry advance, but it was not to be the last. A century later, exactly the same mistake was made in the Crimean War at the Battle of Balaclava, but there the mistake was the consequence of a catastrophic miscommunication rather than a deliberate decision by a general badly wrong-footed by the enemy.

Once they had crossed the Carron Water, Lord George's infantry division marched ahead of Lord John's cavalry, who swept left to right (east to west) behind them to form the second line.

Lord George's division advanced rapidly towards the hills forming the peak of Falkirk Muir, but halted when they saw them occupied by the Hanoverian dragoons. At this point, Lord George ordered his regiments to march west to east to form the front line of the Jacobite Army, in battle order as assembled at Plean Muir that morning. The Clan Donald regiments took the place of honour on the right, as they had at Bannockburn under Robert the Bruce. The Camerons under Lochiel – described as 'the bravest of the clan regiments' by James Wolfe – anchored the left, approximately at the current location of the Obelisk Battlefield Monument.

The position of the Jacobite front line is approximately defined by the public footpath that today links Lochgreen Road and Slammanan Road, with the Lochgreen access commencing close to the location of the Battlefield Monument.

As the Jacobite Army advanced, the weather deteriorated. Rain and sleet were sweeping across the moor, driving from behind the Highlanders and into the faces of the Hanoverian forces. 'Strong wind and rain was at our backs and directly in the enemy's face,' wrote Lord George Murray in *Marches of the Highland Army*.

'We had the cruellest hail and rain that could be seen, but happily it was in our backs,' Colonel Sir John William O' Sullivan commented in his *Narrative*.

The rain, and the softness of the ground, hampered the deployment of the Hanoverian dragoons. The movement of Ligonier's Horse was also impeded by potholes on the moor, mined by local people over the years for clay and stone.

A further problem that Hawley faced was in respect of the deployment of his own troops. His crack regiments were placed on the right, covering the road to Edinburgh, and as they advanced their line of attack was impeded by a ravine forming a deep scar near the current location of Bantaskine Park.

Lord Elcho comments in his account:

> As the Prince's army, in order to gain the top of the hill, marched East, while General Hawley's army for the same reason marched West, when the two armies came to be formed, the Prince outflanked General Hawley on the [Jacobite] right while General Hawley outflanked the Prince's Army on the left, so the Prince's left was opposite Hawley's centre.

This is confirmed by Colonel O'Sullivan's *Narrative*, in which he states that the Jacobite left was dangerously exposed because it was outflanked and outnumbered by Government forces.

The battlefield deployment of the two armies posed the risk of a recurrence of the events thirty years earlier at the Battle of Sheriffmuir. There, the crack regiments of each of the opposing armies were positioned on their right flanks, with their weaker units on the left. The result at Sheriffmuir was that the Jacobite right succeeded in driving back the Hanoverian left while, conversely, the Hanoverian right routed the Jacobite left, and as a consequence no one knew who had won the battle.

> *There's some say that we wan and some say that they wan*
> *And some say that nane wan at a' man*
> *But one thing is sure that at Sheriff Muir*
> *A battle was fought on that day man*
> *And we ran and they ran and they ran and we ran*
> *And we ran and they ran awa' man.*

Between 3.30 and 4 p.m., the Hanoverian dragoons under Colonel Francis

Ligonier sought to draw the fire of the Jacobite infantry by parading across the top of the hill in front of them at a sufficient distance to compromise the accuracy of a musket volley.

Lord George, having now dismounted from his own horse, stood in front of his men to prevent them from firing and ordered them to hold their fire until he gave the signal. The action is described by Geoff Bailey in *Falkirk or Paradise*.

> The noise of the approaching cavalry was deafening. The MacDonalds could almost feel the warm breath from the horse's nostrils as they stared into their wild eyes. Almost every Jacobite eye was transfixed on Lord George as he stood slightly ahead of them. Twenty yards, fifteen yards, thirteen yards – then at just ten yards, Lord George levelled his own musket. The crack of the lone shot rang out giving a hollow peel in the cold winter's air. That was the signal. A devastating volley now echoed along the Jacobite line. It started on the right, by Lord George, and ran up the hill like a rolling wave crashing on the rocks. The second and third ranks of the first line had reserved their fire for this instant, and almost 2,000 guns were aimed at the dragoons at that one brief moment. At least eighty dragoons were instantly killed, many more wounded. Their horses' flesh was ripped and torn. More horses fell, dislodging their riders. A cloud of sulphurous smoke descended over the carnage from the discharge, carried as luck would have it by a sudden ferocious storm blast of wind and hail. It was as though the very elements themselves had declared for the Jacobites.

Among those mortally wounded by that initial volley was Colonel Ligonier himself. Some of the horses reared and bolted in terror, causing confusion among the Hanoverian infantry coming up in their rear. Others charged into the Jacobite front line. What then occurred was recalled by the Chevalier Johnstone, serving as an aide-de-camp to Lord George Murray, in his *Memoir*.

> The cavalry closing their ranks, which had been opened by our discharge, put spurs to their horses and rushed upon the Highlanders at a hard trot, breaking their ranks, throwing everything down before them and trampling the Highlanders under the feet of their horses.

The most singular and extraordinary combat immediately followed. The Highlanders, stretched on the ground, thrust their dirks into the bellies of the horses. Some seized the riders by their clothes, dragged them down and stabbed them with their dirks. Several again used their pistols, but few of them had sufficient space to handle their swords. MacDonald of Clanranald assured me that whilst he was lying upon the ground under a dead horse which had fallen upon him, without the power of extricating himself, he saw a dismounted horseman struggling with a Highlander. Fortunately for him, the Highlander, being the strongest, threw his antagonist and having killed him with his dirk came to his assistance and drew him with difficulty from under his horse.

The resistance of the Highlanders was so incredibly obstinate that the English, after having engaged pell-mell with them, were at length repulsed and forced to retire. The Highlanders did not neglect the advantage they had obtained, but pursued them keenly with their swords, running as fast as their horses and not allowing them a moment's time to recover from their fright.

By this point, Lord George Murray had lost control of the Clan Donald regiments, who were in full pursuit of the retreating dragoons. The terrified horses bolted over their own infantry, the inexperienced volunteers of the Glasgow Militia, causing havoc on the Hanoverian left flank. Lord George was able to advance with the Atholl Brigade, which, he wrote:

kept their line in perfect good order; and having a full view of the confusion the enemy were in, I resolved to attack them upon their retreat, and did all in my power to rally the MacDonalds as I marched down the hill.

It was now after 4 p.m. and darkness was falling.

While the Clan Donald regiments on the right had broken the Hanoverian cavalry attack and were now pursuing them, the picture was very different on the Jacobite left. There, the Camerons under Lochiel were heavily outnumbered by crack Hanoverian infantry regiments under Colonel Howard, Lord Ligonier (older brother of the unfortunate dragoon commander, Colonel Francis Ligonier) and Price in the front line, supported by Fleming, Barrel and Battereau in the second line.

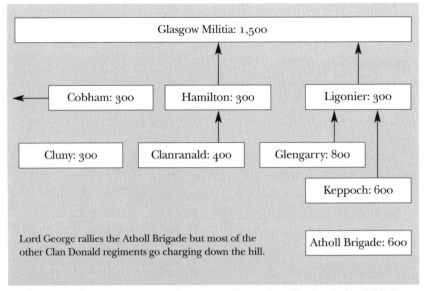

Figure 5: Regimental movements on the Jacobite right flank at Falkirk Muir.

Some of the Hanoverian horse, in particular Cobhams' dragoons, had bolted eastwards across the battlefield, where they were subjected to a volley from the Jacobite front line. But once they reached their own infantry divisions on the eastern flank, they managed to regroup and combined with the infantry to attack the vulnerable Jacobite left.

Colonel O'Sullivan, riding across the battlefield from the Jacobite right flank, recounted the position on the Jacobite left flank in his *Narrative*.

> O'Sullivan went off to regularise the line according to the last movement that Lord George had made [i.e. to line up the regiments that were now extending westwards so they formed a single line]. He repeated the same orders to every Colonel and Major as he went along. His orders were that the second and third rank should only fire as near to the enemy as possible.
>
> While he was giving these orders to Lochiel, one Daniel Cameron answered that he was afraid that they could be outflanked. O'Sullivan did not like that reflection, but reassured him that he would take care of it and went a little farther to the left to examine the right of the enemy's line. There he discovered that they were forming a hollow square of at least four battalions which could destroy us if they came up the height. O'Sullivan did not

know if anybody was aware of what he had observed, or the dread that he was in.

O'Sullivan then states that he sent a messenger with an urgent request for reinforcements from the second line to bolster the Jacobite left wing, by 'bringing up Lord Ogilvy's regiment immediately and posting them on a ravine on our left in case that hollow square should advance onto the heights'.

As O'Sullivan had feared, the hollow square did indeed now begin to advance. O'Sullivan then recounts how he

> went directly to Lochiel to advise him to observe it, keep his ground, and not fire until they were within ten paces of them. Most of the enemy's first line was cavalry [mainly Cobham's Dragoons, who had reformed into battlefield formation after their flight eastwards]. At their right were four battalions, and at the right of these battalions was the hollow square of which I spoke. They detached into two columns to the right and left of their horse, who came on at us at a great trot as boldly as any troops in the world. But our Highlanders stood so firm and managed their fire so well that they could not pierce our lines.

Crucially, Lochiel's Camerons held their ground. O'Sullivan's *Narrative* continues:

> Our left flank, in pursuing their horse, met with the battalions of which I spoke before and received their fire. The Highlanders rushed upon them sword in hand immediately after the discharge and cut them to pieces.
>
> This was perhaps one of the boldest and finest actions that any troops of the world could be capable of, but the cursed hollow square came up, took out our left wing by flanking them, and obliged them to retire in disorder.

O'Sullivan reports that many soldiers in the second line of the Jacobite left flank abandoned the field, and that 'some of them even went to Bannockburn and Stirling where they gave out that we had lost the day'.

At this juncture, there was a very real possibility that the events of the Battle of Sheriffmuir could be repeated, with the Jacobite left routed by the Hanoverians to the east of the battlefield, even as the Jacobite right broke the Hanoverian lines to the west.

The decision to hold the Irish Piquets, the most experienced professional regiment in the Jacobite Army, in reserve now paid dividends. At the critical moment, the Piquets and Lord Ogilvy's cavalry advanced to shore up the Highland infantry regiments on the left flank, thus countering the overwhelming superiority in numbers that the Hanoverians enjoyed on that flank. The reinforcements boosted Jacobite numbers on their left flank to approximately 2,500 men. This was still less than the Hanoverian regiments, but some of the Hanoverian forces, in particular the Argyll Militia under Colonel John Campbell, were impeded by the ravine near the monument.

Who was responsible for rallying the Jacobite left flank? Christopher

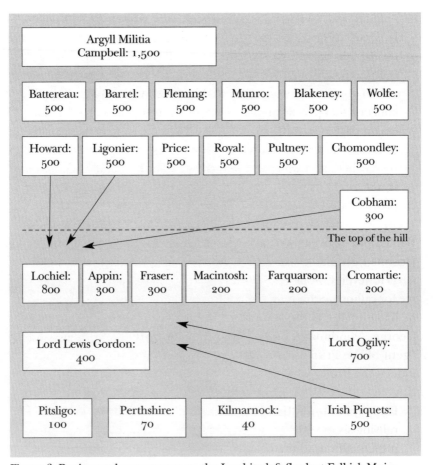

Figure 6: Regimental movements on the Jacobite left flank at Falkirk Muir.

Duffy states in *Fight for a Throne* that credit for sending in the reinforcements at the crucial moment has been variously given to Lord George Murray, Colonel O'Sullivan and Prince Charles Edward Stuart himself. I've considered each in turn and suggest that the vital command could not have been given by Lord George, as he was not in the right place and was not fully aware of what was happening on the Jacobite left. He was too busy trying to rally the right, and in particular organising the advance of the Atholl Brigade and the soldiers of the Clan Donald regiments who had maintained their battle order. Furthermore, he had no command responsibilities over the two key regiments (the Piquets and Lord Ogilvy's), which both fell under Lord John Drummond's division. His own memoir makes no mention of having given commands to them; indeed, in one passage on Falkirk Muir he reflects on the practical difficulties faced by a battlefield general:

> It is not an easy task to describe a battle. Springs and motions escape the eye, and most officers are necessarily taken up with what is immediately near themselves, so that it is next to impossible for one to observe the whole; add to this, the confusion, the noise, the concern that people are in, whilst in the heat of action. The smallest oversights and the most minute incidents are often the cause of the loss or gain of the day; an opportunity, once missed, cannot be recalled; and when a commanding officer commits a mistake, it may perhaps not be perceived but by very few, if any, and yet prove fatal.

While Lord George was fully engaged seeking to maintain control of the Jacobite right flank, Colonel O'Sullivan was focused on shoring up the left. However, Colonel O'Sullivan could not have been directly responsible for calling up the reserves at the crucial moment in the battle because he had even less authority over the two key Jacobite regiments than Lord George. As Adjutant, he only had authority in so far as he acted as an agent of the Prince. His own account states unequivocally that it was indeed the Prince who gave the orders:

> Happily for us, HRH brought up the few regular troops he had, rallying six or seven hundred men [mainly the Piquets] and ordering O'Sullivan to march to a body of horse that was rallied [Lord Ogilvy's] and forming within two musket shots. The enemy's horse,

seeing this body formed and marching towards them, went off as fast as they could, as the rest of their army did, and left us masters of the field.

O'Sullivan's account is corroborated by Alexander MacDonald, who was serving in Clanranald's Regiment that day:

His Royal Highness, whose attention was turned to all quarters, observing that our left wing was outlined by the enemy, sent Brigadier Stapleton with the pickets of the Irish Brigade and some other battalions from the second line, which extended our first line and recovered the disorder we were like to be put into.

The evidence thus appears compelling. The man who saved the day for the Jacobites, by preventing a rout of their left flank, was the army's commander-in-chief, Prince Charles Edward Stuart.

Alexander MacDonald's account of the battle concludes:

both our officers and men behaved with the greatest bravery, and our order in marching and attacking were allowed to be far beyond expectation in the judgement of officers who had been in the wars abroad. It must be acknowledged, indeed, that the Irish officers were of great use to us.

Once the regiments on the Hanoverian right flank retreated, the Jacobites were left in full control of the battlefield. Between 4.30 p.m. and 5.00 p.m., Lord George Murray decided to advance into Falkirk, rejecting an alternative proposal that the Jacobite Army should fall back into Dunipace. 'Tonight, we shall lie in Falkirk or in Paradise,' he said, warning that should the Jacobites fail to take Falkirk, they would give the Hanoverian Army a chance to regroup and strike back the following day. He consulted with the Prince, who agreed to wait on the hillside until the town was properly secured. This decision proved sound, as there were still Hanoverian snipers in the town, one of whom hit Lord John Drummond, who suffered flesh wounds.

During the advance into Falkirk, Lord George secured the enemy's cannon, which they had left behind. The speed with which the engagement had developed during the afternoon was such that neither side had been able to deploy their artillery during the battle.

Lord George entered Falkirk just after six o'clock that night. Sometime between 7 p.m. and 8 p.m., the Prince entered the town. In view of the darkness, the foul weather and the need to reassemble forces scattered across the hillsides and in the town, the Jacobite high command concluded that they could pursue no further that night and must strike camp.

After the battle, there was criticism on the Jacobite side because the victory was not followed up. For example, Christopher Duffy, in his extensive description of the battle in *Fight for a Throne* (in a chapter appropriately entitled Jacobite Apogee), writes, 'The Jacobite victory stopped short of a battle of annihilation. There was much talk afterwards of Lord George Murray having thrown away the chance by ordering a new halt . . .' Christopher then goes on to defend Lord George's actions. The reality was that the army was so exhausted, with the Prince himself succumbing to a severe infection, that it was in no position to pursue the Hanoverians.

O'Sullivan recounts how, on the evening of 17 January, the advancing Jacobites came across

a great many hampers of good wines and liquors and other provisions. The Prince profited of General Hawley's supper which he wanted very much, for he had not a bit of his own, neither had he eaten a morsel that day. A great quantity of bread was found, which was distributed among our men.

The following day was spent in a mopping-up operation and in burying the dead, as O'Sullivan relates:

The Prince gave orders the next day to bury the dead. It is assured that they were near upon a thousand dead found upon the field of battle or on the roads or moors about, among whom were Sir Robert Munro and his brother who were great and inveterate enemies to the cause. [They were buried with full military honours by the Jacobite high command in the Falkirk Old Churchyard.] There were a great many officers killed, for gold watches were at a cheap rate.

There was one further loss, as recounted in a letter written by Lord George Murray to his wife, Amelia, on 22 January 1746:

We hear from Edinburgh by several persons come from it this day
that our enemies are in the greatest confusion, and quarrelling
amongst themselves, holding court martials to try their officers to
throw the blame off the commanders . . .

A most unfortunate accident happened here two days after the
action. Colonel Angus Macdonell, Glengarry's son, who was a
modest, brave, and advisable lad, was mortally wounded by an accidental shot of a miserable fellow of the Clanranald Regiment out
of a window upon the street, of which he died this day, vastly regretted. It is more of a loss to us than all we suffered at the battle.

The 'miserable fellow' responsible for accidentally shooting Young Glengarry was immediately executed in an effort to stop further acrimony
between the Glengarry and Clanranald MacDonalds. His own father was
one of the members of the firing squad, for which he volunteered after
his entreaties for mercy had been unsuccessful in order to ensure that his
son's death was as painless as possible. Young Glengarry himself had
pleaded for clemency as he lay dying, recognising that the shot had been
fired accidentally. In the event, the sacrifice of the man's life was not
entirely successful in preventing bad feeling between the Clanranald and
Glengarry MacDonalds, or in stopping the haemorrhage of men from
the Jacobite Army. In the following weeks there were a large number of
desertions, as the Jacobite Army began to disintegrate.

Perhaps with some self-awareness of the role that he had played in
causing divisions within the Jacobite camp, and perhaps thinking specifically of the fateful decision to turn back at Derby, Lord George concluded
his letter to his wife as follows:

I can say that since I joined I never disobliged any person except
by telling my mind too frankly and sometimes with some warmth,
but only when the service required it. I believe my opinion was
mostly found right in the long run, and always approved of by the
officers that are most regarded and of the most weight . . .

If I be in love with life it is only owing to my love of my dear
Amilie, and nothing else. Otherwise I should not wish to survive a
defeat. Adieu.

*   *   *

Generally, the testimony of those who fought on Falkirk Muir on that bleak winter's afternoon paints a clear and consistent picture of what happened before, during and after the battle.

By 16 January, Hawley's failure to advance was causing concern in the Jacobite high command. As the Jacobite forces were scattered across the countryside, they were vulnerable to a surprise attack by the Government forces. The Prince and his Council of War therefore determined to force the issue by advancing on to Falkirk on 17 January.

Once the decision was taken to advance, the Jacobites comprehensively outmanoeuvred the Government forces. The feint by Lord John Drummond's division, marching directly from the Torwood towards Falkirk, enabled the main body of the Jacobite Army under Lord George to advance unobserved towards the heights of Falkirk Muir. According to Lord George's account, as he advanced there was an unhelpful intervention from Colonel O'Sullivan, who tried to halt the advance until nightfall. O'Sullivan makes no mention of what was evidently a testy exchange in his own narrative, perhaps because Lord George's decision to continue the advance was vindicated by the events that followed.

Brigadier Stapleton, recently arrived from France with the Irish Piquets, appears to have played a key role in mobilising his support behind Lord George's tactics and helping to convince the Prince to overrule Colonel O'Sullivan's proposal to halt the advance. Unusually, Brigadier Stapleton is commended by both Lord George Murray and Colonel O'Sullivan in their memoirs. Stapleton was to fall three months later at Culloden, leading the last stand of the Irish Piquets against the advancing redcoats, when they were providing cover to the retreating Clan Donald regiments which, as a result of Stapleton's sacrifice, were able to escape from the battlefield.

It was only when Lord George's Highland regiments were approaching the heights of Falkirk Muir that General Hawley became aware of what was happening and ordered his cavalry to advance in an attempt to prevent them from achieving their objective.

The decision to send the cavalry into battle ahead of the infantry was contrary to all established battle tactics and evidence of how badly Hawley had been wrong-footed. As an infantry advance would have been too slow to prevent the Jacobites from reaching the top of the hill ahead of his own infantry, Hawley had no option but to throw in his cavalry first, charging directly at the MacDonalds. The defending Highlanders, with the wind and rain at their backs and blowing directly into the faces of their enemy, had overwhelming field advantage and routed the Hanoverian cavalry.

In contrast to the discipline on the Jacobite right under the command of Lord George, the position on the left was confused. O'Sullivan did his best to identify areas of potential weakness, hold the line and rally the Jacobite Army. According to O'Sullivan's *Narrative*, the Prince played the key role in stabilising the position by bringing up his infantry reserves and Lord Ogilvy's Horse, which appears to have been the only cavalry unit in fit condition to fight, reinforcing the crumbling Jacobite left. The Hanoverian attack on the Jacobite left was repelled and the Jacobites secured the field.

All the witnesses agree that a potential opportunity was missed to pursue and destroy the enemy. The two Irish commentators, O'Sullivan and Sir John Macdonald, placed the blame for this on Lord George Murray, but this seems unfair and based on ignorance of what was happening on the right. As Sir John Macdonald himself concedes, he could not see what was happening because of the undulations of the hill. The accounts of Lord George, the Chevalier Johnstone and Lord Elcho seem more balanced and accurate in this regard, as they were aware of the confusion on the right wing.

All accounts agree that by this time darkness had fallen and the weather was appalling. There was general confusion on the field. Johnstone's account makes it clear that he had no idea of the deployment of the Jacobite forces in the immediate aftermath of the battle or the position of the Hanoverians. By this time – between seven and eight o'clock at night – it was pitch dark, the storm was still fierce, and the Jacobite forces were scattered and exhausted. In all the circumstances, the Prince's decision to take shelter in Falkirk that night seems to have been the only rational course of action.

Overall, the Prince led his forces with intelligence and courage throughout the battle. It was he who took the decision to advance that morning and wrong-foot Hawley by initiating Lord John Drummond's feint on the road from Torwood while Lord George Murray advanced, undetected, towards the summit of Falkirk Muir. He supported Lord George's decision to continue the advance, against Colonel O'Sullivan's advice to wait until nightfall. According to O'Sullivan's account, the Prince led from the front, riding among his men to urge on the advance. While the position on the Jacobite right took care of itself, thanks to Lord George's outstanding generalship, the Jacobite left almost disintegrated in the face of an attack from Hanoverian forces superior in numbers and weaponry until the Prince stabilised the situation by sending in reinforcements from the second line. Having secured the field, the Prince entered the town of Falkirk after his two battlefield commanders, Lord George Murray and Lord John Drummond. He did what he could to pursue the fleeing Hanoverians, only giving up the effort when the appalling weather and pitch darkness rendered continued pursuit impossible.

By contrast, it would appear that General Henry Hawley committed blunder after blunder. He failed to attack the Jacobite forces when they were at their most vulnerable during the days leading up to the battle. He was caught napping on the day of the battle itself, failing to recognise the threat that the Jacobites might seize the commanding heights outside Falkirk or posting look-outs to alert him should they try to do so. He then compounded his error by making the tactical blunder of sending his cavalry to charge into a gale of wind and rain at Highland regiments whose position was already secured, leading to an almost inevitable rout that cost many of his officers and men their lives. As Chevalier Johnstone points out in his memoir, Hawley would have been far better advised to take up a defensive position in the town of Falkirk, leaving Prince Charlie's men exposed to a bitter winter's night on the hills outside the town or – possibly even worse – leading them to attack a superior force well dug into defensive positions in the town. Even after the battle, Hawley could have taken up a defensive position in the town, making life very difficult for the Jacobites. Instead, he ordered a full retreat to Edinburgh, leaving the town, cannon, munitions, weapons and plentiful supplies open for the Jacobites to take.

Later commentators have described the Battle of Falkirk Muir as a 'tactical victory but strategic defeat' for the Jacobites. They make the case that, even had the Jacobites successfully pursued the Hanoverian Government forces after the battle, it was unlikely that they could have reversed the retreat on which they had embarked after Derby. Nevertheless, had the Government forces been utterly destroyed after the Battle of Falkirk Muir in January 1746, it is possible that the momentum could have shifted and Prince Charles could have held Lowland Scotland rather than retreat northwards, forcing the Hanoverians to either offer a settlement or face the unenviable prospect of a prolonged and debilitating civil war.

11

Financing the Revolution

The story of the Rising of 1745, as conventionally told, is one of heroes and villains, warriors and poets, and, above all, battles – at Prestonpans, Clifton, Falkirk Muir, and finally at Culloden.

But a question seldom addressed by historians of the period is: How was the campaign financed? Without money, no campaign can long endure, and certainly not a major military venture such as that led by the Prince.

We know how the Hanoverian Government Army was funded – by taxes levied by the British Government from its citizens, including the new Glass Excise Tax raised at the rate of a penny per pound (lb) of glass weight (see Chapter 6). In addition, the Government raised a loan of £1 million from the Bank of England in January 1746, equivalent to approximately £200 million in today's values.

But what about the Jacobite Army? Where did they get the money to fund their venture? Their campaign cost many millions of pounds in today's values. For obvious reasons, there is no official record of the sources of their funding. So I looked up the index of histories of the Rising under 'finance' or 'funding' or 'money'. The references were few and far between and provided little information. I googled 'How did Bonnie Prince Charlie finance the Rising of 1745?'. Again, no answers. On the basis of what you can glean from the standard references of the period, you could be forgiven for thinking that the funds to pay for the campaign descended on the Jacobites like manna from heaven or were gifted to them by some fairy godmother waving her magic fairy money wand.

So, I turned to primary sources written by those who were actually caught up in the Rising. None of them give a complete picture of how the campaign was funded. However, by piecing together the evidence provided by each of them, I was able to build up a consistent account of how the campaign was financed, and why it ultimately ran out of money. I also referred to a small number of secondary sources, which were exceptions to the rule that little has been published on campaign finance. These secondary sources include Ray Perman's 2019 book *The Rise and Fall of the City of Money*, one chapter of which covers the period of the Jacobite occupation of Edinburgh in October 1745.

From these sources emerge four distinct phases in the financing of the campaign: its initial launch in July and August 1745; its second round of financing during the occupation of Edinburgh in October 1745; the period between November 1745 and January 1746 when an expeditionary Jacobite force advanced into England and subsequently retreated back to Scotland, sustaining itself by levies on the populations of the towns and cities through which it where it passed; and finally, the army's progressive disintegration between February and April 1746, when the money finally ran out.

July to August 1745: Campaign Launch

The seed capital for the campaign was provided by Prince Charles Edward Stuart himself. He was not only the leader of this venture, he was also its principal financial backer. He raised £4,000 in gold for his war chest for the campaign and also paid for arms, ships and a small expeditionary force. He raised these funds from Parisian bankers, including Aeneas MacDonald, who was one of the Seven Men of Moidart who landed with him on the isle of Eriskay on 23 July 1745, and the banking house of Waters & Co. As collateral for their loans, he pledged his personal assets, including jewels bequeathed to him by his late mother, Maria Clementina Sobieska.

He applied these funds to hire two ships provided by a Breton of Irish descent, Captain Antoine Walsh – the *Elizabeth* and the *Du Teillay* – which sailed for Scotland from Nantes in early July 1745. As we know, the Prince's venture started to go wrong when his ships were intercepted by Royal Navy vessel HMS *Lyon*, the following engagement forcing the *Elizabeth* to limp back to France, though the Prince continued to sail to Scotland on the *Du Teillay*.

On arrival, he was successful in raising enough support among Highland clans to continue his campaign and march southwards towards Edinburgh. It is not clear how much of his war chest he still had, but his funds were sufficient to meet his campaign expenses until the army reached Perth in early September. However, according to O'Sullivan's *Narrative*, by that time the Prince was down to his last ten guineas.

On arrival in Perth, the Jacobites proclaimed the Prince's father, James Francis Edward Stuart, as the King. Contrary to the impression given by romanticised songs like 'Charlie Is my Darling', this proclamation did not meet with universal adulation. In fact, O'Sullivan says that 'the town in general was not well disposed' towards the Jacobites.

It is not difficult to work out why this might be. The good townspeople of Perth knew perfectly well that the Proclamation of King James had one purpose, which was to give a veneer of legal authority to what the Jacobites did next: collect levies in order to finance their army.

The Jacobites collected £500 from the town's magistrates and secured additional sums from private supporters, many of whom, according to O'Sullivan, preferred to make financial contributions rather than volunteer their services to the Prince's army.

The Jacobites preferred to raise these levies in gold and silver rather than in banknotes. While coin minted in precious metals was acceptable anywhere as a means of payment, not everyone trusted banknotes. In order to accept banknotes, a creditor had to have confidence that the bank issuing the notes would always be ready and able to redeem them for gold.

The banker most trusted by Jacobites in early eighteenth-century Scotland was David Drummond, Bank of Scotland Treasurer for forty years from 1701 until his death in 1740. The Bank of Scotland had been established by an Act of the Scottish Parliament in 1695, a year after the Bank of England, with an initial capital set out in the Act of 'twelve hundred thousand pounds Scots', equivalent to £100,000 Sterling, or approximately £20 million in today's values (see Appendix 1: A Note on the Conversion of 1745 Prices into 2020 Values). It was granted a monopoly on the issue of Scottish banknotes, mirroring the Bank of England monopoly on the issue of banknotes in England. However, the Bank of Scotland's monopoly ended in 1716.

The reason for the termination of the Bank of Scotland's monopoly on banknote issue in Scotland was that it lost the confidence of the Hanoverian Government because of the role it played during the Jacobite Rising of 1715. As Treasurer of the Bank, David Drummond provided financial support to Jacobites imprisoned after the Rising. The Government suspected that his assistance to the Jacobites extended beyond this, to helping to keep their money safe from Hanoverian confiscation and get it out of the country.

Worse was to follow, as far as the old Bank of Scotland was concerned, when King George granted a Charter to a new bank set up in 1727, the Royal Bank of Scotland (RBS). The New Bank, as it became known, then tried to drive its rival out of business by buying up as many Bank of Scotland notes as it could and presenting them for payment in coin and bullion. The Bank of Scotland did not have sufficient gold reserves to redeem these notes because it had lent out a large part of its gold deposits to its borrowers. As a consequence, it was forced to close its doors in March and April 1727 while it raised sufficient gold and silver to honour the notes.

The following year, 1728, the Royal Bank successfully petitioned the Exchequer to prohibit the use of 'unreliable' Bank of Scotland banknotes to pay taxes. Over the next seventeen years, RBS progressively supplanted the old Bank of Scotland as the Government's Bank in Scotland, securing most of the lucrative business of the Hanoverian Government north of the border.

September to October 1745: Second Round Funding

Despite RBS's status as the Hanoverian Government's bank in Scotland, in October 1745 John Campbell of Ardmaddie, RBS's first cashier – effectively, its chief executive – was accused by the RBS's Deputy Governor, Lord Milton, of being a Jacobite collaborator. This allegation has been repeated as if it were an established fact by a number of historians, including Alice Wemyss in *Elcho of the '45* and Desmond Seward, who described John Campbell as a 'crypto Jacobite' in his 2019 book *The King Over the Water*.

So, what is the truth about this sensational allegation made against a man who was a member of the staunchly Hanoverian Clan Campbell and chief executive of the staunchly Hanoverian Royal Bank of Scotland? Was he, in reality, a closet Jacobite?

The key facts pertaining to RBS's financial support for the Jacobite Rising may be briefly summarised.

On Friday, 13 September 1745, word reached Edinburgh that the Jacobite Army had crossed the Fords of Frew and was advancing rapidly on to Edinburgh. The following day, the Old Bank of Scotland transferred its reserves of gold and silver into Edinburgh Castle to keep them safe from Jacobite expropriation. On Sunday, 15 September, the new Royal Bank followed suit.

Their precautions proved timely. In the early hours of Tuesday, 17 September, the Jacobites disarmed the City Guard and breached the Netherbow Port, which was one of the gates protecting the walled city of Edinburgh. On learning that the gold and silver reserves of the two banks were locked inside the castle, the Jacobites immediately demanded its surrender, but without success.

On the following Saturday, 21 September, the Jacobites secured a sensational and unexpected dawn victory over the Government Army at Prestonpans. They then blockaded the castle, trapping the gold reserves of both banks inside, severely hampering the conduct of trade within the city.

In an effort to remedy the situation, the Prince issued a Proclamation on Wednesday, 25 September, in which he declared that the banks could safely return to their former business and that he himself would contribute to restoring public credit by paying for any services required by his army in banknotes rather than coin. As the Prince lacked gold and silver to offer in payment, his ringing declaration supporting the use of banknotes as his preferred means of payment was making a virtue of necessity. In the 1918 edition of his *History of Banking in Scotland*, Andrew William Kerr commented, somewhat tongue in cheek: 'Notwithstanding this polite, but by no means disinterested, manifesto, the bank directors continued to regard the security of the stone walls and cannon of the Castle as more reliable than the words of a prince.'

Irritated by the intransigence of the Edinburgh bankers, the Jacobites now escalated their demands. On 1 October, Prince Charles's Principal Secretary, John Murray of Broughton, presented John Campbell with £857 of Royal Bank notes, along with a demand that they be redeemed for gold and silver. On 3 October, Murray of Broughton presented a further £2,307 worth of notes for redemption. Some of these notes had been raised in Glasgow by John Hay of Restalrig, another of the Prince's secretaries and a former director of the Old Bank of Scotland.

Murray of Broughton was keen to convert the banknotes he held into coin because he knew that, whatever their value might be in Edinburgh, Scottish banknotes would be of no value whatsoever in England, where they would not be accepted as a means of payment.

Murray of Broughton informed Campbell that if he didn't deliver the gold, he would 'protest' the amounts due after forty-eight hours – a legal remedy meaning that he could seize the personal property of John Campbell and other bank directors in lieu of payment.

When John Campbell pointed out that he couldn't convert Murray of Broughton's notes into coin because the Highlanders were blockading the castle where all the coin was kept, Murray helpfully issued him with a *passé port* granting him permission to pass through the Jacobite lines without let or hindrance. Campbell then raised a further objection, pointing out that it would be most dangerous for him to do this since Government forces in the castle were at that precise moment firing cannonballs and muskets at the Jacobites. Upon which Murray of Broughton informed him that if this was an issue, Campbell could always choose the alternative option – military execution.

This was the 1745 version of Hobson's choice. Campbell's Choice was to risk execution by the Jacobites if he didn't pass through their lines, and by the Hanoverians if he did. Moral hazard in banking had slightly different connotations back in 1745!

Such are the principal facts pertaining to John Campbell's decision to transfer Royal Bank gold to the Jacobites in exchange for the banknotes that they presented to him. They do not, in my judgement, support the allegation that John Campbell was a Jacobite collaborator. The fact was that Campbell was in an extremely difficult position. Under the laws of the day, he had an obligation to convert any Royal Bank of Scotland banknotes into gold on demand. He may indeed have suspected that the notes in question had not been secured by legitimate means, and that any gold given by him in exchange for them might be applied to purposes that would not meet with the entire approval of the Hanoverian Government. However, even today a banker presented with a demand for funds which he suspects may be used for nefarious purposes would be ill-advised to try and take the law into his own hands by blocking a withdrawal. The correct course of action would be to alert the relevant authorities of the situation, present supporting evidence and co-operate fully in the ensuing proceedings. Pending such proceedings, a banker could be deemed to be acting illegally by refusing a request for the withdrawal of funds. It was no different for John Campbell in 1745.

In a portrait of John Campbell of Ardmaddie by William Mossman painted in 1749, he strikes a rather diffident and cautious pose, as befits a prudent banker. One would imagine that he struck an even more diffident pose when he emerged from behind the Jacobite lines on the morning of 3 October 1745, leading the three other Royal Bank directors still remaining in Edinburgh. These directors did not include Mr Campbell's chief accuser, Lord Milton, who had ensured his own safety by departing from the city before the Jacobite Army arrived.

Today, the castle Esplanade is the venue for the Edinburgh Royal Military Tattoo and Hogmanay celebrations, when it is always thronging with crowds. Yet, remarkably enough, on that October day in 1745 the Esplanade was completely empty. Not a soul was to be seen taking the morning air. It was completely deserted – deserted, that is, apart from John Campbell, leading his three fellow directors and waving a white flag, which he no doubt earnestly hoped was large enough to be clearly visible to the castle's redoubtable eighty-five-year-old commander, General Joshua Guest, notwithstanding the old man's fading eyesight.

Luckily for John Campbell, General Guest did indeed order his men to hold their fire and he was able to enter the castle. In his diary, John Campbell wrote: 'On our arrival at General Guest's lodgings (the Governor's House), the directors and I went in, and told him our errand in general was to get into the Royal Bank depositories to do some business.'

Once safely inside the castle, Campbell and his fellow directors 'burnt or tore-up as many banknotes as they could', according to Ray Perman, who takes up the story in *The Rise and Fall of the City of Money*:

> with no idea as to who might be the eventual victor, they had to tread a fine line between the two sides of the conflict. Accordingly, they gave General Guest £2,000 'for the public service' and took away £6,000 in gold to meet the requirements of the rebels.

One question that arises is why did General Guest allow Campbell and his fellow directors to withdraw the gold? The most obvious answer – apart from the little matter of the £2,000 donated to him by the directors, equivalent to the not inconsiderable sum of around £400,000 in today's money – is that, had he acted otherwise, he would have been in contravention of the law. The funds belonged to the Royal Bank and its depositors, not to General Guest. They had been placed in the castle for safekeeping and, according to the bank's representative Mr Campbell, were now required by the bank to conduct its normal commercial activities. Had the funds been withheld, General Guest would almost certainly have been held personally responsible for seriously hampering trade in Edinburgh, causing business distress and potentially precipitating the collapse of the bank itself. It was not for General Guest to speculate as to what uses the funds might be put, whatever his private suspicions. Had he refused to release the Royal Bank's reserves to its directors, there was even a risk that he might subsequently be found guilty of theft, a capital crime at the time.

In any event, the Jacobites got their gold. In his essay, 'The Old and New Banks in the '45', Peter Lole states:

> In all, between the 1st and 31st of October, the Jacobite Secretariat presented notes on six occasions, totalling over £6,500, all of which were met; only the first presentation was accompanied by the drama of entering the castle while it was actively responding to the blockade.

During September and October, the Prince also secured contributions from several of his supporters, including 1,500 guineas from Lord Elcho and between £200 and £300 from the Duke of Perth. Lord Elcho understood that his contribution was a loan that would be repaid by the Prince once the Rising was over; the Prince understood it to be a donation. This difference in understanding was later to be the cause of a complete breakdown in relations between the two men. Lord Elcho was to learn an expensive lesson worth bearing in mind today – in any significant financial transaction, always make sure that agreement is made in writing to avoid the risk of any potential dispute.

There was no risk of financial dispute in the case of the Duke of Perth. He died of wounds sustained at Culloden at sea on 8 May 1746 and his body was consigned to the deep, saluted by the guns of *Le Bellone*.

However, these events lay in the future, when the crucial Council of War convened at the Palace of Holyrood on 30 October 1745 and Prince Charles Edward Stuart was able to inform the Duke of Perth, Lord Elcho and his other commanders that they now had the men, the munitions and the money they needed to advance into England. He persuaded the Council to follow his recommendation to march into England by a majority of a single vote.

As for John Campbell of Ardmaddie, he lived to enjoy a long and illustrious career at the Royal Bank of Scotland. Once the dust had settled after the Rising, it transpired that, in his haste to get out of Edinburgh before the Jacobites arrived, Campbell's accuser, Lord Milton, had withdrawn £100 from Royal Bank funds, or around £20,000 in today's money.

This was a not inconsiderable sum in the values of the time, being ten times the annual pay of an ordinary soldier. Lord Milton had made this withdrawal in some haste to help him on his way, without bothering with the minor detail of securing approval from John Campbell or indeed any other director of the Royal Bank.

One suspects that John Campbell may perhaps have mentioned this inconvenient fact to Lord Milton over a friendly cup of tea. There was no further enquiry into the noble Lord's unauthorised withdrawal of Royal Bank funds. It would appear that Mr Campbell was a very understanding fellow. Perhaps he regarded Lord Milton's failure to secure authorisation as an entirely understandable oversight which any chap might make under the circumstances, and nothing more needed to be said about it, provided a mutually acceptable solution could be found.

Coincidentally, nothing more was heard of Lord Milton's allegations against Mr Campbell. Indeed, John Campbell continued to serve as RBS's first cashier for thirty-two years until his death in 1777, leaving behind him a more substantial legacy than perhaps some of his successors as chief executive of the Royal Bank of Scotland.

He received the ultimate accolade of a laudatory poem composed by the great Gaelic bard Duncan Ban MacIntyre, which runs to 192 lines in total. A short extract translated from the original Gaelic may give a flavour of Duncan Ban MacIntyre's high esteem for Mr Campbell:

John Campbell of the Bank,
I give you warm greetings,
To uphold kith and clan,
You strove to act well:
And, with a kind and manly heart,
You surpassed all the rest.

You happy provider of bounty,
It would cheer me up
If I were to see you
Wearing the crown
With joy and grandeur
Instead of King George.

Does one suspects that Duncan Ban MacIntyre might have been seeking a bank loan at the time?

November 1745 to January 1746: To Derby and Back

I now draw on the testimony of Colonel John William O'Sullivan, Quartermaster General of the Jacobite Army, who served on the Jacobite Council of War. Commenting on the crucial Council held on 30 October 1745, which decided to advance into England, O'Sullivan states in his *Narrative*:

> The Army was, about the time we parted for England, at least five thousand men; it was, most certainly, not sufficient to conquer England, but the hope was that the English would join and the French would land. In part, the decision was taken because we had no means of raising enough money to sustain the Army in Scotland.

This Council of War is often portrayed as a debate between one group among the Jacobite leadership, including Lord George Murray and Lochiel, who wanted to break the Act of Union, declare independence and consolidate their position in Scotland, and another group led by the Prince himself and supported by the Duke of Perth, who advocated advance into England on the grounds that the Rising could only succeed if they secured control over the whole of Great Britain. O'Sullivan's *Narrative* suggests another consideration may have entered the equation – the hard fact that the Jacobites did not have enough money to maintain a standing army of 5,000 men in Scotland for any length of time. The Jacobites had to march southwards to secure more treasure, with the ultimate aim of reaching London, winning the English throne and securing the entire revenues of the British Government. As Prince Charlie had written to his father, James Francis Edward Stuart, before his departure from France, there were but two alternatives: to conquer or to die.

In *Fight for a Throne*, Christopher Duffy comments:

> The fact remained that [by late October 1745] all acceptable ways of raising money in Scotland were exhausted. By carrying the fight into England, on the other hand, the Jacobites could appropriate the public monies, fleece the Whigs, and provide the clansmen with all the action they wanted.

On this assessment, the advance on to London was driven as much by financial exigency as military strategy. It was a risk, but staying in Scotland offered only the prospect of dwindling funds while granting the Hanoverian Government the time they needed to build up their forces for a devastating counter-attack.

In reviewing an earlier draft of this chapter, Prof. Charles Munn of Glasgow University raised a question to which I did not have an answer. What were the logistics of transporting money and paying the expeditionary Jacobite Army while it was in England?

It seems a little unlikely that pack horses carried vast numbers of bags filled with silver sixpences to give the men their daily pay. I suggested that perhaps they were paid on a weekly basis in half crowns, but, logistically, it is unlikely that the army carried much of their money in crowns or half crowns. If the Jacobite expeditionary army had between £5,000 and £6,000 in funds when it entered England, that would equate to no less than 40,000 half crowns, which would have been too great a load for pack horses to carry over, in some places, rugged and difficult terrain. Perhaps the Jacobites took most of their money in the form of gold and used moneychangers in Carlisle, Manchester and Derby to convert it into silver coin for payment of their troops.

In any event, it is a mystery that I have not yet managed to solve. Perhaps some future researcher will be able to find the answer.

The Jacobite Army advanced into England in two divisions. The Lowland regiments and most of the cavalry, under the command of the Duke of Perth, carried the army's artillery and baggage and advanced along a westerly route through Peebles. The Highland regiments and the Prince's own lifeguard, under the command of the Prince himself and Lord George Murray, were more lightly equipped and marched along an easterly route as if intending to attack Newcastle. This feint succeeded in wrong-footing the Hanoverian commanders, who as a result kept their main force in Newcastle in preparation for a Jacobite attack that never came. The Highland division then swung west to join the Duke of Perth's division and advance on Carlisle.

Estimates of the numbers in each division vary. Figure 7 gives the estimates provided by Lord Elcho, commander of the Prince's personal bodyguard, in his *Short Account*, and by Frank McLynn in his *Jacobite Army in England 1745*. It will be noted that their respective estimates of numbers differ by some 700 men. The main reason for this appears to be that McLynn's estimates are of the number of men who marched out of Edinburgh in early November, while Lord Elcho's are of the number of men

Figure 7: Estimated strength of the Jacobite Army that advanced into England in November 1745.

Lowland Division under the Duke of Perth	Elcho	McLynn
Atholl Brigade	1,000	1,000
Duke of Perth's	300	750
Gordon of Glenbuchat	200	300
John Roy Stuart's	200	350
Lord Ogilvy's Horse	200	500
Lord Pitsligo's Horse	150	150
Baggot's Hussars	70	80
	2,120	3,130

Highland Division under Prince Charles and Lord George	Elcho	McLynn
MacDonells of Keppoch	450	300
MacDonells of Glengarry	500	450
MacDonalds of Clanranald	200	300
Cluny's MacPhersons	300	300
Appin Stewarts	550	350
Lochiel's Camerons	500	500
Lord Elcho's Lifeguards	150	130
	2,650	2,330
Total	4,770	5,460

Notes to the Table:
1. The figures given for Lord Elcho's Lifeguards include the cavalry units of Lord Balmerino (thirty to forty men) and Lord Kilmarnock (approximately thirty men), as well as Lord Elcho's own unit (seventy to eighty men).
2. There appears to be a difference between the two sources in the allocation of some smaller clan contingents, for example the MacGregors, MacLachlans and MacKenzies, across the Highland Regiments. Lord Elcho may have allocated some of these men to the Appin Stewarts, while Frank McLynn may have assigned them to the Clan Donald regiments.
3. Based upon the numbers provided by the two sources, it would appear that desertions may have been greater from the Lowland Division than from the Highland Division. If my inference is correct, it may reflect the fact that the Lowlanders had less distance to travel to get home and perhaps faced weaker informal sanctions for desertion than the Highlanders. Clan members guilty of desertion could have feared later ostracisation, which might not have been the case (for example) with the hired hands of John Roy's Edinburgh Regiment.

who marched into Carlisle a fortnight later. In his account of the campaign, Lord Elcho commented:

> Upon this march [onto Carlisle], both columns of the Army had a prodigious desertion, and it was computed at a thousand men: for the Army at leaving Edinburgh was 5,500, and at Carlisle it was only 4,500.

According to the account of Norman MacDonald, historian and former president of the Clan Donald Society of Edinburgh, Glengarry Regiment's of approximately 500 men was led by thirty-five officers under their colonel, Angus MacDonell. The officer corps comprised two lieutenant-colonels, four majors, fourteen captains and fifteen junior officers (lieutenants and ensigns). Based on prevailing pay rates for each of the ranks, I estimate that the daily pay of the regiment amounted to approximately 350 shillings or £17 10s, as set out in Figure 8.

Glengarry's Regiment constituted approximately one-tenth of the numeric strength of the Jacobite expeditionary force that entered England in November 1745. Based on this ratio, the daily pay of the entire army would therefore have amounted to approximately 3,500 shillings or £175. In addition, while in England, the army would have to pay for its food, lodgings, clothing and equipment. On the assumption that these overhead costs would have been approximately 50 per cent of the army's pay, the daily cost of sustaining the Jacobite Army in England would have amounted to approximately £250.

In his account of the army's advance to Derby, O'Sullivan does not mention money. I would infer from this that money was not a problem during this period. The gold raised in Edinburgh and Glasgow was sufficient to meet the costs of the Jacobite Army until early December.

However, the rate of cash-burn was rapid. Once the fateful decision was taken to retreat from Derby, the forward momentum of the campaign was lost. The Jacobites collected modest sums from towns through which they passed during their advance, and secured arms, munitions and horses at Carlisle following the surrender of the castle on 17 November. These additional amounts were nothing like enough to replenish the army's coffers, and its cash reserves were running low by the time the decision was taken to turn back on 6 December. At Derby, the Jacobites collected £500 in 'subscriptions' and £665 12s 8¾d in 'public money' on 5 December before they began their retreat. However, at the calculated

Figure 8: Estimated daily pay for the Glengarry Regiment in England.

Rank	Number	Pay rate per day	Total daily pay
Lieutenant-Colonel	2	3s 0d	6s
Major	4	2s 6d	10s
Captain	14	2s 0d	28s
Lieutenant / Ensign	15	1s 6d	22s 6d
Sergeant	40	1s 0d	40s
'Men of Good Name' (Corporals)	150	8d	100s
Ordinary Soldiers (Privates)	280	6d	140s
Total	505		346s 6d

Note: Glengarry's Regiment also included two surgeons and a chaplain.

daily cost of approximately £250, these levies would only be sufficient to sustain the army for about five days. Further sums were reported as raised in Manchester on 9 December, with one account giving the amount as £2,500, which would have kept the army going for a further ten days on my estimates. Nevertheless, by the time the army reached Dumfries on 22 December, it is clear that it was running short of money. There is a note of desperation in the address by Prince Charles Edward to the army there. He reassures his men that, as Lord John Drummond has now landed with reinforcements from France, he will shortly be in a position to give his soldiers

> clothes for a coat, tartan for hose, and shoes at six weeks end from their receiving the last; two shirts and a bonnet for each, and the French Ambassador confirms that the five guineas (per man) shall be paid immediately upon the French landing in England, and a further five guineas on the Restoration.

Given that this payment will shortly be made, the Prince's address then specifically prohibits:

> plundering, which not only has gained us disaffection of all the places we go to, but is likewise a curse against us . . . and therefore,

since our most gracious Prince has been pleased to give us our full pay . . . and now proposes to clothe us, there can be no further excuse for continuing that practice.

The Prince's Dumfries address concludes by warning that anyone found guilty of plunder or desertion will be severely punished. It is clear from the address that discipline was starting to break down. The reality was that the Prince did not have the means to fulfil his promises.

In his *Short Account of the Affairs of Scotland*, Lord Elcho reports:

After the army had passed the water of Esk back to Scotland, the Prince divided it into three bodies. The first, which consisted of the clans, Perth's Regiment and the baggage, he marched himself to Annan; Lord George Murray with the Atholl Brigade, Ogilvys, Roy Stuarts and Glenbuchats marched to Ecclefachan and then on to Moffat. Lord Elcho with all the horse marched to Dumfries with orders to disarm the town and to raise there £2,000 and 1,000 pairs of shoes. Upon his arrival, the militia left the town, and the tax was partly paid. Two hostages were taken for the remainder until the balance was also paid.

In fact, Lord Elcho informed the leaders of Dumfries town council that the hostages would be shot unless the tax was paid. Any pretence of raising funds from an enthusiastic populace keen to welcome back their rightful sovereign had by now been abandoned and the Jacobites had to use force to coerce money from a resentful local populace.

The Dumfries funds lasted long enough to sustain the army during its retreat to Glasgow, where it billeted over the Christmas and New Year period and where the same methods were applied to raise funds, with the same results. Money, supplies and clothing were extorted from a reluctant and resentful population and, after the Jacobite Army had departed, many Glasgow men joined the city militia to exact their revenge by serving with the Hanoverian Army that engaged with the Jacobites on Falkirk Muir on 17 January 1746. The Jacobite victory there enabled the Jacobite Army to secure further funds and supplies in Falkirk, but O'Sullivan's *Narrative* makes it clear their situation was becoming increasingly desperate.

February to April 1746: The Final Disintegration

The Jacobites' French allies tried to get more funds to them. The *Hazard*, a ship which had been captured from the Royal Navy, was refitted, renamed *Le Prince Charles*, and sent to Scotland under Captain Talbot with a sum of 13,000 gold Louis d'Or on board. The Louis d'Or coins minted under Louis XV weighed 8.158 grams, or just under a quarter of an ounce, so were close in value to £1 Sterling and slightly less than a guinea. Applying the Rule of 200, the 13,000 golden Louis d'Or on board *Le Prince Charles* therefore equated to more than £2.5 million in today's values and would have been enough to sustain the army for almost two months. However, on 24 March 1746 *Le Prince Charles* was captured off the Kyle of Tongue by HMS *Sheerness* under Captain O'Brien. Lord Elcho states in his account that 'it was a great loss to the Prince as he was in great distress for want of money'.

There was an attempt to retrieve the gold on *Le Prince Charles* by the MacDonells of Barrisdale, the MacGregors, the MacKinnons and the Jacobite MacKenzies under the Earl of Cromartie. But this venture was unsuccessful and served only to further deplete the strength of the Jacobite Army. As a result of their forlorn quest, none of these regiments were present at Culloden.

There may have been a further problem to add to the army's financial distress. According to James Maxwell of Kirkconnel, the Prince's Secretary John Murray of Broughton was siphoning off the army's funds for his own benefit:

> Though the Secretary managed the direction of everything, he made finances his particular provision, and had so contrived matters that there was no check on him . . . There were very strong presumptions (that) . . . as soon as he and his underlings suspected the opportunity would not last long, they made the best of it, and filled their own pockets with the public money.

By late March 1746, the main body of the army had withdrawn north of the Forth and was encamped around Elgin and Inverness. O'Sullivan says:

> More than 300 Hanoverian prisoners joined us with the Irish Pickets and Lord John's Regiment, which had arrived from France. But money, money, was the word, for there was none to give them. The

French Ambassador just about sustained the regular troops (i.e. the Ecossais Royale and the Irish Pickets, who were part of the French Regular Army), but the Prince had hardly wherewithal to pay the officers. The County of Ross furnished us enough meal, with the little we had before, to give two pecks a week to each man . . . but the scarcity of money made a great many grumble and greatly discouraged everybody.

There was a proposal to print Jacobite banknotes as a means of payment in lieu of gold, but in reality few people were likely to accept notes issued by a bankrupt army. The value of paper money rests ultimately on trust in its issuer; once that has dissipated, it is worthless. O'Sullivan reports that the Prince was finding increasing difficulty in securing help, in money or in kind, from Highland chieftains such as the Countess of Sutherland and the Earl of Cromartie on whom he had thought he could depend. The campaign was disintegrating through lack of funds. O'Sullivan and the Prince both fell ill during this period and desertions were increasing, as O'Sullivan relates:

> If the men are starving, and find themselves in their neighbour-
> hood, most of them would go back to their houses, and you'd have
> no Army. There was no answer to this. It was better to risk a battle
> . . . than give up all for lost, as you would if you retired.

His account is corroborated by Lord Elcho, who, in his *Short Account*, comments:

> There was great distress in his army at this time amongst the officers
> and soldiers. As the money was very scarce with him, he paid his
> troops mostly in meal, which they did not like, and they very often
> mutinied, refused to obey orders, and sometimes threw down their
> arms and went home.

Napoleon observed that an army marches on its stomach, yet the Jacobite Army by now not only had no money, but had no food either. On 15 April, O'Sullivan reports:

> As most of the men had eaten nothing the day before, the Prince
> ordered that the biscuit that was at Inverness should be brought,
> which it was, and delivered; it came to but a biscuit a man.

PLATE 10. Queen Clementina's Cavinet, late 1720s
From the Author's Collection

This devotional image was created by Clementina during her time of troubles, separated from her husband and sons in St Cecilia's Convent. It shows the Sacred Heart pierced by a sword. On the reverse, Clementina has written 'Prego la Cara Mar di racomandar la figlia nel lo cor di Jesu et di Maria' ('I pray to Dear Mary to recommend her daughter to the sacred heart of Jesus and Mary.)'

PLATE 11. James Francis Edward Stuart by Francesco Trevisani, 1720
The National Galleries of Scotland

The Stuart claimant to the British thrones seems to have a rather distant, faraway look in his eyes after a year which has seen the defeat of his supporters at Glen Shiel and his arranged dynastic marriage to Clementina.

PLATE 12. Maria Clementina Sobieska by Francesco Trevisani, 1719
The National Galleries of Scotland

In this portrait, Clementina, aged just seventeen in the year of her marriage, is presented as an immensely wealthy princess adorned with jewels and with the legendary Sobieski Ruby pinned in her hair. Yet, for all her wealth, Clementina is not a free woman; she is an asset to be traded in a dynastic marriage.

PLATE 13. The Solemnisation of the Marriage of James III and Maria Clementina Sobieska by Agostino Masucci, *c.* 1735

The National Galleries of Scotland. Purchased 1977 with assistance from the Art Fund, the Pilgrim Trust and private donors

This painting, commissioned after Clementina's death, was perhaps intended to represent the marriage in a positive light, yet the figure standing behind the couple is believed to be Marjorie Hay, the woman whom Clementina blamed for its breakdown.

PLATE 14. The Baptism of Prince Charles Edward Stuart by Antonio David, 1725
The National Galleries of Scotland

The crowning achievement of the marriage was the arrival of a new Stuart claimant at the end of 1720, yet his mother, Clementina, does not appear in this painting.

PLATE 15. Prince Charles Edward Stuart by Allan Ramsay, 1745
The National Galleries of Scotland. Accepted in lieu of Inheritance Tax by H M Government from the Trustees of the Wemyss Heirlooms Trust and allocated to the Scottish National Portrait Gallery, 2016

This small painting, perhaps a preliminary study for an intended larger painting, shows the Prince at the height of his hopes and his influence in Edinburgh in October 1745, as he prepares to advance into England after his first victory.

PLATE 16. Prince Charles Edward Stuart by Antonio David, 1732
The National Galleries of Scotland

The David portrait of the young prince, commissioned by his father, was part of an ongoing propaganda campaign representing him as the legitimate heir to the throne of England, as symbolised by the Garter Sash and Cross of St George, and the Scottish throne, symbolically represented by the Thistle which can be seen on his chest half obscured under the sash.

PLATE 17. Prince Henry Benedict Clement Stuart by Antonio David, 1732
The National Galleries of Scotland

The partner of the portrait of his older brother shows the future Cardinal York bedecked
in fine clothing and with the Garter Sash and St George Cross confirming his royal status.

PLATE 18. Jacobite fan, 1745
By kind permission of the Tulloch Collection

This fan is typical of those given to ladies attending the Jacobite balls at Holyrood Palace after the victory at Prestonpans, showing the Prince as a triumphant warrior in the centre, lauded (from left to right) by Britannia, the Madonna and Child, the British Lion, Achilles et al. The word 'hubris' comes to mind!

PLATE 19. Fragment of a dress worn by a Jacobite lady, 1745
By kind permission of the Tulloch Collection

This comes from the dress worn by the partner of James Maxwell of Kirkconnel to the Holyrood balls after Prestonpans.

Maxwell of Kirkconnel blames this state of affairs on mismanagement by the Prince's Secretaries, writing:

> There was at that time a provision of meal at Inverness sufficient to maintain the army a fortnight. There was a considerable quantity of salt beef that had been found in the Castle, besides other meat that might have been found in the town and neighbourhood; but such had been the negligence of those whose province it was to supply the army that such as had not servants to bring them victuals were in a downright starving condition . . . (so that) desertions still continued in spite of the endeavours that were used to stop it.

The Highland Army made a desperate Night March on Nairn to attack Cumberland's position under cover of darkness. 'Any troops that are surprised or attacked before they are formed are half conquered,' states O'Sullivan, optimistically. But there is to be no repeat of Prestonpans. The Night March was aborted and the following day the Jacobite Army made its last stand against Cumberland's redcoats on Culloden Moor.

As the Jacobite soldiers awaited their final battle on that bitterly cold morning, they were starving, penniless, poorly armed and physically exhausted.

O'Sullivan concludes in his *Narrative*:

> Nobody that knows anything about military matters could imagine that six or seven thousand men, who for so long had suffered without money or food, and who had been discouraged and harassed as they had been two days before, could resist in a ranged battle against twice that number of regular troops that wanted for nothing.

There are many lessons for us today from the history of the Rising of 1745. One of the most enduring is this: if you want to destroy an insurgency movement, you don't need to sacrifice the lives of thousands of brave soldiers on the battlefield. All you need to do is choke off their access to funds and supplies. Without money, as the disintegration of Prince Charlie's Jacobite Army attests, no insurgency can long survive.

Culloden

Adapted from a nineteenth-century poem by Andrew Lang

Dark was the day when we came on Culloden
And chill was the wind that swept in from the sea,
The moss underfoot was heavy and sodden,
Dull light on the land, damp mist on the tree.

There was wind, there was rain, there was fire in their faces
When the clans broke the bayonets and died on the guns;
But God in his grace guards the desolate places
Where they sleep through seasons of snows and of suns.

Unfed and unmarshalled, outgunned and outnumbered,
All hope and fear gone as fiercely they fought,
As when Falkirk with files of the fallen was cumbered,
Or Gladsmuir ran red with the havoc they wrought.

Where the graves of Clan Chattan are clustered together,
Where MacGillivray fell by the Well of the Dead,
We bowed to the moorland and plucked the pale heather
That blooms where the blood of the clansmen was shed.

And the wind whispered through the wasteland, sighing
Like the voices of heroes who battled in vain,
Saying, 'Not for Tearlach alone the standards were flying
But for the old life, that comes not again.'

12

Was the Rising of 1745 a Just War?

There is an honourable tradition in many of the world's leading philoso-
phies and religions that any act of physical force by one human being
against another is immoral and to be avoided at all costs. If everyone
respected this principle, the world would be a much better place. The
problem is that not everyone does. Those who turn the other cheek and
refuse to retaliate, no matter how great the provocation, risk being bullied
into submission or, in the worst case, being fed to the lions like the early
Christians.

A memory sticks in my mind of an event that happened when I was
working at MINECOFIN, the Ministry of Economics and Finance in
Rwanda, as the republic sought to rebuild after the 1994 genocide. One
day, I was travelling in the north of the country when we came across a
group of ragged people, their ankles manacled together, walking slowly
along the dirt road in the hot sun under the watchful eye of their super-
visors. 'They are the genocidaires,' my driver, Montana, told me. They
were serving their sentences for the crimes they had committed. What
struck me most forcibly was that they did not seem human at all but
looked like wretched husks dressed in rags, stumbling along a road to
nowhere. Perhaps, through their suffering, some among them would find
some measure of redemption.

While it in no way justified their crimes, accounts of the events leading
to the genocide suggest that many of those caught up in it were ignorant
people, brainwashed by evil Hutu extremists into believing that those they
attacked were not humans but cockroaches to be eliminated like vermin.
If this was the case, then some of the genocidaires might also have been
to some degree victims, just as many ordinary Germans hypnotised by
Hitler, who under other circumstances might have led happy and

blameless lives, were victims of Nazism.

What struck me at the moment we encountered the genocidaires was that an act of evil not only destroys the lives of the victims, but also destroys the lives of the perpetrators, who, through their actions, sacrifice their own humanity.

A few days later, sitting in a coffee shop in Kigali, I read an account of a Hutu woman who had saved the life of a Tutsi baby left orphaned by the genocide. For some reason the baby had been overlooked by the genocidaires, and the woman had heard her crying beside the blood-stained bodies of her dead parents. She had taken the baby back to her home and raised her as her own child. Now, some twenty years on, the two were photographed smiling together. It was a moment of hope in the process of truth and reconciliation underway in Rwanda. The orphaned baby girl had been saved by someone whom the genocidaires said should have been her mortal enemy. She had grown into an elegant and beautiful young woman, standing much taller than the illiterate Hutu woman who was her adoptive mother. Her mum stood less than five feet tall, had never been taught to read or write, and had subsisted on $50 a month or less, yet had scraped together enough to feed and support her new daughter.

It occurred to me, as I read the article, that this humble woman had given more in her life than I ever would in mine.

Few would contend that the successful campaign of the Rwandese Patriotic Front to defeat the genocidaires was anything other than a just war, but no war is completely pure. Paul Kagame, the military leader of the RPF in 1994, who is now President of Rwanda, pursued a policy of truth and reconciliation, as Nelson Mandela did in South Africa after the end of apartheid. He also pursued the genocidaires who had fled into the eastern region of the Democratic Republic of Congo. It has been alleged that, during the pursuit, many tens of thousands of people died, including women and children who had no involvement in the conflict.

In any war, atrocities may be committed by both sides. However noble the aspirations of the leaders, soldiers on the ground will act to defend themselves and defeat their enemy, and in the fog of war collateral damage will inevitably be inflicted on innocent non-combatants.

Those who commit men to war should never forget that their decision is almost certain to lead to the deaths of innocent individuals. The question is whether the uncertain benefits of war are sufficient to justify the absolute certainty of its evil consequences.

To this day, Prince Charles Edward Stuart remains the most controversial figure in the whole of Scottish history, and he is among the most controversial in the entire history of Great Britain.

To his supporters, he was an unlucky hero who sought to right historic wrongs and, through vision, courage and charisma, came within an ace of succeeding.

To his detractors, he was a reckless gambler who initiated a war which he had no hope of winning, with scant regard to its possible consequences, leaving a trail of destruction and broken lives in his wake.

Where does the truth lie? Was the Prince, on balance, justified in instigating his Rising?

To inform my judgement on the matter, I sought to consider the Rising against each of the key conditions for a 'Just War' first laid down by St Augustine in the fifth century and further developed in the fourteenth century by St Thomas Aquinas.

The first and most fundamental of the Augustinian principles is that there must be 'just cause' for the war. It must be conducted to avenge wrong or to restore what has been seized unjustly.

Clearly, Charles and his Jacobite supporters believed that the thrones of Great Britain and Ireland had been seized unfairly from his grandfather, James VII and II, back in 1688. By contrast, King James's Whig opponents argued that the coup executed by his son-in-law, William of Orange, was entirely justified to counter the threat that James posed to the established Church of England and his alleged plan to make himself an absolute monarch, overriding the rights and liberties of his citizens.

The balance of evidence does not, in my view, support these allegations, so my conclusion is that King James was unjustly deposed. Therefore, the Jacobites did have just cause in seeking a Stuart Restoration.

Charles put his own case for the Restoration in his Declaration as Prince Regent in Edinburgh on 10 October 1745:

> Our present attempt is not undertaken in order to enslave a free people, but to redress and remove the encroachments made upon them; not to impose upon any a religion which they dislike, but to secure them all in the enjoyment of those which are respectively at present established among them, either in England, Scotland, or Ireland . . .
>
> Our family has suffered exile during these fifty-seven years, everybody knows. Has the nation, during that period of time, been the more happy and flourishing for it? Have you found reason to

love and cherish your governors? Have you found more humanity in those who were not born to a Crown, than in my royal fore-fathers? Have their ears been open to the cries of the people? Have you reaped any other benefit from them, than an immense load of debts? . . .

Why has the nation been so long crying out in vain for redress against the abuse of Parliaments, upon account of the multitude of place-men, which occasions their venality, the introduction of penal laws, and in general the miserable situation of the Kingdom at home and abroad? All these and many more inconveniences must now be removed . . . The King, on his Restoration, will refuse nothing that a free Parliament can ask, for the security of the religion, laws and liberty of his people.

Looking to the next of the Augustinian principles, I questioned whether Prince Charles had 'legitimate authority' to start the war. He failed to secure the prior approval of either his father or his main ally, the King of France. However, Prince Charles would doubtless respond that he himself had the authority to launch a campaign as the rightful heir to the throne, that the principle of supporting a Rising to topple the illegitimate Hanoverian regime had already been approved by the French King in 1744, and that it was subsequently confirmed by the Treaty of Fontainebleau, signed in October 1745.

This treaty was reinforced by the Manifesto of His Most Christian Majesty, drafted for him by Voltaire in December 1745 to counter the suggestion that the Rising was a cover for a French invasion of Great Britain. The Manifesto read, in part, as follows:

His Majesty (the King of France), in giving such just assistance to his kinsman, to a Prince so worthy to reign, only takes this step towards the English nation with the intention and the confidence of thereby bringing peace to England and Europe, fully convinced that the most serene Prince [Charles] Edward places his trust in their goodwill, that he looks to their liberties, the maintenance of their laws and happiness, as the goal of all his ventures, and that, in fact, the greatest kings of England have been those who, raised like him in adversity, have deserved the love of the nation.

Nevertheless, the fact remains that the Prince did not have the prior agreement of either his father or the King of France to launch his campaign, and indeed the lack of such agreement – and the full financial and military support from his main ally this would have secured from the outset – was a key reason that the Rising failed.

The next Augustinian principle concerns 'just intent'. The Prince's actions throughout the campaign indicate that he was not driven by a thirst for vengeance or lust for power. He sought to conduct the war according to Augustinian principles as far as possible, seeking to minimise civilian casualties and instructing his surgeons to care for wounded enemy soldiers. In his speeches and declarations, including his October declaration in Edinburgh, the Prince stated that his mission was to liberate his people and grant them full freedom of religious worship.

Next we look at 'comparative justice', what economists such as myself might term the 'cost-benefit test' – are the likely benefits from the conflict likely to outweigh its costs? The Jacobites naturally believed that this condition was fully met. The Hanoverian view would have been the precise opposite – that the hard-won victory of William of Orange more than half a century before, and the passage of the Act of Union in 1707, had ushered in a period of peace, prosperity and stability which the Prince's arrival in Scotland in 1745 threatened to undo.

The people of Scotland were divided on the matter. The Highlands mainly supported the Prince; the Lowlands were more sympathetic to the Hanoverian case. The majority of the people of England remained loyal to the Hanoverian Government, although there were pockets of support from Jacobites.

Perhaps the reality is that most people didn't particularly care who was on the throne as long as they were left in peace to get on with their lives. Had the Prince reached London and King George fled, the majority of the population would have accepted a change in the monarchy, just as they had accepted William and Mary as their new monarchs after they had forced out Mary's father, King James II, almost sixty years earlier.

Another condition of a just war states that there must be 'a high probability of victory', otherwise a war risks unnecessary loss of life for no purpose.

The Prince's critics argue that his Rising never had any chance of success. Certainly the loss of the *Elizabeth* during the crossing to Scotland tilted the odds against the Jacobites, and perhaps those who advised the Prince to abort his campaign when he landed in Scotland in July 1745 had a fair point.

However, the odds then swung back in the Jacobites' favour after their victory at Prestonpans in September 1745 and the signature of the Treaty of Fontainebleau in October.

On the available evidence, I believe that the Jacobites would have had at least a fifty-fifty chance of success had they continued their advance on to London from Derby. Contemporary memoirs and records of 1745 confirm that there was a genuine belief on both sides of the conflict that the Jacobites could have seized power had they continued their advance.

The 'proportionality principle' requires that the overall destruction expected from the use of force must be outweighed by the good that will be achieved.

With the benefit of hindsight, most would agree that the destruction that followed the failure of the Rising was completely disproportionate in relation to any good that might have been achieved. However, there is no way that Prince Charlie could have anticipated the wholly disproportionate use of force against innocent civilians applied by Cumberland after Culloden. Nor can he be held responsible for it.

In sharp contrast to the Duke of Cumberland, the evidence indicates that Prince Charles sought to apply force proportionately throughout the campaign. The question mark is over whether he should have sought to use force at all to seek a Stuart Restoration in 1745, or whether, as the King of France and his own father would have counselled, he should have had the patience to wait for more propitious circumstances before attempting his coup.

The final principle of a just war is that force should be used only as a last resort, when all peaceful and viable alternatives have been seriously tried and exhausted.

From a Jacobite perspective, the use of force was a last resort, as there was no possibility of the Hanoverian King giving up his throne through a process of negotiation. The only way that Prince Charles was likely to be able to secure a restoration of the Stuart dynasty was through force.

Thus, on consideration of the evidence, I would conclude that the Rising of 1745 was, on balance, a just war. However, the mere fact that a war is just does not mean it will be successful or without significant cost for those who fight for justice. In real life, right does not always triumph and justice does not always prevail.

PART 3
The Aftermath

13

The Prince in the Heather

On 17 April 1746, the day after the Battle of Culloden, there was an attempt to rally the remnants of the Jacobite Army at Fort Ruthven. The Prince advised his supporters to disperse, realising that the campaign was over and no useful purpose would be served by further loss of life.

As he rode away, it is recorded that Lord Elcho said contemptuously, 'There he goes, for a dammed Italian coward!' This remark, uttered in anger as Lord Elcho watched his own hopes and his contribution of 1,500 guineas go up in smoke on Culloden Moor, has been seized upon by Prince Charlie's enemies. Nevertheless, it is grossly unfair. Prince Charlie was no coward. He had manifested great personal courage throughout the campaign and was to continue to do so in the months that followed. Nor, as his November 1746 memorandum to King Louis XV proves beyond doubt, was he proposing to abandon Scotland. His plan was to return to France and raise another army to continue his campaign. As O'Sullivan relates in his *Narrative*:

> His design was to make his way as best he could for France, as he expected his presence there would procure him both men and money and whatever help he could get, and that he'd come back without loss of time.

The Prince reiterated his plan in a letter sent to the clan chiefs on 28 April 1746, writing:

> I am of little use here; whereas, by my going to France instantly, however dangerous that may be, I will certainly engage the French Court either to assist us effectively and powerfully, or at least to

procure you such terms as you would not otherwise obtain. My presence there, I flatter myself, will have more effect to bring this sooner to a determination than anybody else.

This letter suggests that he saw himself like his great uncle, Charles II, who was forced to flee after he lost the Battle of Worcester but later returned in triumph to become one of the most successful monarchs of Great Britain and Ireland.

About the same time as the Prince wrote his letter to the Highland chiefs, two French ships landed in the west Highlands, delivering 3,000 stands of arms and the legendary Loch Arkaig gold. This was enough to convince a few Jacobite diehards, including Lochiel, Cluny MacPherson and John Roy Stuart, that they could continue the campaign. They signed up to the Declaration of Muir Laggan, with a ringing commitment to lead to the Bonnie Prince 'all the able-bodied men every one of us can command within our respective interests or properties'.

However, the number of able-bodied men who actually rallied to the cause on the appointed date was not very many. After that, even the most dedicated Jacobite could no longer deny that the campaign of 1745 was at an end. The only option left was to disperse and seek ships to France and safety.

*   *   *

In order to trace the steps of Prince Charlie during his first two months on the run in the heather, I turn again to the *Narrative* of Colonel O'Sullivan. During this period, the two men were travelling together, masquerading as father and son under the pseudonyms of Mister and Master Sinclair.

O'Sullivan's *Narrative* has been neglected over the years because it is so difficult to read. There is a good reason for this. It is not because O'Sullivan invented the stream of consciousness technique almost two centuries before James Joyce, but because his *Narrative* is an oral rather than a written account. It is precisely this that makes it, in my view, such an important account of the Rising. It is an account told from memory and from the heart, by the man who was closest to the Rising's leader, Prince Charles Edward Stuart. As such, it has an immediacy lacking in official documents or carefully crafted memoirs. O'Sullivan is telling things as he sees them, without fear or favour. And, as he was the Prince's right-hand man and closest ally throughout the campaign, his account is the nearest thing we have to an account by the Prince himself about what happened, day by day, during the months they were together. At times his *Narrative* is so vivid that one can almost imagine sitting listening to him as he tells his story in a Roman taverna in the spring of 1747.

The Prince's sole objective during the period that followed Culloden was to find a ship to carry him back to France. However, as O'Sullivan recounts:

It was no easy matter to get him off [the mainland]. That coast was closely guarded since he landed. There were four or five men of war continually patrolling between the Isle of Skye and Eigg, their longboats and tenders going from one island to another. All the boats they could find in those islands and on the mainland were destroyed, so that there was none to be had, save one owned by the brother of a gentleman in whose house the Prince stayed, which had been sunk, and by that means had escaped the enemy's search. The boat was drawn up out of the water, and repaired as well as possible. The Prince fixed upon the day for his escape, and departed on a Saturday night eleven days after the battle. Sullivan, seeing that the Prince was determined to go off, prayed him to take somebody along with him, in case he fell sick or some accident befall him, so the Prince would not be all alone. Besides, if any misfortune were to happen to the Prince, it would be a cruel situation for Sullivan to be all alone with him. The Prince agreed with Sullivan's reasoning, and asked [Felix] O'Neill, whom the Duke of York [Prince Charles's younger brother, Henry Benedict] had sent to him as a man who could be trusted, to accompany them.

The Prince, O'Sullivan and Felix O'Neill set off in the boat, piloted by Donald MacLeod, on the night of 26 April. However, their voyage had hardly started when a terrible storm started to blow. They took the decision to press on regardless. O'Sullivan takes up the story:

The boat was almost full of water and everybody was for making the first land. MacLeod said that there was no possibility of making any other land but the Isle of Skye, provided we could evade the Men of War. We were not far from them at this time but [the Prince] encouraged everybody and said it was only a squall that would be over soon. He admitted to me very often afterwards that he would have given all he had at that time to be ashore. The wind continued and increased, the sea became mountainous and waves were sweeping over the boat. All hands set to work throwing out the water. There was not a soul in the boat but was as wet as if they were dipped in the sea. We went like the wind, and just before it, luckily, as the least side wind would have overturned us.

The Prince was standing, his hands upon one of the planks across the boat, encouraging the sailors and all those who were helping to throw out the water. Then a furious wave came and threw the Prince flat against the other side of the boat, and the Prince cried out 'there is no hurt, there is no hurt'. As Sullivan and O'Neill went up to help him, another wave came which threw all three of them upon one another. The waves swept over all the boat and made it crack, so that every sailor thought that all was lost. MacLeod, who had spent all his life at sea, trembled like a leaf. The sailors began to pray aloud and call all the saints to their aid. The Prince, being recovered a little, urged the sailors to work and throw out the water, saying that they could pray if there was a Priest on board, but as there was not they should get on with their business. Happily, one of the men was a very good sailor and bold fellow, and he roused up the others.

MacLeod was so frightened that he hardly had strength to hold the helm. The Prince whispered to Sullivan and told him to stay near to MacLeod to encourage him.

Sullivan admitted to me that he had need to be encouraged himself more than anybody else, both to preserve his own life, which is only natural, but above all the Prince's. But his religion gave him great confidence that God would not preserve such a fine Prince in all the dangers he had undergone just to let him perish in such a manner.

Somehow, they made it through the night, as the gale continued unabated. Eventually, the waves died down and, as dawn broke, they caught sight of the island of North Uist and tried to navigate their way onto shore. But the danger was not over.

As we were getting in, as this place is full of little islands and rocks, there was just one landing place before us. The wind blew the boat full upon it, all hands were at work to get the anchor down, but the anchor and cords were so wet that it could not slip along the mast. The danger was evident, so everybody got onto the edge of the boat to throw themselves out when the boat struck the rocks. But, as if God had set his hand to it, when one man touched the anchor it fell down in a minute, when three or four men had not been able to get it down a moment before. The Pilot turned the rudder and avoided the rock by all the good luck in the world. But we were not assured until we saw the rock behind us, as we got in to the shelter of land. The waves were still so monstrous that they would have been looked upon as a high sea in other times. Yet at last we happily got in.

Their relief is palpable: 'When we were ashore we could hardly stand, the wind was so strong, and we struggled to get to a house that was not three musket shots from us.' At least they were safe and able to shelter in a bothy they found:

We were all wet from head to foot, and black with cold, yet everyone, as you may well believe, notwithstanding the condition they were in, was very glad to find themselves ashore. MacLeod and another old sailor with us said that in more than twenty years at sea they had never before been in such danger, nor ever witnessed such a storm . . . We all spoke about the dangers we had gone through, and, at that moment, we were all companions together. 'Come, come,' says MacLeod, 'you'll have time enough to talk about all that. Let's get a fire made; you see the condition that young Sinclair is in.' . . . A fire was made, heather not wanting, and a wooden bowl was put on it to make bread, and an iron pot brought [similar to that depicted in Plate 21], and everybody began to dry themselves by the fire. The pot was filled with half a lamb they had, but when the pot was washed there was a hole as large as half a crown in it. 'I'll shew it up', says one of the men, and takes some rags he had, rolls them up as they were, clean and dirty, and stops up the hole with his rags. The Prince examined this very attentively and laughed heartily to see a hole in the pot that's to go on the fire stopped up with linen rags. It amused him very much. When all that was done, a very good porridge was made in it, and the Prince took some of it as if there were no rags in the pot. The half lamb was not enough to feed all the people there . . . There were cows grazing near the house, so he orders the men to shoot one and that he'll pay for it. He's soon obeyed; the cow is killed and stripped in an instant, they dress meat for themselves and everyone is happy. There is not a house within three miles of us, nor a drop of milk to be had. The storm continued for two full days.

Through May and early June, O'Sullivan and the Prince travelled together. O'Sullivan's *Narrative* describes their efforts to stay out of the clutches of the redcoats and their daily struggle to survive with the help of their friends in the islands, in particular during this period Clanranald, in whose territory they were now hiding.

The Prince, who, just a few short months earlier, had been within touching distance of winning the thrones of Great Britain and Ireland, was now reduced to a fugitive in rags, engaged in a constant quest for food, shelter and clothing.

All the while, Cumberland's brutal campaign of vengeance and retribution progressed unabated across the Highlands.

Their search for a ship to take them to safety in France proved fruitless and the hardship of life on the run in the Highlands began to take its toll on the Prince's health, as O'Sullivan reports:

> We were never a day or night without rain. The Prince was in a terrible condition, his legs and thighs cut all over by briars; the midges and flies, which are terrible in that country, devouring him, and made him scratch his scars, which made him look as if he was covered with ulcers.

Late June found the two men on the island of Benbecula with the Royal Navy closing in. They saw seven Men of War, from which some hundred soldiers descended within their sight, and heard them fire several musket shots. At first, they believed they had been discovered, 'but we found afterwards that they were firing at cattle', O'Sullivan says. Nevertheless, their enemy were getting too close for comfort and the Prince came to the conclusion that it was too risky for him and O'Sullivan to remain together, that they must split up if they were to have any chance of escape.

In the remarkable passage of his *Narrative* that describes their parting on 20 June 1746 it appears that O'Sullivan experienced something close to a breakdown when he parted from the Prince. Though it is not made explicit in his *Narrative*, it is clear that O'Sullivan is genuinely concerned that this could be the last time that he would see the Prince alive.

O'Sullivan's *Narrative* was never intended for public consumption, and this part of his account reads as a private confession to be heard only by his interlocutor and the Prince's own father:

'Sir,' says Sullivan, 'I have followed you until now, and if I abandon you at this in the most critical and dangerous moment, what would the world think of it?'

'Never mind what the world thinks, nobody knows better than I do the services you have rendered me, and nobody can suspect your fidelity and attachment after the proofs you have given me of them. But', says the Prince, 'when you know my plan, you'll find it necessary that we should separate, because I can't execute it unless you stay here to bring me a boat if it be possible to do so. My plan is,' says the Prince, 'to make my way as best I can to Lady Clanranald's house, get myself dressed there in women's clothing, and then, if you can get me a boat, go off immediately to the Isle of Skye . . . I'll go up to the cave that you know is in that mountain, where you can inform me about what is happening. On the other hand, if you don't stay here, the boat men will go off and God knows what will become of us then. Here are a hundred guineas [to put the plan into action]. If I am forced to leave before you can join me, do what you can to follow me, If you are able to go to Ireland and from there to France, please tell the Duke [Prince Henry] and the Court of France about my situation . . .

'So God bless you. There is no time to be lost. I'll take O'Neill with me and send him to you tonight or tomorrow, if you can stay here without being pursued. If you have time or can get some bread baked, send me a little to the Cave. God be with you.'

Sullivan can't contain himself. He burst out crying to quit the Prince and to see the danger and misery he was exposed to. The Prince embraces him, and holds him in his arms for a quarter of an hour, Sullivan talking to him as much as his tears and sobs could permit him, praying him for God's sake, that if he ever had the misfortune to fall into the enemy's hands, never to admit who he was . . . It was a most dismal sight to see Sullivan in the Prince's arms. The sailors hear Sullivan crying and see the Prince go off, they all cry and roar and look upon the Prince as lost. The Prince comes back to them, assures them that there is nothing to fear, that he leaves Sullivan with them, that Sullivan will hear from him that night or the next day, and that 'we will all meet again'.

However, O'Sullivan does not meet the Prince again in Scotland after they go their separate ways. Three weeks later O'Sullivan was able to secure passage on board *Le Hardi Mendiant*, bound for Norway, and after a voyage of ten days landed at Bergen. Once there, he immediately wrote to the King of France, appealing for help in rescuing the Prince. He then travelled by sea and land through the Low Countries to reach Paris in August 1746, where he further pressed his case. His appeals for French support were successful, and two French ships, *L'Heureux* and *Le Prince de Conti*, were dispatched to the western Highlands in September in search of the Prince.

In the meantime, the Prince had put his plan to disguise himself as a woman into effect. He adopted the alias of Betty Burke, a maid to a young woman drafted in to give him cover. Her name was Flora MacDonald, and she provided him with a dress he wore as a disguise (Plate 22).

While he was on the run in the Highlands, the Prince was sustained by faith, hope and, above all, charity – the charity of Highlanders who had nothing to gain and everything to lose by helping him. It remains part of the Jacobite romantic myth that despite the abject poverty of the Highlands not a single Highlander betrayed the Prince for the great reward of £30,000 (equivalent to more than £5 million in today's money), which they would have gained by giving him up.

Flora has become a personification of the Highlanders' loyalty to their fallen Prince in his darkest hour. She had no hidden agenda, no ulterior motive and nothing to gain. Her family, the MacDonalds of Sleat, had not supported the Rising, so there was no reason for her to get involved at all. She came to the Prince's aid inspired by nothing more than common humanity and a desire to save the life of a man she hardly knew, on the run from the redcoats and with a price on his head.

On 27 June, Flora and the Prince sailed from Benbecula to Skye. The following day, the Prince sailed on to the island of Raasay and thence to the mainland, where he was passed into the hands of Cluny MacPherson, who gave the Prince shelter deep in remote clan territory on Ben Alder, well away from the pursuing Hanoverian Government forces that were searching for him on the coast. From there, the Prince was able to board *L'Heureux* when it arrived at Loch nan Uamh, the same location where he had first set foot on mainland Scotland fourteen months earlier. He left Scotland on 20 September 1746 and arrived safely at Roscoff in Brittany ten days later. His point of departure is marked by a cairn that the 1745 Association erected at Loch nan Uamh in 1956.

Flora remained on Skye and was never to see the Prince again. On 12 July 1746, Flora was arrested on information supplied to the authorities by one of the sailors who had accompanied her on the voyage to Skye. She was transported by sea to the Tower of London, where she languished for almost a year until released under a general amnesty in June 1747. By that time, the Prince was safely back in France

One of the most enduring images of Flora has been passed down to us in a painting by Richard Wilson. Wilson was primarily a landscape artist rather than a portrait painter, and in artistic terms his portrait lacks the subtlety and depth of the works of the great Dutch masters, being rather simplistic and two-dimensional. However, Wilson was in the right place at the right time.

By chance, he happened to be on the ship that took Flora from the Highlands to the Tower of London in July 1746. While on the voyage, he was commissioned by one of the officers on board to paint her. Interest in Flora was immense, and Londoners were keen to know what the legendary Jacobite heroine looked like. Wilson's shipboard portrait was the first painting of her from life and was rapidly disseminated through prints that hit the streets of London while she languished as a prisoner in the Tower in 1746 and 1747.

Perhaps somewhat to his surprise, Richard Wilson discovered that, notwithstanding his limitations as a portrait artist, there was a ready market for his paintings of Flora. He wasted little time in producing a few more of them to turn an honest penny.

A vastly superior representation of Flora is given in the portrait of her by Allan Ramsay which today hangs in the Ashmolean Museum in Oxford (Plate 23). Unlike court painters such as Sir Peter Lely and Sir Godfrey Kneller, Ramsay did not go out of his way to flatter his subjects, but rather sought to paint them as they were and, through his skill as a portrait artist, bring out something of their inner character from their appearance, dress and disposition.

The image of Flora by Allan Ramsay reveals a woman who, though not a great beauty in conventional terms, is by no means unattractive. Her blue eyes gaze directly at us from the painting, suggesting someone who is honest, straightforward and unpretentious. This impression is confirmed by her dress of plain blue, covering a white smock and decorated not with jewellery but with white roses pinned on her hair and bodice. Around her shoulders is a shawl made of tartan, the colour and design of which bears a close resemblance to that of the 1745 Association. It's good to know that Flora was an early and loyal supporter!

In all seriousness, the resemblance may not be entirely coincidental. My colleagues in the Association who registered our tartan based it on the Moy Hall tartan given to Lady MacIntosh by Prince Charles when he stayed at her home during his retreat northwards in February 1746, and it may be that Flora or Allan Ramsay also deliberately chose a tartan with a direct connection to the Prince to remind us of Flora's brief time with him at the end of June 1746.

More than a quarter of a century later, in 1773, Dr Samuel Johnson visited Flora on Skye during his tour of the Highlands and Islands with Boswell, shortly before she emigrated to the Carolinas with her husband, Allan. She was to return to Scotland after the American War of Independence, dying in 1790 at the age of sixty-eight, her mortal remains interred in the Kilmuir Cemetery on Skye. Engraved on her memorial is the tribute to her from Dr Johnson: 'Flora MacDonald, Preserver of Prince Charles Edward Stuart. Her name will be mentioned in history and, if courage and fidelity be virtues, mentioned with honour.'

14

The Execution of the Jacobite Lords

While Colonel O'Sullivan and the Prince managed to evade Government forces and escape to safety on the Continent, others were not so fortunate.

The sole Jacobite regiment raised in England during the Rising was the Manchester Regiment, more familiarly known as the Manchesters. They formed part of a garrison that remained in Carlisle after the rest of the Jacobite Army retreated to Scotland in early December 1745, in the hope that they could hold Carlisle Castle until the main army returned. This hope proved misplaced. On 30 December 1745, the garrison surrendered to Hanoverian Government forces. The Irish regulars in the garrison, who formed part of the French Army, were treated as prisoners of war and later exchanged for British POWs.

However, the Manchesters were only granted their lives subject to 'the King's pleasure'. This merely meant that they were granted the right to a trial rather than being summarily executed. Their colonel, Francis Towneley, a member of a prominent Lancastrian Catholic family, was tried on 13 July 1746, found guilty of treason and hanged on Kennington Common on 30 July 1746, along with eight other officers from the regiment. After his execution, he was beheaded and his head placed on a pike on Temple Bar, where it remained as a warning to others who might be tempted to challenge the power of the Hanoverian monarchy.

While the Kennington Martyrs were put to death by hanging, members of the Scottish nobility condemned to death were executed by what was then seen as the more humane and less painful method of beheading.

The Earl of Kilmarnock was arrested by Hanoverian forces as he attempted to escape the battlefield of Culloden, while Lord Balmerino, commander of the Life Guards, surrendered voluntarily the day after the battle, despite earnest entreaties from his cousin and fellow officer David, Lord Elcho, not to do so. Elcho warned him in the strongest possible terms that he could expect little clemency from King George. However, Balmerino had no appetite for escape and exile, and seems to have been resigned to his fate from the outset.

The Earl of Kilmarnock is described thus in *Falkirk or Paradise* written by Geoff Bailey:

> He had all the appearance and bearing of a classical hero. His tall and slender frame was carried with great grace and he always appeared well groomed. His manners were pleasant and his actions and conversation possessed a quiet dignity, combined with wit and intelligence . . . He had been only 12 when his father's death gave him added responsibilities, and his mother's obsessive gambling caused him further problems.

The Earl's financial problems were made considerably worse when, in 1735, an accidental fire started in the kitchen of his ancestral home at Dean Castle, which then spread onto the thatched roof and consumed most of the building. Lacking the money to repair it, the Earl sought to improve his fortunes through his own enterprise, but his efforts had not met with success and by 1745 he had a string of failed business ventures behind him.

These, then, were the circumstances in which Lord Kilmarnock found himself when, on 14 September 1745, an unexpected guest arrived at Callendar House – Prince Charles Edward Stuart, marching southwards at the head of his Highland Army from Glenfinnan to Edinburgh.

Then, as now, there were two main public rooms at Callendar House, the Green Room and the adjacent Pink Room. The Falkirk Community Trust, the current custodians of Callendar House, state that they cannot be certain in which of these two rooms Prince Charlie and Lord Kilmarnock dined in 1745. However, it is my contention that visitors would naturally ascend via the left-hand staircase, as this is the convention in built structures in Great Britain and at railway stations. We tend to ascend from one floor to another on the left and descend on the right. So, visitors to Callendar House in 1745 would naturally ascend the staircase on the left of the main entrance, emerging into the Pink Room, which would have been the main reception or drawing room, and then proceed to dine in the Green Room. Confirmatory evidence that the

Green Room was likely to have been the dining room in 1745 is provided by the fact that the kitchen was below the Green Room. So it would have been physically much easier to carry food directly upwards to this room than to zig-zag the house into the Pink Room.

The nature of the discussion between the Prince and the Earl as they dined on the evening of 14 September is documented in *Fight for a Throne*, the authoritative work on the entire campaign written by my immediate predecessor as chairman of the 1745 Association, Dr Christopher Duffy.

In spite of Lord Kilmarnock's financial difficulties, it would appear that he was able to rustle up a few bottles of claret from the Callendar House cellars, for Christopher reports that the two men, 'after drinking freely', fell to discuss the Prince's campaign.

Already, it can be seen that Lord Kilmarnock was dangerously compromised. The very fact that he entertained the Prince at all could be deemed as disloyal to the House of Hanover. Equally, if Prince Charlie turned up to your house uninvited with a group of heavily armed Highlanders, you too might have thought it a good idea to offer him a glass of wine (or two) and generally be reasonably civil, just to avoid the possibility that there might not be a house to come back to the following day!

Far more compromising, however, was the fact that Lord Kilmarnock then furnished the Prince with information regarding the position and movements of the Hanoverian forces under Colonel Gardiner. Had this become known to the authorities, it would most certainly have been regarded as an act of treason, particularly since Prince Charlie was then able to use this intelligence to outmanoeuvre the Hanoverians. Exactly one week after their meeting, on 21 September 1745, he scored a decisive victory against the Hanoverian forces under Sir John Cope at the Battle of Prestonpans.

It was this victory that finally determined Lord Kilmarnock to throw his lot in with the Prince. If the Prince was successful, his financial difficulties would be over. Reverend Foster, appointed as Kilmarnock's spiritual counsellor while he was awaiting trial in the Tower of London, reported that the Earl had told him that 'his rebellion was a kind of desperate scheme, proceeding originally from his vices, to extricate himself from the distress of his circumstances'.

In early October 1745 Lord Kilmarnock raised a troop of thirty horse and on 20 October they rode to join Prince Charles in Edinburgh. Ten days later, a Council of War was held at the Palace of Holyrood and the decision taken to march southwards into England. Over the next three months, the Jacobites marched 500 miles southwards to Derby, only to halt, turn around and retrace their steps back to Scotland.

After the Battle of Falkirk Muir on 17 January 1746, the Earl of Kilmarnock returned home to Callendar House, almost three months to the day after his departure, to be welcomed by his wife, Lady Ann Livingston, who earlier that day had been playing hostess (albeit perhaps somewhat reluctantly) to her husband's enemy, General Henry Hawley.

The Earl of Kilmarnock's renewed residence at Callendar was not to last very long. The victory at Falkirk Muir was only a temporary hiatus in the long retreat of the Jacobite Army until the final reckoning at Culloden three months later. It was there that Kilmarnock made one final mistake – and this one was to prove fatal.

Disoriented by the smoke and confusion on the battlefield, he approached a cavalry troop believing it to be the Jacobite FitzJames's Horse, only to find he had walked straight into the clutches of a Hanoverian unit and was promptly arrested. It is recorded that his son and heir, Lord Boyd, serving in Hanoverian colours, saw his father being marched away bareheaded and took off his own hat to protect his father's head against the harsh wind that was blowing.

The Earl was taken to London, where he was tried by his peers in the House of Lords in July 1746 as a 'Prisoner of Distinction', alongside Lord Balmerino and the Earl of Cromartie. Unlike Lords Balmerino and Kilmarnock, the Earl of Cromartie had not been present at the Battle of Culloden, and it was this fact that was to save him. His Clan Mackenzie regiment had been intercepted by the Hanoverian Sutherland Militia the day before the battle as they marched from the Kyle of Tongue, where they had unsuccessfully sought to recover the gold from *Le Prince Charles* to rejoin the main Jacobite force at Inverness. Cromartie was captured and several dozen of his clansmen killed during this engagement, thus depriving the Prince of much needed reinforcements.

All three men were duly found guilty and sentenced to death.

*   *   *

On 7 August 1746, the Reverend James Foster was sent to offer spiritual counsel to the imprisoned Earl of Kilmarnock. He recorded these final conversations and published an account of their discussions shortly after Lord Kilmarnock's execution, selling it for one shilling in the streets of London in late 1746. I acquired a copy of this pamphlet at a somewhat

higher price from an antiquarian bookseller in Oxford. The Reverend
Foster begins by explaining the principal points of interest:

> After our general introduction, I thought the next step necessary
> to be taken, in order to awaken [Lord Kilmarnock] thoroughly to
> a due sense of his guilt, was to persuade him to look upon himself
> as a criminal, whose sentence of death was scarce more just, than
> the execution of it was inevitable.

Just in case the Earl of Kilmarnock had not picked up on this point, the
Reverend Foster took it upon himself to leave the noble Lord in no doubt
of his inevitable fate. His account continues:

> Self-preservation and the love of life were not only strong principles
> in human nature, but, to one in his circumstances, very insinuating
> and dangerous principles. I therefore pressed him earnestly not to
> suffer himself to be amused by vain and deluding hopes. I told him,
> that by what I could collect, there was no probability of his obtain-
> ing a reprieve; and that, while his mind was suspended between
> hope and fear, it must be proportionately distracted; and, of conse-
> quence, unable to recollect and exert its whole strength and force
> in such a manner as was necessary to produce in him that deep
> contrition and bitter remorse for his heinous crimes, and that true
> temper of penitence, which alone could recommend him to the
> Divine Mercy.

At this point, I find it difficult not to feel considerable sympathy for the
Earl of Kilmarnock. With friends like the Reverend Foster, one is tempted
to observe, the Earl had little need of enemies. Remarkably, by Foster's
account, Kilmarnock fully accepted his spiritual counsellor's admonitions
and acknowledged the justice of his fate. Yet this is not sufficient for the
good cleric.

> I represented to him that the rebellion in which he had rashly
> engaged was entirely unprovoked and ungrateful, and, of conse-
> quence, most unjust and unnatural; that the King's right to the
> crown was, even in his Lordship's own opinion, incontestable, and
> his government had ever been mild and gracious; and that . . . the
> subject had never enjoyed since the Conquest, that is for near 700

years, such a course of uninterrupted and uncontrolled liberty . . .
I told him farther that, by joining the rebels, he had not only
attacked personal rights of the King and his illustrious house, but
endeavoured to destroy the national happiness, and frustrate the
hopes of posterity; that he had been instrumental in diffusing
consternation and terror through the land, obstructing commerce,
giving a shock to the public credit, in the depredation and ruin of
his country; and ought to consider himself as an accessory to innu-
merable private oppressions and murders.

Lord Kilmarnock appears to have accepted these charges without
comment. He only objects when the Reverend Foster goes on to assert that
the success of the Rising would have led inevitably to religious oppression.

> But when I mentioned to him the consequences of rebellion, that
> its natural tendency was to the utter subversion of our excellent
> free constitution, to extirpate our holy religion, and introduce the
> monstrous superstitions and cruelties of popery . . . Here he at first
> hesitated, and did not seem to have so clear a conviction, as I
> thought was necessary to render his repentance complete. He said
> 'he had considered this as a thing possible but had not looked
> upon it as so closely connected with the success of rebellion as was
> generally imagined. That, as far as he could learn from all the
> conversations he had the Pretender's son, he was not a person that
> had a real concern for any outward profession of religion; he
> thought therefore, that, to introduce popery, he would not run the
> risk of defeating his main design.'

After further urgings from the Reverend Foster, Lord Kilmarnock
concedes even this point and accepts that a victory for the Jacobites would
have led inevitably to the triumph of oppressive Popery.

Reading between the lines, it would appear that Kilmarnock was so
overwhelmed by the calamity that had befallen him that he was in no
mood to argue about anything and accepted full responsibility for his
fate, which he attributed to his own failings. The Reverend Foster reports
that the Earl of Kilmarnock admitted:

> The true root of all was his careless and dissolute life, by which he
> had reduced himself to great and perplexing difficulties; that the

exigency of his affairs was in particular very pressing at the time of the rebellion; and that, besides the general hope he had of mending his fortune by the success of it, he was also tempted by another prospect of retrieving his circumstances, if he followed the Pretender's standard. His love of vanity, and addictedness to impurity and sensual pleasure (he said) had not only brought pollution and guilt upon his soul, but debased his reason.

Having fully acknowledged his guilt, Lord Kilmarnock asked the Reverend Foster to give him communion. The Reverend at first hesitated, asking the Earl to repeat his confession in the presence of 'Mr Fowler, the gentleman-gaoler of the Tower'. The Reverend Foster reports, 'To this, he made no objection.' There then follows a report of the Earl's confession of complete guilt in the presence of Mr Fowler. Duly satisfied, the Reverend Foster administered the Sacrament to the Earl.

On only one point does Lord Kilmarnock deny the charges laid before him – with regard to 'heavy charges of inhumanity and cruelty'. While the Reverend Foster comes across (through his own account) as a prig and apologist for the House of Hanover, he nevertheless impresses me as a reliable witness who endeavours to be fair and honest in his account of his discussions with Lord Kilmarnock. He recalls his questions, and the Earl's answers, on these charges as follows:

Was your Lordship present in the Pretender's Council at Inverness, or any other place, before the Battle of Culloden, where it was proposed to destroy the prisoners taken by the rebels?
I can most sincerely and freely answer: no.
Was you ever present in council where this was proposed? No.
Did you ever move for such an order? No.
Did you ever sign such an order? No.
Did you ever know, or hear, that such an order to give no quarter, was debated, or agreed to, or signed in the rebel army, till you was taken by the King's force? Or do you know yourself guilty of any cruelties, by you authorised or committed, against the King's soldiers or subjects taken prisoners by the rebels? The answer to both these questions was the same as before . . .
I told him, however, that he was charged with an instance of barbarity to the prisoners confined in the church at Inverness. And the account which he gave of the fact is as follows – That there were

orders issued by the Pretender's son, to strip them of their clothing, for the use of some of the highland rebels; that the warrant for executing this order was sent him; that the prisoners, at first, refused to submit, upon which there was a second order and their clothes were taken from them; but that in the meantime, the person styled the French ambassador represented to him that this was an outrage. He therefore, while the clothes were still in heaps in the streets of Inverness, went up to the Pretender's son and represented the matter in the light in which the French ambassador had stated it, and according to what were his own sentiments likewise; upon which the clothes were again restored.

Shortly afterwards, a reprieve came for the Earl of Cromartie, following desperate entreaties from his pregnant wife – a rare example of compassion from the House of Hanover. The rationale behind this decision was that Cromartie had not personally been present at Culloden, and therefore could not be held responsible for the deaths of British soldiers at the battle. However, Kilmarnock's appeals for clemency were rejected and on 11 August the Reverend Foster was given the unenviable task of notifying him that the date for his execution had been set for a week hence. He reports: 'Lord Kilmarnock received this news with the outward behaviour of a man that knew and felt the importance of the scene of death, but without any marks of disorder, without any unbecoming anxiousness or terror.'

In an attempt to console him, the Reverend Foster offers his reflections on human mortality:

> I told him that all mankind were really under sentence of death, though they knew not the manner or precise time; it might be to anyone, as soon or sooner than his own; that they not expecting it, nor having such timely and certain notice of it, might die wholly unguarded and unprepared; while he had warning and the most awakening motives to fit himself, in the best manner possible, for this grand and decisive event.

Lord Kilmarnock's response is remarkable for its stoicism:

> He said that he had not been involved in the fashionable scepticism of the times with respect to Christianity; that he was therefore natu-

rally concerned about the consequences of death, in comparison of which he thought the thing itself a trifle; that as to the particular manner of his death, he thought he had no great reason to be terrified, for that the stroke appeared to be scarce so much as the pain of drawing a tooth, or the first shock of the cold-bath upon a weak and fearful temper.

Over the succeeding days, as the date of the execution drew nearer, Lord Kilmarnock was apprised of the details of the ceremony. He suggested that the coffin might be placed on the scaffold itself, and requested:

That four persons might be appointed to receive the head when it was severed from the body, in a red cloth, that it might not, as he had been informed was the case in some former executions, roll about the scaffold, and be thereby mangled and disfigured: For that though this was, in comparison, but a small circumstance, he was not willing that his body should appear with any unnecessary indecency, after the just sentence of the law was satisfied.

The Reverend Foster reports that the Earl 'talked of these particulars with ease and freedom, though the relation of them, I remember, made me tremble'.

*   *   *

The personal circumstances of the two Jacobite Lords sentenced to execution at Tower Hill on 18 August 1746 were very different. William Boyd, the 4th Earl of Kilmarnock, was forty-two years old and in the prime of life. By his own account at his trial before the House of Lords in July 1746, he had joined the Rising purely for economic reasons – 'For two kings and their rights, I cared not a farthing,' he declared, 'but I was starving . . .' He sent letters of appeal for clemency to the King and the Duke of Cumberland, but without success, and faced his end with trepidation, although the evidence of his spiritual adviser, the Reverend Foster, indicates he approached his end with calm acceptance in his last days.

By contrast, Arthur Elphinstone, the 6th Lord Balmerino, seemed almost to welcome his fate. He was fifty-eight years old at the time of Culloden and had surrendered voluntarily to the forces of King George after the Jacobite defeat. He had already spent a considerable part of his life abroad, having been forced into exile after the Battle of Sheriffmuir in 1715, and he had no desire to repeat the experience. He resisted the efforts of his cousin and fellow cavalry officer Lord Elcho to escape with him after Culloden. Lord Elcho reported in his *Journals*:

> I did all in my power to dissuade him, saying he would lose his head. He answered that of this he was fully aware, but that he was too old to survive such a disaster either by hiding or seeking refuge abroad, and he knew he would meet death with calmness.

On the eve of their execution, the thoughts of both men were with their families. When sentence was passed, Lord Balmerino sought to reassure his wife that he approached death with equanimity:

> Grieve not, my dear Peggy, we must all die one day, and this is but a few years very likely before my death must have happened some other way; therefore, wipe away your tears; you may marry again, and get a better husband.

On the eve of his execution, he wrote a short letter to King James III, appealing to him to support his widow financially:

> Sir, when His Royal Highness the Prince, your son, came to Edinburgh, as it was my bounden and indispensable duty, I joined him, for which I am tomorrow to lose my head on a scaffold, whereat I am so far from being dismayed, that it gives me great satisfaction and peace of mind that I die in so righteous a cause. I hope, Sir, on these considerations, Your Majesty will provide for my wife so as she may not want bread, which otherwise she must do, my brother having left more debt on the estate than it was worth. I am, with the most profound respect, Sir, Your Majesty's most faithful and devoted subject and servant,
>
> Balmerino
> Tower of London
> 17th August 1746.

The Earl of Kilmarnock was similarly concerned to try and secure the future of those whom he would leave behind. His last testament was written to his son and heir, Lord Boyd, who was in the service of King

George's Army at the time of the '45 and whose final meeting with his father had been at Culloden, when he embraced him one last time on the desolate battlefield before watching him being marched away as a prisoner.

Tower of London, 17th August 1746

Dear Boyd

I must take this way to bid you farewell, and I pray that God may for ever bless you and guide you in this world, and bring you to a happy immortality in the world to come. I must likewise give you my last advice. Seek God in your youth, and when you are older he will not depart from you. Be at pains to acquire good habits now, that they may grow up and become strong in you. Love Mankind, and do justice to all men. Do good to as many as you can, and neither shut your ears nor your purse to those in distress whom it is in your power to relieve. Believe me, you will find more joy in one beneficent action, and in your cool mornings you will be more happy with the reflection of having made any one person so, than in the enjoyments of all the pleasures of sense, which pall in the using, and all the pomps and gaudy show of the world. Live within your circumstances, by which means you will have it in your power to do good to others . . .

Love your family and your children, when you have any; but never let your regard for them drive you on the rock I split upon, when on that account I departed from my principles, and brought the guilt of rebellion on my head, for which I am now under the sentence justly due to my crime.

Use all your interest to get your brother pardoned and brought home as soon as possible, that his circumstances and bad influence of those he is among may not induce him to accept of foreign service, and lose him both to his country and his family. If money can be found to support him, I wish you would advise him to go to Geneva, where his principles of religion and liberty will be confirmed, and where he may stay till you see if a Pardon can be procured him. Take care of him on my account.

I must again recommend your unhappy Mother to you. Comfort her, and take all the care you can of your brothers: And may God in his infinite mercy preserve, guide and conduct you and them through all the vicissitudes of this life, and after it bring

you to the habitations of the just, and make you happy in the enjoy-
ment of Himself to all eternity.

His last letter written, the Earl of Kilmarnock faced his execution in a
calm state of mind. The Reverend James Foster, in his account, recalled
that on the morning of 18 August he found Kilmarnock 'in a most calm
and happy temper, without any disturbance or confusion in his mind, and
with apparent marks of ease and serenity in his aspect'. In their last
conversation, the Earl expressed the view that a quick death on the scaffold was preferable to 'dying after a dispiriting and lingering distemper,
in a silent melancholy darkened room, with languid and exhausted spirits,
and his friends standing around him, with lively marks of sorrow and
anguish in their countenances, expecting and deploring his fate'.

Immediately before their execution, the Earl of Kilmarnock had a final
meeting with Lord Balmerino and their conversation is recalled by Foster
'without addition or diminution':

Balmerino: My Lord, I beg leave to ask your Lordship one question.
Kilmarnock: To any question, my Lord, that you now think it
proper to ask, I believe, I shall see no reason to decline giving
an answer.
B: Why then, my Lord, did you ever see or know of any order,
signed by the Prince, to give no quarter at the Battle of Culloden?
K: No, my Lord.
B: Nor I neither: And therefore it seems to be an invention to
justify their own murderous scheme.
K: No, my Lord, I do not think that this inference can be drawn
from it, because, while I was a prisoner at Inverness, I was
informed by several officers, that there was such an order signed
George Murray, and that it was in the Duke's custody.
B: Lord George Murray! Why then, they should not charge it upon
the Prince.

After this exchange, Balmerino leaves, his parting words, as recollected
by the Reverend Foster, 'I am only sorry, that I cannot pay all this reckoning alone; farewell forever.'

At this point, the Reverend Foster asked Kilmarnock to 'allow me to declare in his name to the Sheriffs and all persons there present the substance of the professions and acknowledgements which he had often repeated to me . . . [declaring King George] to be the only rightful and lawful King of these realms'.

This done, the Earl took a final drink from his quaich (Plate 25), then the Reverend Foster accompanied Lord Kilmarnock to the scaffold, where he knelt in prayer with him: 'After having talked with his Lordship a considerable time, to support him in his penitence and resignation, I embraced, and left him in the same calm disposition, having quitted the scaffold some minutes before his execution.'

And with this, the Reverend Foster disappears into the mists of history.

The story is taken up by a Mr T. Ford, whose account, dated 22 August 1746, hit the streets of London within days of the execution, selling at a price of one penny – quite literally, in the light of the events it recounts, a penny dreadful.

Mr Ford, who assisted the Sheriffs on the day of the execution, prefaced his account by stating that he was moved to write it 'in order to silence the many erroneous accounts that have been published, and to take off several cruel aspersions that have been thrown out touching the behaviour of those unhappy Lords'.

Mr Ford relates how, at ten o'clock in the morning of Monday, 18 August 1746 he attended a procession of the two Lords from the Tower of London to their place of execution on Tower Hill, 'where, upon their arrival, they were conducted into separate apartments'. He recounts: 'My Lord Kilmarnock spent his retirement here in a manner suitable to his unhappy circumstances, Mr Foster frequently comforting his Lordship with seasonable exhortations.'

His account of the final meeting between the Earl and Lord Balmerino, between 11.00 and 11.30 a.m. that morning, is consistent with that of the Reverend Foster, 'after which, my Lord having sat down a few moments to refresh himself with a bit of bread and a glass of wine, he, about twelve o'clock, rose, saluted his friends, and proceeded to the scaffold'.

Mr Ford reports that the Earl made no final speech on the scaffold, 'but much better employed his time with Mr Foster in his devotions', then

with a countenance perfectly serene and composed, embraced his friends, and took his final leave of them. After that, the Executioner was introduced to his Lordship, asked for his forgiveness for the painful office allotted to him; which his Lordship readily granted, and gave him a purse of gold, desired him to have courage, and acquainted him that, the signal for the stroke should be the dropping of a handkerchief.

The account relates how the Earl then knelt down at the block, prayed for a few minutes, then gave the signal, upon which the axe fell and his head was severed from his body at one blow. It was 'received into a piece of scarlet baize, and with the body deposited in a coffin, and delivered to his Lordship's friends'.

The scene on the scaffold is depicted in Plate 24. Mr Ford notes that, contrary to tradition, the head was not held up to spectators 'to satisfy the people that the execution had been done'. Instead 'the Sheriffs directed that everybody upon the scaffold should kneel down, that they may might see execution itself performed; a ceremony never practiced before'.

Lord Balmerino's execution was not so straightforward as that of the Earl of Kilmarnock. After being informed that the Earl of Kilmarnock was no more, he 'twice refreshed himself with a bit of bread and a glass of wine, and desired the company to drink him "ain Degrae ta Haiven," but above all, he called frequently upon God, and seemed both willing and prepared to die'.

Mr Ford notes:

When his Lordship mounted the scaffold, he appeared in the very same regimentals he wore at the Battle of Culloden; and, so far was he from having the least concern himself at the fear of death, that he frequently reproved his friends that were about him for showing any. His Lordship walked around the scaffold, bowed to the people, read the following inscription upon his coffin, 'Arthurus Dominus de Balmerino, decollates 18 die Augusti 1746. Aetatis sua 58.' Said it was right, and with seeming pleasure looked at the block, which he called his pillow of rest.

After he had inspected and approved the inscription on his coffin, Lord Balmerino made his final speech, the text of which was to be reproduced in full many years later in *The Lyon in Mourning*, but not in Mr Ford's account. No doubt concerned that any report of the speech could potentially be regarded as treasonous, Mr Ford observes simply, 'whatever may be offered in excuse for his Lordship's making that speech in his last moments, nothing but the highest authority can justify publishing it'.

Lord Balmerino's speech on the scaffold is an unapologetic paean to the House of Stuart, in particular Prince Charles, who, said Lord Balmerino, 'wants no qualifications to make a great man'. He also took the opportunity to deny the charge that the Prince had issued a command to give no quarter before the Battle of Culloden, as he had confirmed earlier that morning during his final conversation with the Earl of Kilmarnock:

> This is such an unchristian thing and so unlike the gallant Prince that nobody who knows him will believe it. It is very strange if there had been any such orders that neither the Earl of Kilmarnock nor I should never have heard anything of it, especially since we were both at headquarters the morning before the battle. I am convinced that is a malicious report industriously spread to excuse themselves for the murders they were guilty of in calm blood after the battle.

His speech completed, Lord Balmerino presented his executioner with three guineas, adding, 'Friend, I never had much money, this is all I have, and I am sorry I can add nothing else to it, but my coat and waistcoat,' which his Lordship instantly took off and placed on his coffin for the executioner.

He then took the axe from the executioner, felt the edge and urged the executioner to strike a clean blow, 'for in that will consist your Mercy'. But it was not to be. Lord Balmerino's signal was so sudden that it took the executioner by surprise.

Mr Ford's account states:

> I wish I could conclude that his head had been taken off at one blow; but the Executioner was so terrified at his Lordship's intrepidity, and the suddenness of the signal, that the force of the blow was not sufficient to sever the head from the body, though happily sufficient to deprive him of all sensation.

Just how Mr Ford could be so confident that Lord Balmerino was deprived of sensation is unclear. Other contemporary accounts state that he turned and looked at the executioner in anguish. In any event, his suffering did not last much longer. Mr Ford's account concludes:

After the first blow, his Lordship's head fell back upon his shoulders, but, being afterwards severed at two more gentle blows, was then received into a piece of red baize, and with his body deposited in his coffin, and delivered to his friends.

The one destiny that all of us share is our own mortality and, almost three centuries on, there is something noble and inspiring in the way in which both the Earl of Kilmarnock and Lord Balmerino met their ends, having made their peace with God and Man, with fortitude, dignity and considerable courage.

*   *   *

So, what is the legacy of the Jacobite Lords executed in August 1746?

Despite the efforts of Hanoverian officials to suppress the words of Lord Balmerino's speech on the scaffold, they lived on and helped to subtly change perceptions of what had happened at Culloden. Perhaps, after all, the Duke of Cumberland was not quite the conquering hero lauded by Handel – and perhaps those he had so brutally repressed were not the sub-human savages portrayed in Hanoverian propaganda.

And what is the final truth about the man whose image looks out upon us today from faded prints? Were the life and career of the Earl of Kilmarnock no more than a series of blunders, leaving nothing in their wake other than unmitigated disaster for himself and those whose lives he had touched?

Well, perhaps the life and death of the feckless Earl were not entirely in vain. If one reads the statements he made at his trial, his conversations with the Reverend Foster in the Tower of London, and the letters he wrote before his execution to his trustees and heirs, one can discern both a genuine love for his wife and family and an element of calculation. Perhaps, if he took full responsibility for his actions, and suffered the full force of the mockery and ridicule heaped upon him, he could salvage something for his family from the catastrophe that had befallen him.

And to a degree it worked. His son James, whom he had met for the last time on the battlefield of Culloden, in due course ascended to become the Earl of Erroll. He did not succeed to any of his father's titles, which were extinguished with him, forfeited by his sentence of treason, but gained his title from his mother's mother. The old Countess of Erroll proved as good as her word, passing on her estate as she had promised to do if Lord Kilmarnock rose with the Prince. As Earl of Erroll, he worked to restore the family's fortunes, dying at Callendar House in 1778.

Two hundred and seventy years after the Battle of Falkirk Muir, the Earl of Kilmarnock's great-grandson seven times removed was the British Prime Minister, David Cameron. As Michael Caine might say, not a lot of people know that. Possibly because Lord Kilmarnock's descendants do not broadcast the fact that their distant ancestor was executed for treason on Tower Hill in the high summer of the Year of our Lord 1746.

But are they right to be so embarrassed about their relationship with the Earl of Kilmarnock?

My case is this: had any of us dined at Callendar House on that fateful evening in September 1745, with all the pressures that Lord Kilmarnock was then under, and encountered the charismatic and dynamic force of Bonnie Prince Charlie urging us to join his cause with promises of great rewards if we did so – which of us might not have made the same decision as Lord Kilmarnock?

So perhaps the most appropriate epitaph for William Boyd, 4th Earl of Kilmarnock, might be Voltaire's aphorism:

Tout comprendre, c'est tout pardonner
To understand all is to forgive all.

15

John Roy Stuart:
The Bard of Culloden

Around the year 1700, a miracle occurred in Strathspey – the birth of a baby boy, baptised John Roy Stuart, or, in the Gaelic, Iain Ruadh Stiubhard. The creation of any human life is a miracle, but what made John Roy so unusual was that his mother, Barbara Shaw, was fifty-two years old at the time of his birth.

Even today it would be exceptional for a woman to give birth to a healthy baby boy at such an advanced age, and when it occurs it is usually with clinical assistance. At the turn of the eighteenth century a natural birth at such an age was almost unprecedented.

So from the moment of his arrival, John Roy was regarded as very special. Indeed, the legend goes that his mother prophesied on the night that he was born that her son would become a great man who would crown the Kings of three nations. This prophecy came to pass when, as a colonel in Spanish service, he attended the coronation of the King of Spain, then, as a colonel in French service, he attended the coronation of the King of France, and finally, as a Jacobite colonel, he crowned Prince Charles as Prince Regent on the day after the Battle of Prestonpans.

His parents sought to secure the very best education for their son, sending him to France and Portugal as a young man to learn French and Portuguese. He had also learnt Latin at school in Inverness and spoke English as well as his native Gaelic. While travelling in France, he met an exiled Highland chieftain, Simon Fraser, Lord Lovat, beginning a friendship that lasted a lifetime.

During this formative period, John Roy developed his skills as a bard, using his poetry as a sort of personal diary to process ideas going through his mind, record key events of his life and learn from his experiences.

The Gaelic Bards played an important role in the hard life of Highlanders during the first half of the eighteenth century. Most people eked out a bare living from the primary activities of farming, fishing, animal husbandry, forestry and hunting. They were also engaged in secondary activities that flowed from them, such as weaving, baking, brewing, distilling, carpentry, joinery and masonry. Often a single person would carry out several of these tasks at different times of the day, or during different seasons of the year, as people do to this very day in remote Highland and Island communities. These activities were undertaken to meet a family's subsistence needs. Any surpluses could be traded with others in the community, frequently by barter rather than monetary exchange.

Much of the work was seasonal and determined by the weather. Men and women worked longer hours in the summer, and longest of all during harvest time. When winter came and the nights drew in, there was more time to spare, but opportunities for entertainment were limited. There were newspapers and books, but only a small minority of educated gentlemen and an even smaller minority of educated ladies were able to read and write. In his book on Shakespeare, Bill Bryson estimates that just 30 per cent of men and 10 per cent of women were able to read and write in seventeenth-century London, and if anything the rate of literacy in the Highlands a hundred years later would have been even lower.

It was also very dreich and damp – as indeed it still is in the Highlands. Traditional Highland dress could serve as a sleeping bag for those caught out on a winter's night, but in reality men and women were used to being cold and wet when outdoors. Only when they got inside could they expect a measure of warmth. On a hard winter's night, there was no better place to be than a local inn or ceilidh house, where they could warm themselves by peat fires, meet their friends, neighbours and cousins to exchange news and gossip, and be entertained by local bards with their stories and songs.

Like popular songs today, these were composed to be heard rather than read, and were repeated from memory. The bard's poems tended to be a lot longer than contemporary songs, often narratives extending to ten or twenty minutes. They covered the eternal themes of love, loss and laughter, and they also served as a medium to communicate news and opinions on current events.

People's memories then were a lot better than they are today. They had to be because most people had no way of recalling information through written records. It is said that one near contemporary of John Roy's, the illiterate Gaelic Bard Duncan Ban MacIntyre, was able to recall many thousands of lines of his poems and songs from memory, so that he could always keep an audience entertained, whatever the occasion.

John Roy was a literate and highly educated man, but in common with the other Gaelic Bards he did not write down his poems on paper, instead composing them in his head and singing them to those who gathered around fires in Highland inns on cold winter nights. For this reason, only a dozen of his songs and poems have survived (see Appendix A for a list of those works).

Memory is assisted by alliteration, rhythm and rhyme, and John Roy's surviving poetry uses all of these mnemonic techniques. His poems are characteristically written in quatrains of alternately rhyming couplets, each line having eight or nine beats. This is the form of one of his early poems, a eulogy for Lady Christian MacIntosh, the wife of William MacIntosh, 21st Chief of the Clan MacIntosh, whose early death was a cause of immense grief. Written around 1735, *Cumha do Bhaintighearna Mhic-an-Toisich* ('The Lament for Lady MacIntosh') serves as a timeless elegy to those who have died before their time. In the poem, John Roy evokes the forces of nature to capture the calamity of her early death, concluding with an expression of his own profound sorrow.

Not long after Lady MacIntosh's death, another crisis occurred in the life of John Roy Stuart when his career in the British Army came to a juddering halt. Piecing together the available evidence, it appears that John Roy sought a commission in the Black Watch, which was refused, possibly because of his known Jacobite sympathies. A year later, in 1736, his regiment, the Scots Greys, was sent to Inverness to apprehend a suspected Jacobite gentleman by the name of Munro of Novar. According to W. Drummond Norrie, writing in the *Celtic Monthly* in March 1895, 'John Roy allowed him to escape, and could give no satisfactory account of his apparent neglect of duty to his superior officers on returning to headquarters without his prisoner.'

John Roy was then arrested, charged with treason and put into jail in Inverness. At this point, his old friend from his days in France, Simon, Lord Lovat, came to his rescue. By this time, Lord Lovat's own fortunes had recovered after he had regained his lands and title as a reward for taking Inverness for King George during the Fifteen. Using his position as Sheriff of Inverness, he connived to get John Roy out of jail and gave him refuge while he arranged his escape to France.

A decade later, these events were to be used in evidence against Lord Lovat at his own trial for high treason before the House of Lords in 1747.

The trial transcript records testimony by a witness by the name of Robert Chevis, in which Chevis testified that John Roy had stayed with Lord Lovat for about six weeks before he escaped to France. During that time, according to Chevis, John Roy and Lord Lovat had amused themselves by 'composing burlesque verses, that when young Charles came over, there would be blood and blows'.

That, as far as I can make out, is the last recorded piece of verse composed by John Roy until after the Battle of Culloden. The reason for this long gap is not difficult to identify: John Roy was, during this period, far away from the ceilidh houses of the Scottish Highlands in a French culture where his considerable talents as a Gaelic Bard had no audience, as few people understood Gaelic. Similarly, an old friend in the 1745 Association, Brigadier John MacFarlane, told me that he didn't speak his native Gaelic for thirty years while serving in the British Army, for the very good reason that there was no one with whom he could speak it. It was only when he retired to the west Highlands that he was able to speak his mother's tongue once more.

After a decade in exile serving as an officer in the French Army, news reached John Roy in August 1745 that the Royal Stuart Standard had been raised at Glenfinnan. He was at that time stationed at Ghent, near the Channel ports, having recently fought at the Battle of Fontenoy (May 1745), where French forces under the Marshal Maurice de Saxe had scored a major victory over the British Army under the Duke of Cumberland.

When John Roy heard that Prince Charles Edward Stuart had initiated his audacious attempt to reclaim the thrones of Scotland, England and Ireland, he immediately secured passage on a merchant vessel bound for Britain to join his army.

As events transpired, John Roy almost didn't make it home at all. When the redcoats got wind that the notorious rebel and outlaw John Roy Stuart was on the high seas sailing for Scotland, they dispatched a welcoming party to arrest him at the Port of Leith.

He never made it that far. The ship's first port of call was Newcastle and it was there that he disembarked. Perhaps he had some inkling that, with Leith crawling with Government troops, he would be better advised to leave the ship at the more lightly guarded port of Newcastle. Perhaps he simply opted to pay a lower fare, covering only the first leg of the voyage. Whatever the reason, once disembarked John Roy made his way overland by coach and horse at his leisure, reaching the Jacobite Army at

Blair Atholl on 1 September 1745, leaving the redcoats at Leith fuming that their quarry had somehow succeeded in evading them.

It was the first, but by no means the last, of John Roy's narrow escapes from their clutches.

Upon arrival at Blair Atholl, he was greeted with open arms by Prince Charles and his senior advisers, as one of the few leading Jacobites with proven military experience. His first job was to travel north to persuade his old friend Lord Lovat to raise his clan for the cause of Prince Charlie.

The Old Fox was conflicted. On the one hand, his personal sympathies were with the young chevalier. On the other, he was old and shrewd enough to know that open support for the Prince carried considerable risks for himself and his clan in the event that the Prince's campaign did not succeed.

The compromise solution that Lord Lovat arrived at was to encourage his son and heir, the Master of Lovat, to raise a Fraser clan regiment for Prince Charles, while at the same time assuring the authorities that he personally remained loyal to King George.

Historians have criticised Lord Lovat for his duplicity, but he was doing no more and no less than a number of other noble families, who hedged their bets by committing one of their sons to Prince Charlie's cause, while the other remained at home. Examples include the Boyd family of the Earl of Kilmarnock; the Earl of Airlie, whose elder son and heir, Lord Ogilvy, rose for the Prince, while the younger son, Walter, stayed at home; and the Atholl Murrays, where the oldest surviving brother, the Marquis of Tullibardine, rose with the Prince, along with the third brother, Lord George Murray, while the second brother, James, remained the 'Hanoverian Duke of Atholl'.

Lord Lovat's decision to connive in raising a regiment for the Prince, while publicly protesting his loyalty to the Government, was to prove the last of a long list of transactional tergiversations in his long and picaresque career.

Back in Duddingston, after successfully recruiting his old friend Lord Lovat to the cause, John Roy was sent on a reconnaissance mission with another Jacobite officer, Captain George Hamilton, to report on the movements of General Cope's troops.

Riding out to Haddington, they encountered two Hanoverian officers, Robert Cunningham and Francis Garden, who had advanced beyond the redcoat lines to enjoy a meal of oysters and white wine at the Crystal Inn. As they fell into conversation, the two Hanoverians asked whether John

Roy and Captain Hamilton were supporters of the Bonnie Prince. Sensing a trap, John Roy declared that, on the contrary, they were loyal subjects of King George, then turned the tables on them by stating that he suspected Cunningham and Garden were themselves Jacobites. They vehemently denied this and boasted that they had entered the Highland camp the evening before and gathered valuable intelligence, which they were about to report to General Cope. At this point, John Roy drew a brace of pistols, revealed his true identity and placed them under arrest. Taking his prisoners back to Duddingston, John Roy helpfully suggested that the pair of them should be hanged to ensure that they didn't pass on any intelligence to Johnnie Cope. Dead men tell no tales.

Calmer counsels prevailed and the two men were merely placed under arrest. After the Rising, both went on to enjoy full and successful careers, Cunningham rising to the rank of General while Garden pursued a career as an advocate and a judge, ending his life as His Honour Lord Gardenstoun.

After Prestonpans, John Roy was appointed commander of a new regiment, the Edinburgh Regiment, formed of fifty Atholl men drawn from John Roy's native Strathspey and 150 new recruits raised in the City of Edinburgh, including deserters from the defeated Hanoverian Army. John Roy drilled these raw recruits into something approaching a professional regiment and they discharged their duties during the campaign with distinction.

On 30 October 1745, when the Council of War was held at Holyrood Palace to decide the next step in the campaign, John Roy was the only regimental colonel not invited to attend. He was still complaining about his exclusion almost two years later, claiming that it was because the Prince knew he would oppose his proposal to march into England. In a letter dated June 1747 to James Edgar, Principal Secretary to James Francis Edward Stuart, John Roy writes:

> The first great error committed (during the campaign) was going into England at the time and in the manner we did. The authors of that inaccountable scheme (for I must call it so) have much to answer for to God, the King, the Prince and the Country. I was not then admitted to their Councils and was the only Colonel debarred and for no reason I could ever imagine but that I spoke too warmly against such a step.

Was John Roy right to think that he was excluded from the vital Council of War on account of his known opposition to an advance into England?

My suspicion is that there might be an alternative explanation. Just as the cry of the American revolutionaries was 'no taxation without representation', so on the Jacobite Council of War the principle was 'no representation without taxation'. Uniquely among the regimental colonels, John Roy was not a clan chieftain and had brought no money, men or resources to the campaign. That might explain why he wasn't given a seat at the top table.

Notwithstanding John Roy's reservations, the Jacobite Army marched into England and advanced to within 120 miles of London before another Council of War held in Derby on 6 December 1745 (from which John Roy was also excluded) decided to turn back.

During the retreat, John Roy performed his usual sterling service. At Clifton, his Regiment was deployed on the left flank and succeeded in causing the redcoats to retreat with the bloodcurdling cry of 'Claymore'.

At the time of the Battle of Falkirk Muir in January 1746, John Roy's Regiment was deployed under the Duke of Perth at the Siege of Stirling. John Roy himself was commissioned by the Prince to undertake reconnaissance and gain intelligence on the position of General Hawley's redcoats. The story goes that he came across an old comrade from his days in the Scots Greys, a certain Colonel Shugborough Whitney, then serving in Ligonier's dragoons. Whitney recognised John Roy and cried out, 'Ha – You there! We shall soon be up with you.' To which John Roy shouted in reply, 'You're more than welcome. We'll give you a warm reception!' The story concludes that these words were barely out of his mouth when Colonel Whitney was struck by a chance shot and fell dead from his saddle.

Personally, I find this story rather hard to swallow. Had John Roy been riding about in no-man's-land on Falkirk Muir, it seems more likely that he would have received a volley of musket shot for his pains rather than be left to exchange pleasantries with an old comrade from his days in the British Army. However, this story has been repeated so often in so many histories of the period that I reproduce it here and leave others to form their own view of its veracity.

Despite the victory at Falkirk Muir, the momentum of the campaign of 1745 had shifted irrevocably against the Jacobites as they retreated ever further northwards. They were short of money, munitions and supplies, and more and more men were deserting as their wages went unpaid. In one last desperate throw, the Jacobite high command decided to launch a night-time attack from their base at Culloden against the Duke of Cumberland's redcoats eight miles away at Nairn, whom they confidently expected to be drunk after celebrating the Duke's birthday.

The night march ended in disaster. Many of the men were now starving and went in search of food. Their local guides got lost in the dark. The two Jacobite columns, one under Lord George Murray and the other under the Prince, became separated and communication between the two columns was lost. As dawn broke, Lord George, concluding that the essential element of surprise had now been lost, gave orders to his men to return to camp.

The Prince was furious. He was convinced that the attack could have succeeded. In his mind, Lord George was entirely to blame for the fiasco.

John Roy took the Prince's side in this dispute. There seems to have been a serious argument between the two men, which ended with Lord George threatening John Roy with arrest. From that day on, John Roy conceived a visceral dislike of Lord George and convinced himself that he had betrayed the cause.

The following day, the redcoats advanced from Nairn to the Jacobite encampments on Culloden Moor. John Roy's Edinburgh Regiment was positioned between the Stewarts of Appin, his blood relatives, and the Clan Fraser Regiment under the Master of Lovat, son of his old friend Lord Lovat. Apart from the Camerons, these three were the only Jacobite regiments that succeeded in charging over the moorland to reach the Hanoverian front line – and almost broke it.

Overwhelmingly outnumbered, their attack faltered. For the only time in the campaign, the Highland Charge was broken. Within half an hour, the Battle of Culloden was over.

After the battle, one of Cumberland's captains was quoted as saying that 'if all of the Highlanders had fought as well as the officer with the red hair and the little hand [later identified as John Roy], the issue might very well have been different'.

For John Roy, as for others who had risked all for the Jacobite cause, the battle was an unmitigated disaster.

*　　*　　*

Swiss psychologist Elizabeth Kübler Ross identified five stages that, she said, all humans experience after a catastrophic loss. The first is denial, then anger, followed by bargaining, then depression and, finally, some kind of acceptance. When we examine the work of John Roy, we can see these different emotions in relation to the grief he felt at the loss at Culloden.

Two weeks after the battle, in May 1746, two French ships landed in the west Highlands, delivering 3,000 stands of arms and sufficient gold to convince John Roy and a few other Jacobite diehards that they could continue the campaign.

The Loch Arkaig money was not too little, but it was too late. Had it arrived before Culloden, it could have been of considerable assistance in feeding, re-arming and paying the Jacobite Army, and could have enabled them to fight on – although without military support from France in the form of boots on the ground, how long the campaign could have continued, even with this assistance, is questionable. As it was, the surviving Jacobite soldiers made up their own minds and came to the same conclusion as their Prince: the campaign of 1745 was over, and it made no sense to risk further lives in a lost cause. Very few able-bodied men turned up to Muir Laggan, and after that even John Roy could no longer deny that the Campaign of 1745 was over. He headed for the hills of his native Strathspey.

During this period, he wrote his least known surviving poem, '*Latha Chuilodair nan Siol*' ('Culloden's Day of Dust'). The only version of this poem of which I am aware is that provided by Neil MacGregor in his dissertation on John Roy Stuart, published in Volume LXIII of the *Transactions of the Gaelic Society of Inverness*. The problem with the poem is not just that it is a work of denial, but that it amounts to little more than a rant of rage and frustration. John Roy goes on at considerable length in expressing his contempt for the Duke of Cumberland and swearing revenge, without actually saying much of any interest or insight. The general tone of the poem can be gathered from its fourteenth stanza:

> *Though I am now in clefts and caves,*
> *With your bloodhounds on my trail,*
> *Should I survive for times to come*
> *I shall meet you yet.*

The following month, in June 1746, John Roy composed '*Oran Eile Air Latha Chuilodair*' ('The Silk of Clan Chattan'), which opens as follows:

I am in utter torment!
My spirit has fallen to the earth,
And tears teem from my eyes.

This is no mere poetic artifice written in some academic ivory tower or the traditional garret attic of the impoverished bard. This is a cry of despair uttered from the depths of the soul of a man whose world has come crashing down around him.

'The Silk of Clan Chattan' is not so much a poem as a series of staccato sobs, whose fractured and fragmented structure reflects John Roy's own mental disintegration at this time. His greatest anger is reserved for William, Duke of Cumberland, of whom he says:

May William, the son of George,
Be as a tree without leaves,
Without a twig, without a branch, or even the shoots of a branch!

John Roy's diatribe against the Butcher Cumberland extends over the last four verses of the poem.

May your hearth be bare,
Lacking wife, brother or son,
Without the sound of a harp or candlelight!

And lacking joy, happiness or prosperity,
May grief, misfortune and plague
Such as beset the Children of Egypt come upon you!

And we shall yet see your head
Rising into the air on a gallows
And the birds of the sky mocking it.

While we, both old and young,
Will be under the rightful King
To whom we owe allegiance.

Even three centuries later, the contempt and bitterness that John Roy feels for the Butcher is palpable.

The curse that he visited upon the Duke of Cumberland did indeed come to pass. Cumberland did die like a tree without leaves or branches, unmarried and childless, his military career after Culloden one of failure, and his reputation in tatters as the truth about the atrocities committed after the battle came to light.

At this point, if John Roy was to succumb to the anger and despair of 'The Silk of Clan Chattan', then his ultimate fate was inevitable – capture and death, and not the swift death of a warrior in battle, struck down by the stroke of a sword or the shot of a musket ball, which he had faced many times, but the most agonising and humiliating death yet devised by man: hanging, drawing and quartering.

So another emotion begins to overwhelm John Roy, an emotion even more powerful than anger – fear, and a fear bordering on terror. We know this because in the one poem which John Roy wrote in English that survives to this day, 'John Roy's Psalm', the words 'I shall not be afraid' are repeated twice in the opening two verses. He is like a child in the dark, using the power of auto-suggestion and repetition to overcome his primeval fear.

As the Psalm progresses, we can almost hear John Roy's shattered nerves begin to steady; he uses repeated incantations expressing his determination to overcome negative emotions and build his fragile confidence until the song concludes with a statement of ringing defiance.

But despite the bargain he has struck, John Roy is not restored to the devil-may-care troubadour of his younger days. His next poem, '*Urnuigh Iain Ruaidh*' ('John Roy's Prayer'), is another conversation with the Good Lord, his only companion during the long days and nights he spends alone on the run in the mountains. John Roy is clearly still feeling very sorry for himself, but he is past the utter despair of 'The Silk of Clan Chattan'. 'The Prayer', as it is known, composed in twelve four-line verses of alternately rhyming couplets, opens as follows:

By a streamlet, tired and worn,
The good Christian John Roy sits alone,
A weary warrior, utterly forlorn,
In wretched spirits and with a fractured bone.

As he moves from cave to cave to stay one step ahead of the pursuing redcoats, John Roy is not a happy camper. He is distinctly grumpy. He is passing through the fourth stage of grief and is depressed.

His depression only starts to lift when he is reunited with his Prince in

PLATE 20. Prince Henry Benedict Stuart by Maurice Quentin de la Tour, conventionally dated 1746/47
The National Galleries of Scotland. Purchased with aid of the Art Fund 1994

I believe that La Tour actually painted Prince Henry's portrait in Paris in November 1745, as the Prince awaited mobilisation of an army of 11,000 men which he would then lead into England. If so, this portrait was painted not in commemoration of the failure of the Rising of 1745, but rather in anticipation of its imminent success, and it is this which makes it one of the most important and poignant Jacobite portraits of all.

PLATE 21. Cooking pot used by Prince Charlie, 1746
By kind permission of the Tulloch Collection

Iron cooking pot reportedly used by Prince Charles Edward Stuart while on the
run after Culloden.

PLATE 22. Piece of Betty Burke's dress, 1746
By kind permission of the Tulloch Collection

A piece of the dress given to Prince Charles Edward Stuart by Flora MacDonald
to disguise him as Betty Burke. Many years later, he gave it to Lady Mary Stuart,
wife of Lord Fortrose.

PLATE 23. Flora MacDonald by Allan Ramsay, 1749
Image copyright © Ashmolean Museum, University of Oxford

This beautiful 1749 portrait of the Jacobite heroine shows her as a straightforward,
honest and unpretentious woman, elegantly accoutred in 1745 tartan. 'Her name will
be mentioned in history and, if courage and fidelity be virtues, mentioned with honour.'

PLATE 24. The Beheading of the Jacobite Lords on Great Tower Hill, August 1746
From the Author's Collection

The text below the print includes a poem, which begins: 'At this sad scene which blood must deeply stain ,/ Scarce can the pitying Eye the Tear restrain: / But that same instant call to mental sight ,/ Those heroes bleeding in their country's right.' These rather clumsy lines suggest some doubts as to the justice of the execution, which are then dismissed and the sentences justified as retribution for the deaths of Government soldiers.

PLATE 25. The Earl of Kilmarnock's quaich, August 1746
By kind permission of the Tulloch Collection

Taken down to London and used by the Earl of Kilmarnock for his final drink before his execution on Tower Hill.

PLATE 26. The Prince's Cairn. Erected by the 1745 Association, 1956

The Cairn marks the Prince's traditional place of departure from Scotland in September 1746.

PLATE 27. The Kennington Martyrs' Plaque. Installed in St George's Gardens, London, by the 1745 Association, 2015

The Plaque commemorates the men executed on Kennington Common in 1746 who are buried in the gardens.

A man traduced by history? Condemned by the Jacobites as a turncoat; condemned by the Hanoverians as a traitor; condemned by the bar of history as 'wicked Lord Lovat', during his final hours the Tower of London he said that all he had ever sought was the protection and preservation of his family and clan, and beyond that the restoration of the Royal House of Stuart.

PLATE 29. The Trial of Lord Lovat, 1747
By kind permission of the Tulloch Collection

Alone and unaided, Lord Lovat was left to defend himself against the finest lawyers in
England before his peers in the House of Lords. Betrayed by the Prince's secretary,
Murray of Broughton, the result was a foregone conclusion.

PLATE 30. Alexander Murray of Elibank by Allan Ramsay, 1742

National Galleries of Scotland. David Laing bequest to the Society of Antiquaries of Scotland. Gifted in 2009

This portrait of Elibank captures both the intelligence and the naivety of the man who, ten years later, instigated the plot that bears his name and marked the end of Prince Charles' attempts to regain the throne for the House of Stuart.

Cluny's Cage at Ben Alder and sails with him on 20 September 1746 to France, and to safety, on board *L'Heureux*. It is during this period, I believe, that John Roy composed his most complete poem about the battle, '*Latha Chuilodair*' ('The Day of Culloden'), which shows the clear influence of his conversations with the Prince. It is John Roy's last and greatest poem, and marks a degree of acceptance about what had occurred. John Roy makes it clear, however, that he remains determined to continue the fight, convinced of the ultimate justice of his cause.

Today, John Roy Stuart's poems can only be understood in the Gaelic language in which they were composed by a few thousand people. There is no monument to his memory other than a modest cairn that we in the 1745 Association built during the dying days of the last millennium. The Jacobite cause to which he dedicated his life ended in abject failure. The sacrifices he made and the risks he took were all for naught. And he died in poverty and in exile. So you might be forgiven for concluding that the life of John Roy Stuart was not exactly one of unalloyed success. Yet he did leave a legacy in the few of his poems that survive.

The Regimental Colonel who served with such valour at Culloden is, above all, the bard of the boulevard of broken dreams, who speaks for all who have suffered catastrophic loss for reasons beyond their control or comprehension. And the message he sends to us today through his surviving poems is this:

Whatever troubles we may face,
however desperate things may seem,
however bleak our prospects may be,
as long as there is life there is hope,
and as long we have hope we are never defeated.

16

John Roy's 'The Day of Culloden'

If my dating is correct, '*Latha Chuilodair*', 'The Day of Culloden', was composed during the six-week period that John Roy Stuart spent with Prince Charles in September and October 1746, when the two men were hiding together in Cluny's Cage on Ben Alder and then when they both escaped on *L'Heureux* back to France.

There are several clues that support this dating. First, in the poem John Roy refers to the destruction of Castle Dounie at the hands of Cumberland's troops, which occurred in May 1746. However, the poem does not refer to the subsequent capture of his old friend Lord Lovat, which occurred in March 1747. He almost certainly would have referenced Lord Lovat's capture had the poem been composed after that date, so we can infer that it was written between those dates. Second, 'The Day of Culloden' develops many of the themes of John Roy's other poems about the Battle of Culloden, but is more completely developed and structured, which suggests the poem was written after 'Culloden's Day of Dust' and 'The Silk of Clan Chattan'. Third, the reasons given in the poem for the final Jacobite defeat mirror the Prince's opinions almost exactly, suggesting that the poem could have been heavily influenced by John Roy's conversations with the Prince during September and October 1746. So, although John Roy was the poet who composed 'The Day of Culloden', the ideas it expresses about what went wrong were shared (and maybe even inspired) by the Prince himself.

In the third verse, John Roy says that the redcoats won the battle thanks 'to westering winds and showers that came over us up from the lowland plain'.

In the fourth verse, he writes that 'evil witchcraft and spells were worked upon us before the engagement', and that it was a pity the battle was fought in Scotland, where the clansmen could easily disperse to their homes and families, and not in England, where they would have fought to the death. This reflects the Prince's own view that the Jacobite Army should never have turned back at Derby but should have continued to advance on London.

In the sixth verse, John Roy tells us that 'Castle Dounie's a fire-black-ened ruin – Dishonoured its bare silent walls'. I wonder whether, as he wrote these words, he felt a tinge of guilt at the role he had inadvertently played in the razing of the castle. Had he not paid his fateful visit to Castle Dounie a year earlier, then Lord Lovat might not have thrown in his lot with the Prince, and Cumberland would not subsequently have reduced his family seat to ashes.

In the poem's eighth verse, the defeat is blamed on the treachery of Lord George Murray. This is a wholly baseless calumny, unsupported by any evidence of which I am aware, but by that time Lord George had become a convenient scapegoat for the Prince, and John Roy had fallen out with the headstrong Jacobite general after they had argued about the fiasco of the Night March on Nairn.

Anything and anyone is blamed for the disaster, in fact, except for Prince Charles Edward Stuart. John Roy does not concede even the remotest possibility that, on the day, the Hanoverian regulars were more than a match for the disintegrating and starving Jacobite Army, and that it just might have been a major strategic error on the part of the Bonnie Prince to attempt to stand and fight on an open plain. Indeed, as far as John Roy was concerned, the Jacobites were never fairly defeated in battle at all.

Yet, whatever its limitations as a work of historical analysis, there is no doubt that 'The Day of Culloden' is a very powerful work of catharsis and grief.

My Translation of 'The Day of Culloden'

'The Day of Culloden' runs to a total of ninety-six lines, comprising twelve verses of eight lines each. Each verse is made up of two quatrains of alter-nately rhyming couplets, with each couplet ending in a single downbeat syllable reflecting the poet's own sadness, as he reflects on the battle.

There have been several attempts to translate the poem into English for wider appreciation, with mixed results. This is no surprise. Poetry is notoriously difficult to translate from any language. It can be translated literally, word-for-word, as Elizabeth E. Mackechnie did in her booklet *The Poems of John Roy Stewart* (1947). However, it is then reduced to blank prose, losing its rhyme and musicality. Alternatively, a translator can opt to retain the metre and rhythm of the original, but sacrifice its meaning. This is the path generally taken by translators of popular songs, such as the Elvis Presley classic 'It's now or never', which retains the musicality of the Neapolitan aria '*O Sole Mio*', while abandoning its literal meaning.

John Lorne Campbell, in his *Highland Songs of the Forty-five* (1934), comments:

> Gaelic poetry involves the assonance of accented vowels in stressed metres . . . an exceedingly musical form of verse, very agreeable to the ear, but not possible to render into English . . . (so that) a part at least of the poet's ability can never be conveyed to anyone unable to read the original.

John Lorne Campbell rejected the option of trying to retain the rhyme of John Roy's original Gaelic on the grounds that the use of English rhyme would demand frequent padding or clumsy expressions. He therefore opted for a blank verse translation as the least bad of the available options, preserving the rhythm of the original but not its literal meaning.

My translation of 'The Day of Culloden' draws both on the literal word-for-word translation of Elizabeth Mackechnie and the blank verse translation of John Lorne Campbell. It also benefited from discussions with John MacFarlane, a native Gaelic speaker who served as president of the 1745 Association when I was chairman. I have sought to replicate the rhyming structure of John Roy's Gaelic original and retain its rhythmic beat as far as possible. This means foregoing a literal word-for-word translation of the original, while seeking to convey the essential meaning of each of the verses. As in John Roy's original, the poem concludes with a reference to the hoot of the barn owl, echoing the poet's sense of sadness and foreboding. This reference may be obscure to a modern urban audience. To John Roy's ear, the hoot of a barn owl, cutting through the silence of a dark night, would have sounded very ominous, for in the eighteenth century the barn owl's cry was widely believed to be a harbinger of death.

The translation was uploaded onto the 1745 Association website, along with a rendition of some lines from the poem in Gaelic and English by John MacFarlane, in April 2020. This marked the anniversary of the battle in a year when the annual commemoration at the battlefield site itself was cancelled to help stop the spread of the Covid-19 coronavirus. The poem, composed as it was by an officer wounded at the battle who saw many of his men fall around him and the cause to which he dedicated his life destroyed within a single hour, served as a reminder that, no matter how dark the outlook might sometimes seem, life goes on and better times will come.

Latha Chuilodair

Gura mór mo chùis mhuliad,
'S mì ri caoineadh na guin atà 'm thìr;
A Rìgh! Bi làidir, 's tù 's urrainn
Ar nàimhdean a chumail fo chìs;
Oirnne is làidir Diùc Uilleam,
An rag-mheirlaeach, tha guin aige dhuinn;
B'è sud salcahr nan sgeallag
Tighinn an uachdar air chruithneachd an fhuinn.

Mo chreach, Teàlach Ruadh bòidheach
Bhith fo bhinn aig Rìgh Deòrsa nam biasd,
B'è sud dìteadh na còrach,
An Fhìrinn 's a beòil foipe sìos;
Ach, a Rìgh, ma's è 's deòin leat,
Cuir an rìghachd air seòl a chaidh dhinn,
Cuir Rìgh dligheach na còrach
Ri linn na tha beò os ar cinn.

Mo chreach, armailt nam breacan
Bhith air sgaoikeadh 's air sgapadh's gach àit',
Aig fìor-bhalgairean Shasuinn
Nach do ghnàthaich bonn ceartais 'nan dàil;
Ged a bhuannaich iad baiteal,
Cha b'ann d'an cruadal no 'n tapadh a bhà,
A ch gaoth aniar agus frasan
Thighinn a nìos oirnn bhàrr machair nan Gall.

Is truagh nach robh sinn ans Sasunn
Gun bhith cho teann air ar dachaidh's a bhà,
'S cha do sgaoil sinn cho aithghearr,
Bhiodh ar dìchioll ri sesamh na b'fhearr;
Ach 's droch-dhraoidheachd us dreachdan
Rinneadh dhuinne nu'n deachas 'nan dàil,
Air na frìthean eòlach do sgap sinn,
'S bu mhì-chomhdhail gun d'fhàirtlich iad oirnn.

The Day of Culloden

Great are the depths of my sorrow
As I mourn for the wounds of my land;
My King, stay strong so you are able
All of our foes to withstand;
Over us Duke William is a tyrant,
A vile rogue with hate for us all;
As foul as fetid black straw
That strangles wheat in its thrall.

I weep for handsome fair Charlie
At the mercy of George and his brutes,
While around us corrupted and sullied
Are justice and honour and truth;
But, Lord, should you but will it,
The kingdom will come back into our hands,
Through a leader royal and righteous
Who reigns fairly over our land.

I weep for the Army of Tartan
Now scattered and spread everywhere,
Battered by England's base villains
Beaten by methods unfair;
Though in battle they were victorious
It was through no courage or merit of theirs,
But westering winds and rains that swept on us
From the lowlands, to our despair.

It's a pity we were not in England
But close to our homes as we fought,
For we'd never have scattered so quickly,
Were it not for the homes that we sought;
Spells and witchcraft were cast upon us
As we marched into battle in gloom,
Across the bleak moor were we scattered
As ill fortune led to our doom.

Mo chreach mhòr! na cuirp ghlé-gheal
Tha 'nan laigh' air na sléibhtean ud thall,
Gun chiste, gun léintean,
Gun adhlacadh fheéin anns na tuill;
Chuid tha beò dhiubh an déidh sgaoilidh
'S iad 'gam fògair le gaothan thar tuinn,
Fhuair na Chuigs an toil féin dinn,
'S cha chan iad ach 'reubaltaich' ruinn.

Fhuair na Goill sin fo 'n casan,
Is mòr an nàire 's am masladh sud leinn,
An déidh ar dùthaich 's ar n'àite
An spùilleadh 's gun bhlaàths againn ann;
Caisteal Dhùinidh an déidh a losgaidh,
'S è 'na làriach lom, thosdach, gun mhiadh;
Gum b'è 'n caochladh goirt è
Gun do chaill sinn gach sochair a b'fhiach.

Cha do shaoil leam, le m'shùilean
Gum faicinn gach cùis mar a thà,
Mar spùtadh nam faoilleach
'N am nan luibhean a sgaoileadh air blàr;
Thug a' chuibhle car tionndaidh,
'S tha iomadh fear gu h-aimcheart an càs,
A Rìgh! Seall le do chaoimhneas,
Air na fir th'aig na nàimhdean an sàs!

Is mór eucoir 'n luchd-orduigh
An fhuil ud a dhòrtadh le foill;
Mo sheacdh mallachd air Mhoirear Deòrsa,
Fhuair e 'n là ud air ordugh dhà féin;
Bha an dà chuid air a mheòirean,
Mar an gìoghan gun tròcair le foill
Mheall e sinne le 'chomhradh,
'S gun robh ar barail ro-mhór air r'a linn.

I weep for each of the white corpses
That lie on the side of the hill,
Abandoned, unhonoured, unshrouded,
Untouched and unburied still;
And those who survived the disaster
Are shackled in ships across seas,
For the Whigs now are the masters,
To do with us just as they please.

Oppressed are we now by strangers,
Great the shame and disgrace that we feel
As our homes and our country are plundered
Crushed under a foreigner's heel;
Castle Dounie's a fire-blackened ruin,
Dishonoured its bare silent walls;
The wheel of fortune is changing
With no comfort found in her halls.

I never thought that my own eyes
Would see things as they are now,
As if the tempests of Springtime
Had laid all the wild flowers low;
Fortune's wheel has turned against us,
Many brave men are now in distress,
May God look with kindness and mercy,
And save them from foreign duress.

Our leaders that day betrayed us.
And treacherously spilt of our blood;
I curse Lord George seven times over,
For leading us into the mud;
Two choices were at his disposal,
That flatterer of merciless guile,
And he chose the road of deception,
Concealed by a treacherous smile.

Ach fhad's is be sinn r'ar latha
Bidh sinn caoi na ceathairn' chaidh dhinn,
Na fir threubhach bha sqairteil
Dheanadh teugmhail le claidheamh's le sgiath;
Mur bhiodh siantan 'nar n-aghaidh
Bha sinn sìos air ar n-adhairt gu dian,
Us bhiodh luchd-Beurla 'nan laighe
Ton air cheann, b'è sud m'aighear 's mo mhiann.

Och nan och! 's mì fo sprochd
'S mì an dràsda ri h-osnaich leam fhìn,
Ag amharc feachd an dubh-Rosaich
'G itheadh feur agus cruithneachd an fhuinn;
Rothaich iargalt us Cataich
Tighinn a nall oirinn le luchd chasag us lann,
Iad mar mhìol-choin air acras
Siubhal chrìochan, chàrn, chlach, agus bheann.

Mo chreach! tìr air an tàinig,
Rinn sibh nis clàr rèidh dhith cho lom,
Gun choirce gun ghnàiseach
Gun sìol taight' ann fàsach no 'm fonn;
Prìs na circ' air an spàrdan,
Gu ruige na spàinean thoirt uainn,
Ach sgrios na craoibhe f'a blàth dhuibh,
Air a crìonadh f'a bàrr gus a bonn.

Tha arc inn fo na choille,
'S eiginn beanntan us gleanntan thoirt oirnn,
Sinn gun sùgradh, gun mhacnus,
Gun èibhneas, gun aitneas, gun cheòl;
Air bheag bìdh no teine
Air na stùcan air an laigheadh an ceò,
Sinn mar Chomhachaig eile
Ag èisdeachd ri deireas gach lò.

As long as we live, till our days' end
We will mourn the men we have lost,
Valiant and brave-hearted heroes
Who fought fiercely with sword, shield and cross.
Had the gale not been in our faces
We'd have charged with no fear at the foe,
And scattered the English before us
And ended our poor country's woe.

I am plunged into grief and sadness
As I weep bitter tears all alone,
Watching the host of black roses
Devour the wheat of the land;
Savage Munros and wild Sutherlanders
Crawl towards us like ravenous hounds,
Scouring moors, clefts and hollows
Their gluttony knowing no bounds.

I weep for the land you've invaded,
The scorched earth you've left in your wake,
Crops stripped from our fields and hillsides,
No seeds sown so the land may awake;
You've taken the hens from the hen roosts,
Stolen our last spoonful of soup away,
May the curse of the fig tree be upon you,
From root to top may you wither away.

Now we are reduced to mere outlaws,
And must take to the hills and the glens,
Without sport, without mirth or diversion,
With no songs, joy or pleasures of sense;
With little to feed or to warm us
On the rocks where the cold mist lies,
Hearing the haunting hoot of the barn owl
As of death and disaster she cries.

17

Lament for Lord Lovat

The hoot of the barn owl that John Roy heard during the dark night of his soul did indeed prove to be a harbinger of death. But it was not John Roy's death. It was the death of his old friend and consigliere, Simon Fraser, Lord Lovat.

The redcoats finally caught up with the Old Fox in a cave where he was hiding on 18 March 1747. From there, he was taken down to London, tried by his peers in the House of Lords, found guilty and executed on Tower Hill a month later on 19 April, the last man to be publicly beheaded in Great Britain. As he was approaching London, the cartoonist William Hogarth came across him in a barbershop, and took the opportunity of sketching him, representing him as a toad-like figure, feeding Hanoverian propaganda that he was a monster undeserving of pity. In reality, far from being the monstrous figure of Hogarth's grotesque caricature, contemporary portraits of Lord Lovat reveal him as a tolerably good-looking man (Plate 28). No matter. In the fervent atmosphere of the time the demonisation of Lord Lovat had begun.

In the aftermath of the Rising the London mob needed a villain to despise and, in the absence of Prince Charles Edward Stuart himself, Lord Lovat fitted the bill very well. For the catchpenny journalists of Grub Street, his trial and execution offered easy money from penny dreadfuls like *Memoirs of the Life of Lord Lovat*, published in London and Dublin in 1746, a concoction of sensational tales and fabrications purporting to be from the lips of the Noble Lord himself. If it made a few guineas for its anonymous author and its publishers, where was the harm? After all, Lord Lovat had more immediate concerns, and he was hardly in a position to complain about any libels published about him, was he?

And so the stories circulated and grew about Lord Lovat, painting him as a duplicitous rogue whose wickedness knew no bounds. Why, even at his execution, it was said that when the news came to him that one of the stands holding spectators who had come to see his execution had collapsed, killing several of them, he had merely chortled, 'The more the mischief, the greater the sport!' What sort of man could behave like that in the face of his own imminent death?

The only problem was that there was no evidence that Lord Lovat ever made such a remark. It was a story made up about him after his death, which has been repeated so often that it has become accepted as fact.

In *Anchored Narratives: The Psychology of Criminal Evidence*, authors W.A. Wagenaar, P.J. van Koppen and H.F.M. Cromberg write, 'A good story is better than half of the proof. Once the story as told by the prosecution is recognisable as the way things usually happen, anchoring the story in hard evidence becomes of secondary importance for its acceptance.'

In other words, if you can make up a good story about someone, you can condemn them without worrying about trivial matters like hard evidence. Give a dog a bad name and you might as well hang him.

As I researched more deeply into the career of Lord Lovat, I became increasingly concerned that he was the victim of just such a syndrome. The truth about his life had been sacrificed for the sake of a good story, and no one over the three centuries that had elapsed since had had much reason to take the trouble to redress the balance.

Don't get me wrong. I'm not trying to represent Lord Lovat as some kind of plaster saint. I don't doubt that, on occasion, he could be a bully. Equally, in the fervid environment of the Scottish Highlands in the early eighteenth century, no gentle liberal seeking to govern by consensus would have survived very long. Any sign of weakness would have been ruthlessly exploited. A man had to be tough to survive.

Yet Lord Lovat was a man who had won the respect of Duncan Forbes of Culloden, the Lord President of the Council and the Hanoverian Government's leading public servant in the Highlands. He regarded Lord Lovat as a capable clan chieftain who had maintained law and order within his territory highly effectively. He had done so by winning the loyalty of his clan, who supported him as a just and able leader. He was regarded with affection by those closest to him, including his piper, David Fraser, who composed a poignant lament to mourn his passing. And he was the man who enjoyed the lifelong friendship of John Roy Stuart.

Would such a diverse range of people really have given their loyalty, affection and friendship to the duplicitous thug of legend?

As so often, reality may be more complex than the simple narrative of historians with an axe to grind. In seeking the truth about Lord Lovat, I decided that uncorroborated assertions about him could not be accepted as proof of his character or actions. Eyewitness statements also needed to be handled with some care. The memory can play tricks. Even where eyewitness accounts reconcile, it is important to back them up, if possible, with forensic evidence.

And, crucially in the case of Lord Lovat, even if evidence was corroborated by several eyewitnesses and supported by forensic evidence, so that the facts pertaining to a particular event were agreed, there may be very different interpretations of the implications of those facts.

Thus, in this case, the facts indicate that Lovat navigated carefully through the treacherous waters of eighteenth-century Scottish politics and changed his loyalties to the Crown on several occasions. The case for him is that he had to do so in order to protect the Clan Fraser and ensure the survival of his own family. The case against him is that he was a ruthless opportunist who would stop at nothing to promote his personal interests, with no thought of the possible consequences for anyone other than himself.

Both interpretations are consistent with the facts. My point is that only the case against Lord Lovat has been passed down in history. Perhaps it is time for someone to put the case for him. In the absence of anyone else likely to volunteer after 270 years, I decided to say a few words on his behalf at the place of his execution in 2017. My late friend Brian Whiting, then editor of *The Jacobite*, cautioned against this, concerned that the arrival of a few men in Highland dress, extolling the virtues of the Jacobite Lords who had been executed there, might be seen by some as provocative and lead to trouble, even though, as peace-loving people, we were going to leave our sgian dubhs at home.

'Brian,' I said, recalling a couple of lines from Shakespeare (which were so apt I included them in the eulogy itself), 'cowards die a million times before their end; the valiant never taste of death but once!'

So it was that, on a crisp autumn morning in September 2017, the 1745 Association gathered on Tower Hill to remember with respect the Jacobite Lords who had met their end there almost three centuries before. Glen MacDonald said a few words of introduction. David McNaughton spoke the words of Lord Balmerino on the scaffold. I then stood up to say a few words in support of the man of whom it was said, with some justice, that 'he lived like a fox and he died like a lion'. Here is my eulogy for Lord Lovat, delivered 270 years after his passing at his place of execution.

'Cowards die a million times before their end;
The valiant never taste of death but once.'

Today, we remember the Jacobite Lords, valiant men who each of them tasted of death but once, here on Tower Hill, during the dark days after the Battle of Culloden, when the drumbeat of war echoed across Great Britain for the last time.

On a morning such as this, on the 18th day of August 1746, William Boyd, Earl of Kilmarnock, was led from his place of imprisonment in the Tower of London to his place of execution, here on Tower Hill, followed shortly thereafter by Arthur Elphinstone, Lord Balmerino. Then, on December 8th 1746, by Charles Radclyffe, Earl of Derwentwater. And finally, on April 9th 1747, by Simon Fraser, Lord Lovat, the last man to be publicly beheaded in Great Britain.

Lord Lovat was condemned by the Jacobites as a turncoat; condemned by the Hanoverians as a traitor; condemned by the bar of history as 'the wicked Lord Lovat'. Even his most recent biographer, Sarah Fraser, subtitles her book The Last Highlander *as the story of* Scotland's Most Notorious Clan Chieftain, Rebel, and Double Agent.

Surely, no man merited his fate more than this duplicitous rogue.

No one knows exactly where or when he was born, although most authorities place his birth somewhere between 1670 and 1675. What is known is that he enjoyed the classical education of a gentleman of that time, who, upon graduation from the University of Aberdeen, gained a commission as a captain in the British Army, having at that time no great expectations of inheritance.

None of us can choose the hands we are dealt in this great adventure of life; all we can do is play the cards as they fall. And, for Simon Fraser, the cards of life began to fall in his favour. His elder brother, Alexander, fell at the Battle of Killiecrankie. The 9th Lord Lovat, Hugh Fraser, died young at the age of just thirty. Upon his death, Simon's father, Thomas Fraser of Beaufort, became the 10th Lord Lovat, with Simon as his heir.

But there was one problem. The Marquis of Atholl, head of the Murray Clan and father-in-law of the 9th Lord Lovat, claimed that Hugh Fraser had left his title and estate to an ally of the Murrays, a certain Lord Saltoun. Simon Fraser responded by kidnapping Lord Saltoun, then, according to Moray McLaren in his Life of Lord Lovat, 'humorously erected gallows on which the unfortunate nobleman was told he was to be hanged in two days' time' unless he renounced his claims.

Just how much humour the Noble Lord saw in the situation is not recorded. However, when Lord Saltoun had quite recovered from his mirth, he signed papers revoking all claims to the Lovat estate, with some considerable alacrity. This, Moray McLaren declares, was 'an old Highland victory in the old Highland style'.

The 'old Highland style' clearly being similar to the new Glasgow kiss, but not quite as subtle.

Simon Fraser then moved to consolidate his grip on the Lovat estates by proposing marriage to his cousin's widow, the Dowager Lady Lovat, Amelia née Murray.

Amelia did not share his enthusiasm for matrimony, suggesting that her father, the Marquis of Atholl, might not be entirely in favour of such a match.

What happened next remains a subject of controversy to this day.

The story goes that Simon Fraser marched up to Castle Dounie, seat of the Clan Fraser, where the Dowager Lady Lovat was in residence, with a drunken minister in tow, who duly performed a perfunctory wedding ceremony.

Later that same night, as a storm raged and the rain lashed down outside, Simon Fraser entered Amelia's bedchamber and consummated the marriage, while outside bagpipes played ever louder to drown out whatever sounds were emanating from the bridal chamber.

This lurid tale of debauchery and bodice-ripping on a dark and stormy night at Castle Dounie has grown so much with the telling that the full truth of what happened may never be known.

But seven facts are beyond dispute.

1. Despite the immense pressure placed upon her by the Murrays, Amelia resolutely refused to press any charges against Simon Fraser.

2. With Amelia refusing to testify, the Murrays charged Simon Fraser with the capital crime of 'Hamesuken', violent entry into and taking possession of the home of another.

3. With the Edinburgh judges in the pocket of the all-powerful Murrays, Simon Fraser was found guilty, and sentenced to be hung, drawn and quartered.

4. When Simon Fraser, for some unfathomable reason, proved somewhat reluctant to give himself up so that sentence might duly be carried out, the Murrays raised a Commission of Fire and Sword, sending 800 men into the Fraser lands to track him down.

5. The Frasers, believing it was the Murrays, and not their own clan chieftain, who were guilty of Hamesuken through their outrageous land grab, rallied behind Simon Fraser.

6. The invading Commission of Murrays was surrounded by a force of Frasers at Stratherrick. The Murrays, believing that they were heavily outnumbered and with no means escape, duly surrendered.

7. Perhaps the most remarkable fact of all, this occurred six years after the Massacre of Glencoe. Yet while to this day there remains some bitterness between Campbells and MacDonalds, the clan feud between the Atholl Murrays and the Frasers has been long forgotten. Why? Perhaps because no blood was shed.

Instead, with the Murrays at his mercy, Simon Fraser obliged each man among them to kneel before him, kiss the naked tip of his sword and swear an oath that he had composed especially for the occasion, by which, and I quote:

They renounced their claims in Jesus Christ
And their hopes of heaven.
And damned themselves to the torments of Hell for all Eternity
If ever they returned into the territories of Lord Lovat.

It may surprise you to learn that they did not return into the territories of Lord Lovat – not while Simon Fraser was around at any rate! But with the redcoats hunting him down like a fox, the Murrays sworn to vengeance, and his father now dead, the Highlands had become too hot for Simon Fraser to handle.

And so, as the eighteenth century dawns, Simon Fraser arrives at the Stuart Court in exile in St Germain-en-Laye, seeking to curry favour with the councillors of the fourteen-year-old James Francis Edward Stuart, in the hope that, were James to win back the British throne, he would be pardoned.

Sadly, he fell out with James's advisers and after a period of imprisonment was ordained as a Catholic priest in Saumur in France.

And there the story might have ended, with the exiled Lord Lovat living out a life of quiet spiritual contemplation, had not, one day, his cousin, Major Fraser of Castleleathers, arrived in the town with a desperate plea for Lord Lovat to return to the Scotland and save the Frasers from the oppressive yoke of the Atholl Murrays and their allies.

So, in 1715, Simon Fraser returns to Scotland, capturing the town of Inverness at the head of a division of loyal Fraser Clansmen – not for King James, but for King George – and for his services during the Fifteen, King George granted him a general pardon and restored the Lovat estates to him. And for the next quarter century Lord Lovat ruled over the Fraser lands like a feudal lord, with his tacksmen swearing allegiance to him at clan feasts held in the Great Hall of Castle Dounie, master of the Clan Fraser. Until one day in the high summer of 1745, Prince Charles Edward Stuart landed on the shores of Scotland to reclaim its crown and Lord Lovat took the fateful decision to throw in his lot with him.

After the Prince's defeat at Culloden, Lord Lovat was captured, tried by his peers in the House of Lords [Plate 29], left to defend himself unaided without any legal assistance against the finest advocates in England, betrayed by the Prince's secretary, Murray of Broughton, who turned King's evidence to save his own skin, and was duly found guilty.

When asked whether he had anything to say after the verdict, he replied:

Nothing but to thank your Lordships for your goodness to me.
God bless you all, and I bid you an everlasting farewell.
We shall not meet all in the same place again, of that I am sure.

Well, if ever any man devised a more elegant way of subtly suggesting that his unjust persecutors could all go to hell, then I for one am not aware of it.

In his final days in the Tower, Lord Lovat said that his paramount priority had always been the preservation and protection of his family. That, second only to this, he had always striven for the restoration of the Stuart Dynasty, claiming he 'had never betrayed another man in his life; nor ever shed a drop of blood by his own hand; nor ever struck a man, save one young nobleman for his impertinence and impiety'.

So, to the end, Lord Lovat remained faithful to the motto he had adopted after his victory over the Atholl Murrays at Stratherrick:

Sine Sanguine Victor
Victor without bloodshed.

Unlike Lord Balmerino, he made no final speech on Tower Hill, having been warned in no uncertain terms that it would be much the worse for his family if he did. As he mounted the scaffold, he did, however, quote the words of the Roman poet Horace:

Dulce et decorum est, pro Patria mori.
It is a sweet and proper thing to die for one's country.

Yet no one can ever be sure whether, as he put his head on the executioner's block, Lord Lovat really did see himself as a great Scottish patriot laying down his life for his land, or whether his last words were just a final sardonic comment uttered by an old cynic playing his audience right up to the very end.

But he did make one startling admission during his final hours in the Tower, which throws some light on his character and motivation, when he said that all he had ever really wanted was to have been the greatest Lord Lovat that ever there was. A pathetic ambition which he evidently felt he had failed to achieve and which has been widely mocked and derided ever since.

Perhaps, happily, it is not given to any of us on this side of Paradise to pass final judgement on any man. Yet, standing here today at his place of execution, what I would say is this:

> *for his audacity in saving the Fraser lands from annexation;*
> *for his courage and indeed his cunning in securing the Lovat estates;*
> *for his ability, through sheer force of personality, to bring peace, stability and a measure of prosperity to the turbulent and troubled Highlands of Scotland for quarter of a century between 1720 and 1745;*
> *for his decision, in 1745, to take the considerable risk of raising his clan for the cause of Prince Charlie in his endeavour to reclaim the thrones of Scotland, England and Ireland for the Royal House of Stuart;*
> *and for the composure, the courage and the dignity with which he met his fate here on Tower Hill when that risk didn't pay off*

For all these things, perhaps, after all, Simon Fraser really was the greatest Lord Lovat that ever there was.

* * *

As I was coming to the end of my eulogy, church bells began to ring nearby. Perhaps it was not entirely surprising that, on a Sunday morning at 10.30 a.m., the bell ringers would be calling the faithful to prayer. But I did find it a little discombobulating.

After I concluded my eulogy, Roddy Livingstone stepped forward to play 'Lord Lovat's Lament'. It was a most poignant rendition of the pibroch composed by his own piper to mourn his passing, played at the slow pace of Lord Lovat's final march of 300 paces from the Tower of London to Tower Hill. As the pibroch was playing, I noticed a white butterfly fluttering briefly before me, before rising into the sky and disappearing from sight.

What was a white butterfly doing on Tower Hill on such a Sunday morning?

If one were superstitious, one might almost believe that it was the soul of Lord Lovat, finally released after 270 years.

But, of course, that wouldn't apply to me.

I'm not superstitious at all.

18

The Last Hopeful Epistle of Bonnie Prince Charlie

After Prince Charlie landed in Roscoff at the end of September 1746, he travelled to Paris, where he was reunited with his younger brother, Prince Henry. This was, by Prince Henry's account to his father, a most joyous occasion. The Rising might have failed, but Prince Henry's paramount concern was the safe return of his beloved older brother.

Prince Charles's physical condition after more than five months on the run and a difficult sea crossing to France was poor. He was covered with sores, midge bites and lice when he arrived. But, with the help of baths, clean clothes and no doubt excellent French food and wine, he rapidly recovered both in body and spirit. Before long, his thoughts turned to a continuation of the campaign to restore his father to the throne.

The myth propagated by his Hanoverian enemies was that Prince Charlie abandoned Scotland after Culloden. The memorandum written by the Prince to the King of France on 5 November 1746 provides evidence, in the Prince's own hand, that directly contradicts this myth. In the memorandum, the Prince sets out his own account of the Rising, which he says very nearly succeeded. He states:

> I never lacked Scottish subjects ready to fight. What I did simultaneously lack was money, supplies and a handful of regular troops; with but one of these three, I would today still be master of Scotland and probably the whole of England.

He concludes that 'these setbacks can still be redressed' if the King could see his way to confer on him a corps of 20,000 regular troops.

The Prince's letter and memorandum were passed by King Louis XV to his Minister of War, the Marquis d'Argenson, who was one of the strongest supporters of the Rising within the French Government. Although several of the King's other counsellors were less enthusiastic, the position of the Marquis was vindicated when the withdrawal of British forces from the Continent to quell the Rising in Britain enabled French forces to capture Brussels in February 1746, secure control of the Low Countries, and eventually force Britain to sue for peace under the terms of the Treaty of Aix-la-Chapelle in 1748.

The Prince's memorandum remained in the d'Argenson family archives for nearly 250 years until it was loaned to the University of Poitiers in 1990. In 2002, the d'Argenson family put this and other letters from the Prince up for sale by auction in London, and it was then that they came into my possession after a successful bid. They remained in my own archives until 2014, when I sold them by auction at Lyon & Turnbull in Edinburgh.

Granted, his memorandum reveals a certain characteristic over-optimism on the part of the Bonnie Prince. However, it is also testimony in his own hand that proves beyond doubt that he believed a Stuart Restoration was still eminently feasible. He saw himself like his great uncle Charles II, who lost a battle but later returned in triumph to restore the Stuart dynasty. It confirms that the Prince's decision to advise his supporters to disperse after Culloden was not a betrayal but rather a wholly rational decision intended to minimise loss of life pending his efforts to mobilise further support from France.

Yet the memorandum is also very poignant, as we know how the story was to turn out, as the Prince did not when he sat down to write it in November 1746.

The Prince's submission comprised three sections. The first is a covering note to d'Argenson requesting him to forward the letter and memorandum to the King. The second, reproduced at the beginning of this book, is a covering letter from the Prince to the King, presenting his memorandum and requesting a meeting to discuss next steps. The third and most important is the memorandum itself, reproduced here with my translation.

La Situation dans la quelle J'ay Laissé l'Ecosse
a mon depart merite toutte la tention de Votre
Majesté ce Roiaume esta la Veille de se voir
aneantir et le gouvernement d'Angleterre est re=
solu de Confondre les Sujets qui etoient restez fi=
deles avec ceux qui ont pris les Armes pour moi,
d'ou il est aisé de conclure que le meconten=
tentement de cette Nation est general
et que j'y trouverois aujourd'huy trois par=
tisant pour un que j'ay trouve en debar=
quant.

Ce cera tromper Votre Majesté que de la
flatter que je pourrois encor Soulever
l'Ecosse, si le Parlement a le tems cet
Jyver d'y metre les Loix penales en
Execution et Votre Majesté d'oit renon=
cer pour Jamais au secours d'une revolution
dans pays la, Et moi, je n'aurai de ressource
que dans les Cours des Sujets du Roi mon
Pere, quant il plaira a la providence de le
rappeller.

Le Nombre des Sujets aguerris ne m'a jamais
manqué en Ecosse, J'ay manqué tout a la fois,
d'Argent, de Vivres, et d'une poignée de
Troupes regulieres, avec un Seul de ces
trois secours, Je serois encor aujourd'uy
maitre de l'Ecosse, et Vraisemblablement
de toute l'Angleterre.
Avec trois mil Hommes de Troupes Reglées
Je penetrois en Angleterre immediatement
apres avoir defait le Sieur Cope, et rien ne
s'opposoit alors a mon Arrivée à Londres,
puisque l'Electeur etoit absent et que
les Troupes Angloises n'avoient pas encor
repassés.
Avec de vivres J'eus été en etat de poursui=
vre le Sieur Hawley a la Bataille de
Falkirque, et de detruire tout Son Armée
qui etoit la Fleur des Troupes Angloises.

Memorandum

The situation in which I left Scotland deserves your Majesty's full attention. This kingdom is on the eve of annihilation, as the English government refuses to distinguish between those who remained loyal to it and those who took up arms for me, from which it is easy to conclude that discontent is general throughout the nation and I would find three partisans today for every one I found on leaving.

But His Majesty would be mistaken to believe that I could raise Scotland again if Parliament has the time to put penal laws into execution this winter, without Your Majesty's assistance for a revolution in this country. For I will only have the resources of the King my father's subjects when it will please Providence to recall him.

I have never lacked Scottish subjects ready to fight. What I did simultaneously lack was money, supplies and a handful of regular troops; with but one of these three, I would today still be master of Scotland and probably the whole of England.

With three thousand regular troops, I could have penetrated England immediately after defeating General Cope, and nothing would then have opposed my arrival in London, since the Elector would have been absent and the English troops would have resisted no further.

With adequate supplies, I would have been in a position to pursue General Hawley at the Battle of Falkirk and to destroy his entire army, which was the flower of the English troops.

Si J'eus recu deux mois plutot la Moitié
seulement de l'argent que Votre Majesté
m'envoye, J'eus Combattu Le Prince
Guillaume, d'Hannover avec un nombre
égal et je l'eus surement battu puisq' u'
avec quattre mil hommes contre douze
J'ai longtems fait pancher la Victoire,
et que douze cens hommes de troupes
Reglez l'eurent decide en ma faveur
au vû et teu de toute mon armée.
Ces Contre tems peuvent encore se re=
parer, Si Votre Majesté veut me Confier
un Corps de dix huit ou Vingt mil hommes
C'est Dans son sein seul que je reposeray
l'usage que j'en veu faire; Je l'employeray
utilement pour ses interets et pour les
miens; Ces interets sont inceperables,
et doivent etre regardez Comme tels
par tous ceux qui ont l'Honneur d'ap=
procher de Votre Majesté et qui ont
Sa gloire, et l'avantage de Son Royaume
a Coeur.

If I had received two months earlier just half of the money that Your Majesty sent me, I would have fought Prince William of Hanover on equal terms, and would surely have beaten him, since with four thousand men against his twelve thousand I pressed for victory for a long time, and just 1,200 regular troops would surely have decided the conflict in my favour and that of my entire army.

These setbacks can still be redressed. If Your Majesty wishes to confer a corps of twenty thousand men upon me, they will be deployed purely in his interests. I will employ them for his interests and for mine; these interests are inseparable and must be regarded as such by all those who have the honour of approaching Your Majesty, and who have the glory and benefit of his Kingdom at heart.

*   *   *

The King did not respond positively to the Prince's request for further support.

Worse was to follow, from the Prince's viewpoint, when his younger brother, Prince Henry, was ordained as a Cardinal Deacon of the Roman Catholic Church on 30 June 1747, with the full support of his father. Prince Charles described the ordination as 'a dagger through my heart', which, he believed, seriously compromised any hope of a Stuart Restoration, as it bound the Stuart dynasty irrevocably to the Catholic Church in a way that would be unacceptable to the ruling class in England. The Prince was never to see or speak to his father again, and only made contact with Prince Henry, now Cardinal York, after his father's death in 1766.

Prince Charles was expelled from France in December 1748 as part of the peace deal between King George and King Louis, which concluded two months earlier. As far as the French Government were concerned, Prince Charles and his Highland supporters had served their purpose as pawns in their wider political game. The Prince had now become an embarrassment to them and was of no further value.

While the French may have given up on Prince Charles, the Prince had certainly not given up on his plans to regain the thrones of Great Britain and Ireland. Recognising the futility of seeking to overthrow the Hanoverian regime by military means without French support, the Prince opted for a more direct alternative – a coup in London. If King George could be deposed and replaced by himself, surely (he optimistically believed) enough influential supporters would rally to his cause to effect a bloodless revolution. After all, as he had written to King Louis in his memorandum, he had never lacked supporters and, since discontent was general throughout the nation, he 'would find three partisans today for every one I found on leaving'. It was just a great pity (in Prince Charlie's view) that his commanders under the malign influence of Lord George Murray had opted to retreat from Derby in December 1745, when one final push would have sent the Hanoverian regime toppling. But all was not lost. Perhaps his appearance in London would be all that was needed to spark a revolution.

In her meticulous research on 'The last great Jacobite councils in England (1750 and 1752)', published in the *Royal Stuart Society Journal* in 2009, Victoria Thorpe provides compelling evidence that the Prince made a brief secret expedition to London in 1750 and she presents further evidence that he returned at the end of 1752. Of the first occasion, she writes:

> On the evening of September 16th 1750, the Prince reached London and appeared without warning in the drawing room of a house in Essex Street near the Strand, home of one of his most influential English friends, Lady Primrose.

The Prince remained in London for six days, during which time he held meetings with his supporters and abjured the Catholic faith in a belated attempt to redress the damage caused by his brother's ordination and reassure the English ruling class that a Stuart Restoration would threaten neither Parliamentary Democracy nor the Established Church.

In 1752, the Prince was party to a serious attempt by one of his supporters, Alexander Murray of Elibank, to kidnap the King.

The enduring image of Alexander Murray of Elibank (Plate 30) is the portrait of him by Allan Ramsay that hangs today in the Scottish National Portrait Gallery. The twinkle in Elibank's eye suggests a blend of cunning and naivety – the very features that characterised the plot forever associated with his name.

Elibank's cunning plan was to enter St James's Palace, kidnap King George and his family, and declare Charles as Prince Regent. Meanwhile, an army under James Keith, younger brother of the Earl Marischal, would arrive from Sweden and join up with the Jacobite clans in the Highlands.

186

Dr Archie Cameron, younger brother of Lochiel, was dispatched to Scotland, ostensibly to track down and recover the Loch Arkaig gold but in reality to coordinate efforts there.

Things started to go wrong on the night of 10 November 1752, the date chosen by Elibank for the kidnap of King George, when the 2,500 men whom Elibank had recruited for the operation failed to turn up. Fearing betrayal, capture and the same fate as Guy Fawkes a century and a half earlier, Elibank panicked, aborted the plan and told his friends that he was going to France to consult further with the Prince.

Once in France, Elibank informed the Prince that he suspected that information about his plot had been leaked to the Hanoverian Government by the Prince's mistress, Clementina Walkinshaw, and urged the Prince to get rid of her.

Intelligence about the plot had indeed been passed to the Government, as Elibank suspected, but not by Clementina Walkinshaw. The double agent in the Jacobite camp was identified by Andrew Lang in his 1897 book *Pickle the Spy* as Alasdair MacDonnell of Glengarry, older brother of the Young Glengarry accidentally killed the day after the Battle of Falkirk Muir.

What happened next remained shrouded in mystery until new evidence came to light in 2009 in the form of the Prichard Letters. These were a series of five letters written between April and August 1822 by Mrs Anne Prichard née Preston (1732–1829) to her grandson Richard. In 1905, Richard's son, Charles Edward Prichard, 'selected from them such letters as, besides having a family interest, may be of interest to others'. In 2009, Charles's great nephew, David Prichard, forwarded them to the then editor of *The Jacobite*, Peter Lole, who published extracts from them in the journal's Winter 2009 (No. 131) and Spring 2010 (No. 132) editions.

The first letter, dated 1 April 1822, opens as follows:

My dear Richard,

You have often asked me to tell you what I know about our Young Prince Charlie and, as your birthday is just approaching and our good friend and Member of Parliament, Mr Hornby, is coming to London, I avail myself of his kind offer to take charge of this letter to you, so that it may reach you on or about your birthday. I have always taken pleasure in the interest you have shown respecting the

Prince, whom as a girl, I almost worshipped . . . I propose in this letter to relate what I personally know of the Prince.

Mrs Prichard then relates how she first saw him as he marched into Preston on 27 November 1745:

As he passed your Great Grandfather's house, he looked up and smiled such a light happy smile as if he was going to his wedding or his coronation. I was nearly wild with delight at seeing him, and leaning out of the window I showed my hands full of white cockades. He smiled again and said something to a young officer near him. This young man approached, and, holding out his hands, took my cockades and returned to the ranks. Prince Charles smiled again and I had the delight of seeing him fix one on his arm and the others were quickly distributed.

She was to see him again ten days later during the retreat from Derby, 'but alas how changed'. Gone was the carefree smiling Prince she had seen during the advance. 'I only caught a glimpse of him as he passed sitting moodily back in the carriage,' she writes.

And that was the last that she saw of him until December 1752.

Mrs Prichard recounted how she was introduced by a cousin to Lady Anne Primrose, 'well known as the protector of the heroic Flora MacDonald and ardent follower of the Stuarts', and was attached to her as a young lady companion 'and spent many happy days at her home in Essex Street off the Strand in London'.

Then, one evening after Christmas 1752, they were playing cards together when a mysterious stranger arrived. Mrs Prichard writes, 'I knew him for the Prince, but I do not think that anyone else did, for one thing he was a good deal changed.'

After the other members of the party had left, Mrs Prichard reports that Lady Anne remonstrated with the Prince for his recklessness in coming to London. Nevertheless, she agreed to give him protection, and for two or three days he remained in Lady Anne's house. But on the third day, Mrs Prichard says, 'the Prince began to show signs of restlessness and I felt that Lady Anne was very anxious'.

The Prince then disappeared, and 'the next morning early, Lady Anne came to me in great alarm, the trusted manservant had been to his room and found that the Prince was not there'.

He did not return until about ten o'clock in the morning, when 'we saw him coming hastily up the street from the direction of the river'.

The story that he had to tell was so remarkable that Mrs Prichard's account is reproduced in full below:

His dress was dishevelled and his eyes wild with pain.

He addressed no word of explanation to us but hurried to the sitting room and, throwing himself on a chair, covered his face with his hands and sobbed aloud. Too shocked for words, we could do nothing but watch him. Presently he looked up. 'Give me some brandy quick,' he said, and he gulped down a quantity undiluted. He then seemed more himself. 'Forgive me, my dear friends, for the pain I know I must have caused you,' he said, giving his hand to Lady Anne. 'I will not offend again.'

'What has happened?' she said.

He shuddered and seemed unwilling to speak, but at last he said that he would tell us.

It appeared that, being unable to sleep and feeling restless, he had risen early and gone out roaming the streets north of the Strand. Returning at what he fancied would be breakfast time, he emerged from a side street just north of Temple Bar. He had been stopped by a man with a telescope. 'Have a look,' said the man, 'only a penny.' Not desiring to stop, he passed him with a shake of the head, but the fellow was not to be put off. 'Come on, Sir, only a penny, well worth having a look.'

'What is there to see?' said the Prince.

'You'll see, Sir, on the bar there,' said the man, handing him the telescope. 'The rebels' heads, Sir, that one on the left is Colonel Towneley. He was a great rebel, and the worse for being English.'

With a cry, the Prince dropped the telescope on the ground. 'Curse your carelessness,' said the fellow, but, seeing the look on the Prince's face, he said with an oath, 'Why, I believe you are a cursed Jacobite,' and, calling to several other men who plied a similar hideous trade to his own, a crowd quickly collected.

To argue was ruin, and the Prince quickly took to his heels, but fortunately did not lose his presence of mind. Several men followed him as he went quickly down Fleet Street away from our house. Seeing that he would be overtaken as the men were beginning to gain on him shouting 'Rebel, Traitor, Jacobite', he turned and, flinging a handful of mixed gold and silver amongst them, turned quickly up an alley leading to the river. As he hoped, they stopped with loud laughter and scrambled for the coins. The Prince did not slacken his pace, but dived down one court after another until, tired out, he had at last ventured to find his way to Essex Street from the river side.

As he told us, his voice shook, and when he had finished he again buried his face in his hands. 'Oh God,' he said, 'that that wretched black thing should be all that is left of poor Towneley. And I would gladly have died to save him. Towneley should never have been left at Carlisle and would not have been could I have but had my way. It was a useless sacrifice.'

And then he told us, what has never been stated, but which I for one do not doubt, that after Culloden when a price of £30,000 was on his head and he hunted through Scotland, he had written to the Duke of Cumberland, stating that, if he would give King George's word that all slaughter would cease and that his friends should be set free, he would surrender himself. The Duke never answered the letter, being so beset on bloodshed and revenge and making sure of capturing Charles as well. 'I would have saved them if I could,' he said. It was all very painful.

He did not go out again. We made private enquiries to find out whether the incident had been reported, but could not find that it had. Lady Anne however was so alarmed that she urged her friends to induce him to leave us as soon as possible and the next day or the day after he left us.

I shed bitter tears when he had gone. He had been so kind to me, as indeed he had been to everyone with whom he came into contact.

A note on the fate of the Manchester Regiment, the only Jacobite Regiment raised in England: Whig historians blame the Prince for the decision that it should remain in Carlisle, while the main body of his army retreated back to Scotland. Contemporary accounts suggest that this version of events is not correct. In his essay on the Manchester Regiment, published in *A Jacobite Anthology* (1995), Edgar Wyard writes:

Being Englishmen, the Manchester Regiment were made the special objects of a bloody revenge. Nearly all of the officers and sergeants were hanged, and the men transported. Colonel Francis Towneley was executed on Kennington Common on July 30th 1746. Captain John Daniel, in his 'Progress with Prince Charles Edward', states that it was never the intention of the Prince to leave the Manchester garrison to face Cumberland at Carlisle, and that Colonel Francis Towneley not only petitioned the Prince in his own name but in the name of all the officers that they should remain in the city.

This account of the events leading to the decision to leave the Manchester Regiment at Carlisle is consistent with the Prince's own testimony, as quoted in Mrs Prichard's letter. The decision was taken against the Prince's better judgement, and one that he later regretted.

Anne Prichard was to see the Prince once more, in Florence, during a visit there in the 1770s. She writes:

I only saw him for a minute, and I do not like to dwell on it . . . Directly that he heard some English loyalists wished to pay their respects to him he rose from his chair (he was sitting at a table drinking). 'Don't let them see me thus' he said twice over, and then, seeing we were in the room, he hurled the cup across the room and dashed out of a side door.

Did the events recounted by Mrs Prichard in her 1822 letters actually take place? Using the same set of conditions to test the truth of the story as I did for Lord Lovat, I assert that no unsubstantiated assertion by a single individual can constitute proof that an event has occurred. However, if the events recounted by Mrs Prichard did not take place, one can only admire her extraordinarily vivid imagination. And why would she have written her account of his visit in private correspondence to a family member, sixty years after the event, if it weren't true? Normally, an individual fabricates an account in order to avoid loss or secure gain. Mrs Prichard had nothing to gain from her account, and indeed other sections of her letters to her grandson show her in a poor light. For example, Mrs Prichard confesses in one of her letters that she went against her own father's wishes and caused considerable distress to her family by encouraging her own brother to join Prince Charlie's Army.

There is supporting evidence that suggests Mrs Prichard's account was not a figment of her imagination. Mrs Prichard's statement that the

Prince travelled to London in secret in December 1752 gains some support from Victoria Thorpe. She states in 'The Last Great Jacobite Councils in England (1750 and 1752)' that 'Frustration at the sudden unexpected postponement of the Elibank Plot may have drawn the Prince back to England at the end of 1752 in order to try and reassess the situation.'

Peter Lole, who published the letter, was a leading authority on the Rising and its aftermath, and his opinion, as expressed in *The Jacobite* (No. 131), was that the letter:

> although penned so much later [than the events it recounts] has a ring of truth about it, and, whilst the fact that it was written so long after the event by an 89-year-old makes one uncertain if all the detail is correct, the general tenor and broad facts are both fascinating and extremely important.

That there is no other eyewitness account of the Prince's 1752 visit is understandable. The other main witness to the events recalled by Mrs Prichard was Lady Anne Primrose. It would have been extremely unwise for Lady Anne to have committed any account of the Prince's visit to her home to paper. Had such an account ever fallen into Government hands, it would have constituted compelling evidence of Lady Anne's guilt on a charge of high treason. This would have carried very severe consequences, as evidenced by the fate of Dr Archie Cameron.

Dr Archie Cameron was the main victim of the Elibank Plot. Sent to Scotland by the Prince to coordinate activities there, he was captured on 20 March 1753 on the basis of the intelligence supplied to the Hanoverians by Pickle the Spy. Condemned without trial for his part in the Rising under the 1746 Act of Attainder and executed on 7 June 1753, Cameron became, in the words of a monograph by Sonia Cameron Jacks, 'The Last Jacobite Martyr'.

In an article marking the bicentenary of his execution in 1953, the then secretary of the 1745 Association, Marion Cameron, wrote that Dr Archie was 'a man of steadfast principles and kindly character. His was a zeal untainted by rancour, and at Prestonpans he tended the wounded on both sides.'

Despite his status as a non-combatant medical officer, his method of execution was, even by the often brutal standards of the Hanoverian Government, egregiously cruel. He was drawn through a crowd of spectators on a sledge to Tyburn, hanged for twenty minutes in an agonisingly slow death, and then cut down and beheaded.

Commenting on his execution, Sonia Cameron Jacks wrote:

> The government of George II preferred to carry out the execution of one of the Prince's most valuable agents on the seven-year-old charge of High Treason rather than risk revealing the intelligence sources supplying them with information regarding Charles Edward's most secret plans. So long after Culloden, even the hardened populace of mid-18th century England felt this act smacked more of vengeance than justice, and, in order to avoid trouble, the Jacobite doctor's funeral was carried out secretly, and he was laid to rest in the Chancel Vault of the Savoy Chapel by the Strand on the ninth of June at midnight.

Conventional histories, if they mention the Elibank Plot at all, tend to dismiss it as a rather insignificant coda to the Jacobite Wars which never had a serious chance of success. The treatment of Dr Archie would suggest that the Hanoverian Government of the day was not quite as sanguine. Perhaps they feared that the Prince was right in thinking that King George's hold on power was not as strong as his supporters represented, and the loyalty of his people was more tenuous than Whig historians cared to admit. Viewed in this light, the treatment meted out to Dr Archie Cameron, while still indefensible, at least becomes slightly easier to comprehend. It begins to explain why the Hanoverian Government was so keen to send an unambiguous message of the likely consequences for anyone tempted to try and dislodge it.

Whatever the truth of the matter, after the failure of the Elibank Plot and the execution of Dr Archie Cameron, Prince Charles never launched another attempt to regain the thrones of Great Britain and Ireland. His extreme distress at the terrible fate of Dr Archie is well documented. Mrs Prichard's testimony is that he had been very badly shaken by coming face-to-face with the severed head of Colonel Francis Towneley in the Strand just after Christmas 1752. Both events brought home to him the terrible consequences that any further attempt to secure the Crown might have for those who dedicated their support to him.

Abandoned by the French King, deserted by his own father and brother, and discouraged by those closest to him, the Prince finally gave up. It was the beginning of his decline into alcoholism and progressive psychological disintegration.

Today, his supporters and sympathisers, of whom there are many in the 1745 Association, prefer to remember the Prince not as the broken alcoholic of later years but as he was portrayed by Allan Ramsay at the very height of his hopes at Holyrood Palace in October 1745. A man to be admired for the audacity of his vision, the clarity of the strategy he devised to achieve it, and the courage he manifested in forging the Highland clans, Lowland volunteers and regulars of the Ecossais Royale and the Irish Piquets into a victorious army that very nearly succeeded in conquering Great Britain.

A Final Toast

That the 1745 Association has survived for three-quarters of a century is in large part down to the efforts of three redoubtable women: Marion Cameron, the Association's first secretary, who served from 1946 to 1975; Betty Stuart Hart, who served as secretary between 1975 and 1982; and her successor, Christian Aikman, secretary between 1982 and 2010. In addition to discharging their duties as Association secretary, Betty and Christian collaborated with Alistair Livingstone of Bachuil, the Association's chairman between 1981 and 1991, in compiling *No Quarter Given: The Muster Roll of Prince Charles Edward Stuart's Army, 1745–46*. This major work of scholarship endeavoured to list the names of each of the men who served in the Jacobite Army of 1745 by their regiment and their fate, whether imprisonment, death on the field of battle or execution, so that they might never be forgotten.

Reviewing the book in *Scottish History*, Professor Martin Margulies noted:

> [It] explodes several common misconceptions about the Jacobite forces. Though they wore Highland dress, they were not a Highland army. Fewer than half were actually Highlanders; the rest were Lowlanders, or French regulars of Irish or Scottish origin, or the hapless Manchesters. Nor were they a clan army; rather, they were organised into regiments by skilled professional officers. Nor were they necessarily down-and-outers: on the contrary, the *Muster Roll* records some substantial occupations such as merchant, innkeeper and writer even among the rank-and-file, and most seem to have had employment of one sort or another . . .

Of their ultimate destinies, the book tells us a great deal, and a

poignant tale it is. The Manchesters led by Colonel Francis Towneley were hardest hit. Taken at Carlisle, they paid the price for being
English and mostly Catholic. Of the 166 officers and men of the
Manchester Regiment whose names appear in *Muster Roll*, 27 were
executed, including 18 officers and sergeants, 39 were banished
or transported, and numerous others are believed to have died in
captivity . . .

Above all, the *Muster Roll* stands to this day as a memorial to the remarkable achievement of Prince Charles Edward Stuart in recruiting, financing
and organising a volunteer army built on nothing more than his personal
charisma and vision, which very nearly succeeded in pulling off the most
sensational victory in British history.

When I first joined the Council of the 1745 Association as its treasurer,
Christian was in the final years of her long term of office. Towards the
end of her term, her hearing was not as good as it had been, and she got
into the habit of bringing an antiquated cassette recorder into Council
meetings, so that she could replay tapes of the discussions afterwards in
order to ensure that her record of proceedings was as accurate as possible.
She finally stepped down in 2010.

A few years later, in 2016, I took up the chairmanship, and in her last
letter Christian wished me well. She passed away on 17 July 2016. A few
days later I attended her modest funeral at Ardgour Parish Church, watching her small coffin decked with white roses being lowered into the earth
overlooking Loch Linnhe as a steady drizzle fell like teardrops from the
sky.

During my term as chairman, I sought to build upon her legacy and
the legacy of all the other women and men who had dedicated their time
on an entirely voluntary basis over many years to improve our understanding of the Jacobite era. This seems, if anything, even more important
today than it was in 1946, in an increasingly intolerant age where many
people seem to be not just unwilling to make the effort to understand
the views of others, but not even prepared to listen to them.

The conventional representation of history is a narrative told by historians sitting as godlike figures above the events of which they write, delivering their conclusions as if they represent some objective truth. Reality
is more complex. There is not a single truth. The Hanoverian loyalists
who saw the Prince and his cause as an existential threat to the stability
and unity of King George's realm were speaking the truth, just as much

as the most ardent Jacobite supporters who believed that victory for the Prince could usher in greater hope, prosperity and opportunity for them. Both opinions were equally true from the perspective of those espousing them. But only one has been handed down as conventional wisdom.

We can never know what sort of country we might be living in today, had the Jacobites followed the earnest entreaty of their Prince to continue the advance from Derby on to London, instead of retreating back to Scotland. Would his revolution have ended in success, with his father restored to the throne? Would a restored Stuart dynasty have been more tolerant of minority opinion? Would Ireland today be united and part of the United Kingdom, with its own parliament, much like Scotland? Would London and the south-east be quite so dominant, or would the traditional Jacobite heartlands of Scotland, North Wales, Lancashire and Northumberland have a larger share of population and resources within a more balanced United Kingdom? Would we have enjoyed greater cultural diversity and wider acceptance of different dialects, traditions and cultural practices during the nineteenth and twentieth centuries, as perhaps we are beginning to see in the twenty-first?

If, over the years of its existence, the 1745 Association has made some modest contribution to challenging the conventional view that the Rising of 1745 was a foolish venture, initiated by a reckless gambler, supported by knaves and condemned to inevitable defeat from the outset, then perhaps it has, at least in part, fulfilled the mission set by its founders back in 1946.

There is an historical truth to be gleaned from official documents, minutes of Government meetings, and memoirs of politicians and officials choosing their words carefully to protect their reputations. These sources no doubt seek to tell the truth. But is it the whole truth, and nothing but the truth?

Or is there a deeper truth to be gleaned from poems and from paintings, from private diaries and letters never intended for publication, written by people about events in which they personally participated, unvarnished by policy considerations?

During my quest for truth, I benefited greatly from the stories of the men and women caught up in the Rising, from visits to the houses where they lived, the inns where they drank and the battlefields on which they fought, and above all from discussions over the years with friends and colleagues who had researched the Jacobite era more extensively and deeply than I ever could.

Now many of those with whom I shared my journey have passed on. Sometimes it seemed to me, as I chaired meetings of the Association Council in the Stirling Art Gallery and Museum, that it was still populated by the ghosts of those who had attended meetings alongside me over the years, imbued with the Jacobite spirit of loyalty to legitimate authority, fidelity to family above financial gain, magnanimity in success and courage in adversity. All now passed from this side of Paradise, but living still in my memory, and no doubt in the memories of others who had travelled with them, and laughed and loved life alongside them.

One day early in 2020, just before the time of the coronavirus, I went down to the Old Chain Pier overlooking the Firth of Forth accompanied by Uisce, my West Highland terrier, and my baby granddaughter, Elsa. The inn was almost deserted that winter afternoon, and we sat alone in the conservatory overlooking the sea, which beat on the rocks beneath us, sending spray splashing against the windows as darkness fell.

As I watched the waves crash onto the rocks below, my mind was taken back to Jacobites I had known, and other Jacobites long since gone, who existed only in my mind – Queen Clementina, Prince Henry, John William O'Sullivan, Lord George, the Earl of Kilmarnock, John Roy, Lord Lovat, and of course the tragic-heroic Prince himself – and was moved to say something to mark the occasion.

'I would like to raise a toast,' I said portentously, addressing the terrier and baby girl. They both looked me expectantly, as if conscious of the great solemnity of the occasion. 'To those I have I loved who are with us no longer, and to those I have loved who are with us still. And may God bless them all, wherever they may be!'

And with that, I demolished a bumper of red wine, just like the brave Lord Balmerino before he began his long, slow march to the scaffold.

Perhaps overcome by the sudden sensation of the wine flowing into my system, I added, in a moment of exuberant optimism, 'And who knows, perhaps someday we shall all meet again!'

Wee Elsa gurgled and clapped her hands in appreciation. Uisce, for her part, cocked her head to one side with a quizzical expression, as if to say sceptically, 'And maybe we won't!'

Then again, maybe we will.

_____

A Note on the Conversion of 1745
Prices into 2020 Values

_____

In 1745, a silver crown (five shillings in old money, or 25p today) weighed one ounce of silver. As at late July 2020, an ounce of silver costs almost £20. So, on this basis, 25p in 1745 values would convert into £20 today, an eighty-fold increase. By contrast, a guinea weighing a quarter ounce of gold had a value of twenty-one shillings in 1745 or £1.05 in today's money. In late July 2020, a quarter ounce of gold commanded a price of approximately £375. From these conversions, it can be seen that gold has increased in price relative to silver over the past three hundred years. So, in converting 1745 values into 2020 values, should we use the Gold Standard or the Silver Standard?

I have also considered the price of other products, such as glass, ceramics, food and beverages of similar specification in 2020 as in 1745. Based on these comparators, as a rule of thumb I multiply 1745 prices by a factor of two hundred to arrive at equivalent values in 2020: i.e. higher than a conversion of 80 times applying the Silver Standard but lower than a conversion of about 350 times using the Gold Standard..

Testing this 'Rule of 200' against the records in the Prince's Household Book, which kept note of daily expenditure during the campaign, we find that:

- two bottles of brandy were purchased at a price of half a crown, which would convert to a 2020 value of £25, or £12.50 a bottle;
- a pint of ale cost threepence in the money of the day, where a shilling comprised twelve pennies and there were twenty shillings or two hundred and forty pennies to the pound. This equates to 3/240, or 1.25p in today's decimal currency, which would convert to £2.50 applying the Rule of 200;
- nine gallons of ale is recorded as costing nine shillings, equating to £1.25 a pint. This wholesale price suggests a 100 per cent mark-up to the retail price per pint charged at the inns of the time, similar to the retail mark-up one would expect today;
- four turkeys cost ten shillings, converting to a price per turkey of approximately £25 in today's prices;
- eggs are quoted at various prices, including one shilling sixpence for eight dozen and two shillings for six dozen, the differences presumably depending on their size and availability. The average cost of a dozen

eggs is thus around threepence a dozen in old money, converting to £2.50 today.

While the prices quoted in the Prince's Household Book indicate that the price of farm produce such as milk and eggs has fallen in real terms since 1745, the book records that the household purchased 600 oysters at a cost of half a crown (2s. 6d), equating to less than 5p per oyster in today's prices.

Today, an oyster served in a restaurant would cost fifty times more than in 1745. Conversely, commodities regarded as staples today, such as tea, oranges and other tropical fruits, were expensive luxuries in 1745, and the Prince's Household Book records not a single purchase of these rare delicacies. However, of all the hardships that the Prince had to bear during his campaign, perhaps he would not have regarded the lack of pineapple as among the more arduous.

No attempt to convert prices to equivalent values almost three centuries later can be regarded as precise, given changes in tastes, technologies and product availability over that period. However, the Rule of 200 seems a reasonable guide to get some idea of what 1745 values mean in today's money, as follows:

- A 1745 farthing would be worth about 20p today, while a halfpenny would equate to about 40p and a penny about 80p
- Sixpence in 1745 (the basic daily pay of a soldier) equates to approximately £5 in today's values
- A silver shilling (5p in new money) would equate to around £10
- A silver crown (five shillings) to around £50
- A golden guinea (£1.05) to around £200.

The Fourteen Land Battles of
the Jacobite Wars

I define a 'battle' as a premeditated engagement between two organised armies, each comprising at least a hundred men, under an identifiable commander on each side, and resulting in significant material damage and casualties, with the number of fatalities at least in double figures.

By contrast, a 'skirmish' is an engagement between a few combatants on two sides of the conflict (normally less than a hundred), who may come across each other accidentally during the course of the campaign and briefly exchange fire before disengaging, having suffered light casualties, with the number of fatalities in single figures.

On this definition, the engagement at Clifton in December 1745, often described as a 'skirmish', is more accurately classified as a battle. By contrast, the engagement at Highbridge in August 1745, the first land engagement of the '45, and the Rout of Moy in February 1746 are correctly described as skirmishes and therefore not included in this list.

Applying the above definition, fourteen land battles were fought during the Jacobite Wars, the first being at Killiecrankie in 1688 and the last at Culloden in 1746.

The Williamite War of 1689–91

27 July 1689: Killiecrankie, Scotland.
A Highland Army supporting the restoration of King James VII and II under John Graham, Viscount Dundee ('Bonnie Dundee') defeated Williamite forces commanded by Major-General Hugh Mackay, but their victory was marred by the death of Dundee himself, shot by a sniper's bullet at the end of the battle.

21 August 1689: Dunkeld, Scotland.
A Williamite Cameronian Regiment led by Lieutenant-Colonel William Cleland defeated Jacobite forces under Colonel Alexander Cannon.

30 April – 1 May 1690: Cromdale, Scotland.
Williamite forces led by Sir Thomas Livingstone engaged with Jacobite forces under Major-General Thomas Buchan. Although the result was inconclusive, the

Jacobites lost more men and the battle effectively ended the Jacobite campaign in Scotland.

1 July 1690: The Boyne, Ireland.
A Jacobite Army personally led by James VII and II was decisively defeated by William of Orange near the town of Drogheda, turning the tide in James's attempt to regain the British crown and ensuring continued Protestant ascendancy in Ireland.

12 July 1691: Aughrim, Ireland.
The last battle of the Williamite War in Ireland, the bloodiest ever fought on Irish soil, and the most destructive battle of the entire Jacobite Wars, with at least 6,000 soldiers killed (4,000 Jacobites and 2,000 Williamites). Although the city of Limerick held out for King James until the autumn of 1691, the defeat marked the effective end of James's campaign in Ireland.

The Rising of 1715

13 November 1715: Sheriffmuir, Scotland.
An indecisive battle. The Jacobites under the Earl of Mar ended the battle with a significantly larger army than the Hanoverians under the Duke of Argyll, but Mar failed to press home his advantage, and the capture of Inverness the same day by a Clan Fraser Regiment led by Simon Fraser, 11th Lord Lovat, swung the balance of advantage towards the Hanoverians. In recognition of his support for the Hanoverian Government, on 10 March 1716 King George signed a document confirming that Lord Lovat was a free and lawful British subject and that the capital charges found against him twenty years earlier were annulled.

9–14 November 1715: Preston, England.
Jacobite forces under the Northumbrian Thomas Forster were defeated by Hanoverian Government forces under General Charles Wills when Forster surrendered following the siege of the town of Preston in which Jacobite forces were trapped.

The Rising of 1719

10 June 1719: Glen Shiel, Scotland.
Hanoverian Government forces under Major-General Joseph Wightman defeated a Jacobite Army under the Marquis of Tullibardine to bring the Jacobite campaign in Scotland to an end. The wider war between Great Britain and Spain was ended by the capture of the Spanish port of Vigo by British naval forces under Lord Cobham in October 1719.

The Rising of 1745

21 September 1745: Prestonpans, Scotland.
Jacobite forces led by Prince Charles Edward Stuart inflicted a decisive defeat on Hanoverian Government forces under Sir John Cope.

18 December 1745: Clifton Moor, England.
The retreating Jacobite rearguard commanded by Lord George Murray defeated pursuing Hanoverian Government forces under General Bland and were able to continue their retreat in good order back to Scotland. This was the last battle fought on English soil.

23 December 1745: Inverurie, Scotland.
Jacobite forces under Lord Lewis Gordon defeated Hanoverian forces under MacLeod of MacLeod.

17 January 1746: Falkirk Muir, Scotland.
A Jacobite Army under Prince Charles Edward Stuart inflicted a decisive defeat on Hanoverian Government forces under General Henry Hawley in the largest battle in terms of the number of combatants fought on Scottish soil during the Jacobite Wars. However, bad weather, the need to re-gather their forces and Prince Charles's illness after the battle prevented a complete rout of the Hanoverian Government forces, which were able to regroup in Edinburgh. This was the last Jacobite victory.

15 April 1746: Little Ferry, Golspie, Sutherland, Scotland.
Jacobite forces from the Clan Mackenzie, Clan Gregor and Clan Mackinnon returning from the Kyle of Tongue to rejoin the main Jacobite Army at Inverness were intercepted and defeated at Little Ferry by two Independent Highland Companies from the Clan Sutherland and the Clan Mackay.

16 April 1746: Culloden Moor, Scotland.
The Jacobite Army of Prince Charles Edward Stuart was decisively defeated by the Hanoverian Government Army under the Duke of Cumberland. This was the last battle fought during the Jacobite Wars, and the last battle fought on British soil.

Timeline of the Rising of 1745

3 July 1745
Prince Charles's ships, the *Elizabeth* and the *Du Teillay*, depart from Nantes in Brittany bound for Scotland.

15 July 1745
The *Elizabeth* engages HMS *Lyon* on the high seas, is badly damaged and forced back to France.

23 July 1745
Prince Charles and seven of his supporters (the Seven Men of Moidart) land on the Hebridean island of Eriskay.

25 July 1745
Prince Charles and his seven supporters land in mainland Scotland at Loch nan Uamh.

16 August 1745
Skirmish at Highbridge, Lochaber. The first action of the Rising. The Hanoverian Captain Scott of the Royal Scots surrenders to Major Donald MacDonald of Tirnandris.

19 August 1745
The Stuart Standard is raised at Glenfinnan in the presence of the first recruits to Prince Charles's Jacobite Army, including Lochiel's Camerons.

20 August 1745
Hanoverian Government forces under Sir John Cope march northwards from Stirling to intercept the southward advance of the Jacobites.

27 August 1745
The Appin Regiment under Charles Stewart of Ardshiel and the MacDonalds of Glencoe join the Jacobite Army, increasing its total strength to some 2,000 men.

29 August 1745
The Jacobites fail in an attempt to capture the Ruthven Barracks in Kingussie.

3 September 1745
James Francis Edward Stuart is proclaimed as King James VIII of Scotland at Perth.

11 September 1745
The Jacobite Army leaves Perth to advance on Edinburgh.

16 September 1745
'Canter of Coltbrig': Jacobite forces rout Hanoverian dragoons at Coltbrig on the outskirts of Edinburgh.

17 September 1745
The Jacobites take the City of Edinburgh but not the castle, which remains in Government hands under the command of General Joshua Guest.

21 September 1745
A Hanoverian Government Army under the command of Sir John Cope are surprised by a dawn attack by Jacobite forces at Prestonpans and overwhelmingly defeated.

24 September 1745
The Hanoverian officer Colonel James Gardiner, who was killed at Prestonpans, is interred in the kirkyard of Tranent Parish Church.

28 September 1745
Audiences at the Drury Lane and Covent Garden theatres in London sing 'God Save the King' for the first time after news arrives of the Government defeat at Prestonpans. The anthem calls for the victory of Marshall Wade in the notorious and now discontinued stanza, 'May he sedition crush/And like a torrent rush/ Rebellious Scots to crush/God save the King!'.

9 October 1745
Pitsligo's Horse commanded by Alexander, 4th Lord Forbes of Pitsligo, joins the Jacobite Army in Edinburgh.

Cluny's Regiment of 350 men, led by Ewan Macpherson of Cluny, join the Jacobite Army in Edinburgh.

18 October 1745
William Boyd, 4th Earl of Kilmarnock, joins the Jacobite Army in Edinburgh.

27 October 1745
A force of Jacobite Frasers tries but fails to seize the Lord President of the Council, Duncan Forbes of Culloden.

30 October 1745
The Jacobite Council of War meets at the Palace of Holyrood in Edinburgh and decides by a majority of a single vote to advance into England. Hanoverian supporters besiege Oliphant of Gask, Jacobite depute governor of Perth, and drive David Fotheringham, Jacobite governor of Dundee, out of the city.

31 October 1745
The main body of the Jacobite Army marches from Edinburgh to Dalkeith en route to England.

2 November 1745
Hanoverian forces based in Edinburgh Castle retake the City of Edinburgh from depleted Jacobite forces, while the main Jacobite Army continues its march south from Dalkeith.

8 November 1745
The Jacobite Army crosses the Scottish Borders into England.

10 November 1745
The Jacobite Army reaches Carlisle and lays siege to the city, which surrenders five days later on 15 November. On 17 November, Prince Charles Edward Stuart enters Carlisle.

20 November 1745
Lord George Murray leaves Carlisle with the first division of the Jacobite Army. Prince Charles follows with the second division on 21 November.

23 November 1745
The Duke of Cumberland is appointed supreme commander of the Hanoverian Army in England.

28 November 1745
A Jacobite Sergeant named Dickson, accompanied by a single drummer and a young woman, takes Manchester for the Jacobites ahead of the arrival of the main army.

3 December 1745
Prince Charles Edward Stuart declares his father King of England, Scotland and Wales at Ashbourne, north of Derby.

6 December 1745
The Jacobite Council of War in Derby decides to turn back to Scotland against Prince Charles's proposal to continue the advance on London.

10 December 1745
An assassination attempt is made on Prince Charles in Wigan.

18 December 1745
Battle of Clifton Moor: retreating Jacobite forces under Lord George Murray defeat General Bland's Hanoverian troops and continue to retreat in good order to Scotland.

20 December 1745
The Jacobite Army crosses the River Esk back into Scotland.

21 December 1745
The Hanoverian Army under the Duke of Cumberland commences its siege of Carlisle, where 400 Jacobites, mainly of the Manchester Regiment, remain. The Jacobite garrison surrenders a week later.

23 December 1745
Battle of Inverurie. Jacobite forces under Lord Lewis Gordon defeat Hanoverian forces under MacLeod of MacLeod.

2 January 1746
Prince Charles reviews his army on Glasgow Green.

3 January 1746
The Jacobite Army leaves Glasgow in two columns by Kilsyth and Cumbernauld.

8 January 1746
The Burgh of Stirling surrenders to the Jacobite Army, but Stirling Castle remains in Hanoverian hands.

13 January 1746
MacPherson of Cluny's Regiment, under the command of Lord George Murray, seizes provisions intended for the Hanoverian Army at Linlithgow.

17 January 1746
Battle of Falkirk Muir. The Jacobite Army commanded by Prince Charles Edward Stuart inflicts a decisive defeat on the Hanoverian Government Army under General Henry Hawley in the largest battle in terms of number of combatants fought during the Rising.

31 January 1746
The Hanoverian Army, now under the command of the Duke of Cumberland, advances from Edinburgh to Linlithgow.

1 February 1746
The Jacobite Army evacuates Stirling to begin its retreat to the Highlands.

2 February 1746
A Jacobite Council of War held in Crieff decides to retreat northwards in three columns.

11 February 1746
Ruthven Barracks surrenders to Jacobite forces.

16 February 1746
The Rout of Moy: Lord Loudoun leads a private initiative to seize Prince Charles at Moy and claim the £30,000 on his head, but is surprised and routed by a handful of Jacobites.

18 February 1746
The Jacobite Army captures Inverness.

27 February 1746
The main Hanoverian Army under Cumberland arrives in Aberdeen.

17 March 1746
The Atholl Raids: before daybreak, Jacobite forces under the command of Lord George Murray capture more than thirty Hanoverian military posts between Dalwhinnie and Blair Castle, and commence the siege of Blair Castle.

20 March 1746
The Jacobites capture Captain Aeneas MacIntosh of MacIntosh, 22nd clan chieftain, who is paroled by Prince Charles into the hands of his wife, Lady Anne.

25 March 1746
The Jacobite sloop *Le Prince Charles* (formerly the *Hazard*) is captured by the Hanoverians, who seize money and supplies on board intended for the Jacobite Army.

31 March 1746
Lord George Murray abandons the siege of his ancestral home, Blair Castle, and retreats northwards with his Atholl Regiment.

3 April 1746
Cameron of Lochiel abandons the siege of Fort William, which began on 20 March.

12 April 1746
The Hanoverian Army under the Duke of Cumberland crosses the Spey.

15 April 1746
Night March on Nairn: an attempt by the Jacobite Army to make a pre-emptive dawn strike on the Hanoverian Army is aborted by Lord George Murray when it fails to achieve its target before sunrise.

16 April 1746
The Battle of Culloden: the final defeat of the Jacobite Army by Hanoverian Government forces.

20 April 1746
Remnants of the Jacobite Army rendezvous at Ruthven Barracks but disperse after receiving instructions from Prince Charles to 'let every man seek his safety in the best way he can'.

4 May 1746
Following assurances from their clan chieftain, Ludovic Grant, sixteen Grants of Glenmoriston and sixty-eight Grants of Glen Urquhart surrender at Inverness. Instead of the safe return to their homes that they had been promised by their chieftain, they are transported to Barbados and all but eighteen are dead by 1750.

11 May 1746
Death of the Duke of Perth at sea while seeking to escape to France after Culloden.

28 May 1746
Destruction of Achnacarry, the seat of Lochiel, by Hanoverian forces as part of their campaign of vengeance, which also includes the razing of Castle Dounie, Lord Lovat's seat, and Linlithgow Palace.

30 July 1746
Francis Towneley, Colonel of the Manchester Regiment, is executed at Kennington.

18 August 1746
The Earl of Kilmarnock and Lord Balmerino are executed for high treason on Tower Hill.

5 September 1746
Prince Charles Edward Stuart joins Cluny Macpherson in his hideout on Ben Alder, where he remains until news comes through of the arrival of a French frigate on the west coast of the Highlands.

20 September 1746
Prince Charles Edward Stuart sails from Loch nan Uamh to safety in France on board the French frigate *L'Heureux*, along with other leading Jacobites, evading Royal Navy ships under cover of fog.

9 April 1747
Simon Fraser, Lord Lovat, is executed for high treason at Tower Hill in London, the last man to be beheaded in Great Britain.

7 June 1753
Dr Archie Cameron is hanged at Tyburn, the last man to be executed for his part in the Jacobite Rising of 1745.

APPENDIX 4

Poems and Songs of John Roy Stuart

Original Title of the Poem	English Title	Estimated Date of Composition
Oran A'Bhranndaidh	An Ode to Brandy	c. 1725
Oran do Mac Ailpein an Duin	A Song for the Laird of Tulloch	c. 1730
Mairi Grant	Mary Grant	c. 1730
Oran do Leannan	A Song for a Loved One	c. 1730
Cumha do Bhaintighearna Mhic-an-Toisch	Lament for Lady MacIntosh	c. 1735
D' Bharbara à Dùnaid	To Barbara of Dounie	c. 1735
Oran Eadar e Fhein Agus Leanabh Nighean	A song between me and my girl	Early 1745
The Culloden Poems		
Latha Chuilodair nan Siol	Culloden's Day of Dust	May 1746
Oran Eile Air Latha Chuilodair	The Silk of Clan Chattan	June 1746
John Roy's Psalm	John Roy's Psalm	July 1746
Urnuigh Iain Ruaidh	John Roy's Prayer	August 1746
Latha Chuilodair	The Day of Culloden	September 1746

APPENDIX 5

1745 Association Memorials

Over the years, the 1745 Association has built a number of memorials to mark people and places of particular significance in the Jacobite story. A complete list of Association memorials is given here, in chronological order, according to the date of their construction, and images can be viewed on the Association website itself. My colleague Paul Macdonald has created a helpful map of the monuments, which can be accessed through the Association website. I am also grateful to him for supplying the Ordnance Survey (OS) map references of their locations, as below.

CAIRNS

Prince's Cairn, Loch nan Uamh
The Prince's Cairn marks the place where, according to tradition, Prince Charles Edward Stuart departed for France after his wanderings in the Highlands and Islands following the defeat of the Jacobite forces at the Battle of Culloden on 16 April 1746. The cairn was erected by the 1745 Association in 1956. Loch nan Uamh is also where the Prince first set foot on mainland Great Britain on 25 July 1745. The cairn is located near the A830. Ordnance Survey Map 40 (Mallaig & Glenfinnan). Ref. NM 72005 84435.

Ardgour Cairn (The Seven Men of Moidart)
This cairn was erected in 1990 and is dedicated to 'The Seven Men of Moidart', who arrived in Scotland along with the Prince and included the Marquis of Tullibardine, Colonel John William O'Sullivan and Aeneas MacDonald, the Parisian financier who helped to bankroll the Rising. The cairn is on the roadside on the A861 a mile or two west of Kinlochmoidart, overlooking seven oak trees originally planted in the 1800s to represent the Seven Men. A few years ago, new trees were planted to replace those that had died, of beech rather than oak. Ordnance Survey Map 40 (Mallaig & Glenfinnan). Ref. NM 70338 72887.

Cairn at Highbridge
Erected in 1994, the Highbridge Cairn is close to Spean Bridge and was the main crossing point over the River Spean from 1736 until Thomas Telford built a new bridge in 1819 over the river at the place that is now Spean Bridge. The cairn

marks the location of the skirmish at Highbridge, the first engagement in the Rising of 1745, and can be located on Ordnance Survey Map 34 (Fort Augustus & Glen Albyn). Ref. NN 19964 81922.

Cairn to John Roy Stuart

Erected in 1998, the cairn dedicated to John Roy Stuart, Gaelic Bard and colonel of the Edinburgh Regiment that fought at Culloden under the Green Flag of Kincardine, is located half a kilometre north of Auchgourish, along the B970 on the banks of the River Spey. Ref. NH 94085 16582.

Sheriffmuir Cairn

The Association's cairn commemorating the Battle of Sheriffmuir was erected in 2002. The plaque reads:

> On this moor on 13 November 1715, a Jacobite Army composed largely of Highlanders under the command of the Earl of Mar met a Hanoverian army consisting mainly of regular British soldiers under the Duke of Argyll ... The result was indecisive, but Mar's failure to take advantage of Argyll's weakened position in the closing stages of the conflict and subsequent withdrawal from the field contributed to the failure of the Rising.

Ref. NN 81571 01934.

PLAQUES

1982: Dalilea House, Loch Shiel

A plaque to commemorate the bicentenary of the Repeal of the Dis-clothing Act in 1782 is located at Dalilea House, the home of the Gaelic Bard Alexander MacDonald. This plaque has twice been renewed. Ref. NM 73403 69310.

1988: Cille Choirill Church

Two plaques, one commemorating Colonel Alexander Macdonald, 17th Chief, and the other Major Donald Macdonald of Tirnadris, are placed at Cille Choirill, a fifteenth-century Roman Catholic Church in Lochaber. The church, dedicated to St Kerrill, is at Roy Bridge, Glen Spean, PH31 4AP. Ref NN 30697 81212.

2000: Sancerre de Berry

Erected in 2000, this plaque marks the house in which the 3rd Lord Nairn, who fought in the Rising of both 1715 and 1745, lived during his exile, following his escape to the Continent after Culloden. It is at 9 bis, Rue Porte-Oison, Sancerre, France.

2003: Callander

A plaque to the memory of James Drummond, Duke of Perth (1713–46), is placed in South Ancaster Square. The Duke was Lieutenant-General of the Jacobite Army alongside Lord George Murray and the only member of the Council of War that met in Derby on 6 December 1745 to support the Prince's proposal to continue the advance on to London. Ref. NN 62840 07886.

2005: Cairn Tree Site, Brampton, Cumbria
A plaque in memory of six Jacobites executed in 1746 is fixed onto an existing stone cross dating from 1904. Ref NY 52739 59776.

2012: Flodigarry
The Flodigarry Plaque commemorates the Highland heroine Flora MacDonald (1722–90), who lived in this cottage in the period 1751–59. Famous for her part in the escape of Prince Charles Edward Stuart after the Battle of Culloden in 1746, she married Allan MacDonald of Kingsburgh in 1750 and five of their seven children were born in Flodigarry Cottage. Ref. NG 46410 71907.

2015: St George's Gardens, London
Erected in 2015, the plaque in St George's Gardens commemorates the men executed on Kennington Common in 1746, who are buried in the gardens. The inscription reads:

> In Memory of The Officers and Gentlemen of the Army of Prince Charles Edward Stuart who were executed on Kennington Common in July, August and November 1746. Nine of the Manchester Regiment and seven Scots are buried here. Francis Towneley, Colonel of the Manchester Regiment, lies in the churchyard of Old St Pancras Church.

Ref. TQ 30453 82481.

2015: Castlegate, Aberdeen.
This plaque commemorates the involvement in the '45 of Jacobites from the area. Ref. NJ 94493 06404.

2018: Young Glengarry
The Young Glengarry plaque was erected to commemorate the accidental shooting of Young Glengarry, Colonel of the Glengarry Regiment, after the Battle of Falkirk Muir. The plaque is located on Falkirk High Street at the entrance to the Old Church (Falkirk Trinity). Young Glengarry rests in the tomb of John de Graeme. The plaque was unveiled by Ranald MacDonell, 23rd Chief of the MacDonells of Glengarry and patron of the 1745 Association. Ref. NS 88701 79986.

2019: Kyle of Tongue
The Kyle of Tongue plaque commemorates the capture of *Le Prince Charles* (formerly HMS *Hazard*) on 25 March 1746, along with the gold sent to help the Jacobite cause. It is located on the wall of the Craggan Hotel, Skinnet, Melness, Sutherland, IV27 4YP. Ref. NC 58773 61529.

Sources and References

Chapter 1: The Rise and Fall of the House of Stuart
This chapter is based on a talk given during the 1745 Association tour of the Stuart and Jacobite portraits at the National Portrait Gallery in London in September 2017. The quotation from Count Nikolai Tolstoy is from a letter published in the *Daily Telegraph* of 1 May 2000, entitled 'Foreign "rulers" and the bill of rights'.

Chapter 2: Remembering Dunkeld
This chapter is based on a talk given to commemorate the 330th Anniversary of the Battle of Dunkeld outside Dunkeld Cathedral in August 2019. Links to this and the other videos referenced are on the 1745 Association's website at https://www.1745association.org.uk/.

Chapter 3: The Tragedy of Queen Anne
This chapter is based on talks given at the Scottish National Portrait Gallery in Edinburgh in 2016, 2017 and 2019 to commemorate the anniversary of the Jacobites' decision to turn back at Derby on 6 December 1745. These talks considered different aspects of the Jacobite story, as revealed by the paintings that hang there. In the 2019 talk, entitled 'The '45 in 45 Minutes', Part One covered the overthrow of James VII and II and can be seen on YouTube at https://www.you tube.com/watch?v=EgP7i4DR8vs&t=1s.

Chapter 4: Glen Shiel, The Forgotten Battle
This chapter is based on a presentation given at the Scottish National Portrait Gallery to mark the 300th anniversary of the battle on 19 June 2019. It was originally published in *The Jacobite*, No. 160, Summer 2019. It draws on a number of sources, including Jonathan Worton, *The Battle of Glenshiel*, Helion, 2018. A report of the talk by Jody Harrison, entitled 'The "forgotten" battle of Scotland' was published in *The Herald* on 16 June 2019.

Chapter 5: Queen Clementina's Cavinet
This chapter is based on Part Three of 'The '45 in 45 Minutes' given at the Scottish National Portrait Gallery in March 2019, which can be seen on YouTube at: https://www.youtube.com/watch?v=cIURfVvPgWk&t=1s

Chapter 6: Keeping the Flame Alive

My analysis of Jacobite portraiture draws particularly on the work of Professor Edward Corp, including *The King Over the Water,* and on Robin Nicholson's *Bonnie Prince Charlie and the Making of a Myth: A Study in Portraiture, 1720–1892.* My personal view of the truth behind some of the Jacobite portraits in the care of the Scottish National Portrait Gallery is set out in my talk 'The '45 in 45 minutes: Fifteen Myths and Misconceptions Challenged' (March 2019). Parts One and Three are referenced above and Part Two is at https://www.youtube.com/watch?v=gmuRt777c9M&t=1s.

The authoritative work on Jacobite glass is Geoffrey Seddon's *The Jacobites and their Drinking Glasses.* In his introduction to this work, Dr Seddon readily acknowledged his debt to the extensive research carried out by Peter Lole, my immediate predecessor as treasurer of the 1745 Association. Following his passing in November 2018, I synthesised Peter's research and the conversations I had with him over the years in 'Peter Lole on Jacobite Glass and the Jacobite Clubs', published in *The Jacobite,* No. 159 (Spring 2019) and in *The Fifteen,* No. 20, February 2020. The main references on which this article drew are as follows (in chronological order):

F. Peter Lole, 'Northern England Jacobite Clubs of the 18th Century', *The Jacobite,* No. 75, Spring 1991
F. Peter Lole, 'The Scottish Jacobite Clubs', *The Jacobite,* No. 81, Spring 1993
F. Peter Lole, 'A Digest of the Jacobite Clubs', *Royal Stuart Society, Paper LV,* 1999
F. Peter Lole, 'The Gask Amen Glass', *The Jacobite,* No. 109, Summer 2002
F. Peter Lole, 'Mid-18th Century Pictures of the Exiled Stuarts at Traquair', *The Jacobite,* No. 115, Summer 2004

Chapter 7: The Road to Prestonpans: The Quartermaster's Story

This chapter is based on the first-hand account of Colonel John William O'Sullivan, reproduced in *1745 and After,* edited by Alistair Taylor and Henrietta Taylor (Thomas Nelson & Sons Ltd, 1938).

Chapter 8: Decision at Derby

My analysis of the La Tour portrait was reported in *History Scotland* on 12 December 2016 at https://www.historyscotland.com/news/has-the-mystery-of-the-lost-portrait-of-prince-henry-benedict-stuart/.

Neil Jeffares' comment on 'La Tour's Stuart Copyists', April 2016, can be found at https://neiljeffares.wordpress.com/2016/04/02/la-tours-stuart-copyists-the-kamm-family-and-others/.

A contemporary account of what happened at Derby is given in the memoir of the Hanoverian double agent Dudley Bradstreet in *The Life and Uncommon Adventures of Captain Dudley Bradstreet,* published in Dublin in 1755, although this needs to be treated with caution, as Bradstreet's account may be somewhat self-serving.

Chapter 9: Retreat to Scotland

My analysis of the events leading up to the Battle of Falkirk Muir, and the battle itself, is based as far as possible on first-hand accounts written by those who served at the battle, including the *Narrative* of Colonel O'Sullivan; Lord George Murray's memoir, *Marches of the Highland Army*; Lord Elcho's diaries, as cited in Alice Wemyss's *Elcho of the '45*; Lord Elcho's *Short Account of the Affairs of Scotland in the years 1744, 1745, 1746*; the memoirs of the Chevalier de Johnstone; and the account of Sir John Macdonald, published in *1745 and After* (1938).

The story of Lady Ann Livingston draws on Barbara Graham's paper, 'Did Lady Kilmarnock die of a broken heart?' published in *The Jacobite*, No. 153, Spring 2017.

The story of Wolfe's refusal to shoot Major Charles Fraser of Inverallochy after Culloden is recounted in Christian Aikman et al., *No Quarter Given: The Muster Roll of Prince Charles Edward Stuart's Army*.

Chapter 10: The Last Jacobite Victory

In addition to the primary sources cited for Chapter 9, my analysis of the Battle of Falkirk Muir draws on the research and analysis of two contemporary historians, Christopher Duffy, in particular *Fight for a Throne*, and Geoff Bailey, *Falkirk or Paradise*. The quote from Alexander Macdonald is on p. 372 of Norman MacDonald, *The Clan Ranald of Garmoran*, 2008.

Chapter 11: Financing a Revolution

This chapter evolved from a talk given at the Royal Museum of Scotland on 5 December 2019 to mark the anniversary of the arrival of the Jacobite Army in Derby in 1745. Thanks are due to Russell Napier, founder of the Library of Mistakes in Edinburgh, an invaluable resource on financial and economic history, where I was able to refer to a range of sources to help piece together how the Jacobite Rising of 1745 was financed, and to Professor Charles Munn of Glasgow University, for his comments on an earlier draft of this chapter. Key primary sources in alphabetical order by author surname are as follows:

The Diary of John Campbell of Ardmaddie. Campbell was the first cashier of the Royal Bank of Scotland at the time of the Rising
Lord Elcho, *Short Account of the Affairs of Scotland, 1744–46*
James Maxwell of Kirkconnel, *Narrative of Charles Prince of Wales' Expedition to Scotland in the year 1745*
Narrative, Colonel John William O'Sullivan, Quartermaster-General of the Jacobite Army
Prince's Household Book, recording daily expenditure during the campaign
In addition, I drew on the following secondary sources:
Christopher Duffy, *Fight for a Throne. The Jacobite '45 Reconsidered* (Helion, 2015)
F. Peter Lole, 'The Old and New Banks in the '45', *The Jacobite*, No. 119, 2005
Ray Perman, *The Rise and Fall of the City of Money: A Financial History of Edinburgh* (Birlinn, Edinburgh, 2019)
Francis Wilkins, *James Maxwell and Prince Charles' Expedition 1745–46* (Wyre Forest Press, 2008)

Chapter 12: Was the Rising of 1745 a Just War?

The analysis in this chapter is based on my personal experience and understanding of the seven conditions for a just war, discussed with members of the 1745 Association during the September 2017 Annual Gathering.

Chapter 13: The Prince in the Heather
This chapter is based largely on the *Narrative* of Colonel O'Sullivan. In addition, I have drawn on Malcolm Seddon's *The Escape of Bonnie Prince Charlie* (2016), which gives a most helpful day-by-day account of the Prince's movements while he was a fugitive in the Highlands and Islands after Culloden.

Chapter 14: The Execution of the Jacobite Lords
This chapter was originally published in two parts in *The Jacobite* under the title 'Eyewitness Accounts of the Behaviour of the Earl of Kilmarnock and Lord Balmerino in August 1746'. Part One, 'Events Leading up to their Execution', was published in *The Jacobite*, No. 128, Winter 2008. Part Two, 'The Day of their Execution', was published in *The Jacobite*, No. 129, Spring 2009. Key sources for these articles were:

David, Lord Elcho, *Journal*, reproduced in Alice Wemyss & John Sibbald Gibson (ed.)
Elcho of the '45, Edinburgh, The Saltire Society, 2003
An Account of the Behaviour of the late Earl of Kilmarnock after his Sentence and on the Day of His Execution, by the Reverend James Foster, London 1746. This includes the text of Lord Kilmarnock's last letter to his son.
T. Ford, *An Account of the Behaviour of William, late Earl of Kilmarnock, and Arthur, late Lord Balmerino, From the Time of their being delivered into the Custody of the Sheriffs of London, to the Time of their Execution*, London, 1746.

Chapter 15: John Roy Stuart, the Bard of Culloden
This chapter is based on a privately printed monograph that I wrote on John Roy's life and poetry, and on talks given at the Clan Donald annual dinner at the Culloden commemoration in April 2018, the Queens Arms in Edinburgh in July 2018, and Dilston Chapel, Northumberland, to members of the Fifteen (the Jacobite Northumbrian Society) in November 2019.

An edited version of the Clan Donald talk was published in their magazine, *A'Bhirlinn*, No. 18, Autumn 2018, while my translations of some of John Roy's poems were published in 'The Life, Poems and Extraordinary Adventures of John Roy Stuart, Colonel of the Edinburgh Regiment', in *The Fifteen*, No. 20, February 2020.

An extensive account of John Roy's life and poems is provided by Neil MacGregor in 'John Roy Stuart: Jacobite Bard of Strathspey', in Volume LXIII of the *Transactions of the Gaelic Society of Inverness*. Other references used include:

Elizabeth E. Mackechnie, *The Poems of John Roy Stewart* (1947)
'John Roy Stuart – The Soldier-Poet', *The Jacobite*, No. 99, Spring 1999
John Lorne Campbell, *Highland Songs of the Forty-five* (1934)

Chapter 16: The Day of Culloden
The source of the Gaelic version of 'The Day of Culloden' is John Lorne Campbell's *Highland Songs of the Forty-five* (1934).

Chapter 17: Lament for Lord Lovat
There are multiple accounts of the life and supposed misdeeds of Lord Lovat.

Two of the more reliable accounts are Sarah Fraser's *The Last Highlander* and Moray McLaren's *Life of Lord Lovat*. I sought to cross-check and validate incidents from his life as far as possible, quoting his own words rather than words ascribed to him by others. My Tower Hill eulogy was published in *Strawberry Leaves*, the journal of the Clan Fraser Society of Australia, No. 139, September 2019, and in *Fraser*, the newsletter of the Clan Fraser Society of Scotland and the United Kingdom, No. 59, March 2020.

Chapter 18: The Last Hopeful Epistle of Bonnie Prince Charlie

This chapter draws on the Prince's own account of the Rising in his memorandum to King Louis XV of France in November 1746, which gives an insight into his state of mind immediately after his escape from Scotland and helps to explain his subsequent return in secret to London in 1750 and 1752. A key reference for these visits is Victoria Thorpe's meticulously researched paper 'The Last Great Jacobite Councils in England (1750 and 1752)', published in the *Journal of the Royal Stuart Society* in 2009.

The Prichard Letters, containing Mrs Prichard's first-hand account of the Prince's secret visit to Lady Primrose between Christmas and New Year 1752, were published in *The Jacobite*, No. 131 (Winter 2009) and No. 132 (Spring 2010).

The account of the life and death of Dr Archie Cameron draws on the bicentennial commemoration of his execution, written in 1953 by the then Secretary of the 1745 Association, Marion Cameron, and published in *The Jacobite*, No. 69, Spring 1989, on the monograph on *The Last Jacobite Martyr* by Sonia Cameron Jacks, and Sonia's related article in *The Jacobite*, No. 112, Summer 2003.

Index

The 1745 Association

Over and above published sources, this book could not have been written without the considerable benefit of travels, conversations and adventures with friends and colleagues who served on the Council of the 1745 Association over the years. They include (in alphabetical order) Christian Aikman, Sheila Barcroft, Colin Brien, Peter Brown, Michael Cook, Maggie Craig, Louie Donald, Dr Christopher Duffy, Barbara Graham, John Graham, Rev. Canon Dr Robert Harley, Siân Johnson, Maureen Lipscomb, Peter Lole, Stephen Lord, John McCulloch, Glen MacDonald, Norman H. MacDonald, Paul Macdonald, Brigadier John MacFarlane, David McNaughton, Janet Niepokojczycka, the Very Rev. Dr A. Emsley Nimmo, Kevin Smith and Brian Whiting. In addition, thanks are due to my Italian colleagues Stefano Baccolo and Benedicta Froelich for having organised visits to Rome and Florence, and Geoff Bailey and Guy Wedderburn for their contribution to the commemoration and interpretation of the Falkirk Muir battlefield.

Their immense fund of knowledge about the events and personalities of those caught up in the Jacobite Wars, drawing on unpublished letters, diaries and memoirs, and on their own investigations and family connections, goes far beyond anything that I could have learned from history books alone. One final reference is *Walking with Charlie*, by Stephen Lord, in which Steve recounts his own odyssey in retracing the Prince's steps both during the campaign and during his subsequent flight in the Highlands and Islands. Steve's own experiences walking in his footsteps proves beyond doubt that, far from being the effete and effeminate figure of Hanoverian propaganda, the Prince was, at the time of the Rising of 1745, a remarkably resilient and determined man.